CW01666582

© Hannal

Hannah Jackson has asse

as the author of this W

Copyright, Designs and Patent Act 1988

ISBN 978-1-9997562-4-6

First published 2018 by Fear Gone Publishing, UK.

Photography by Katharine Davies.

Cover design by Hannah, Anton & Umar.

ROOM READER

HOW TO MIND-READ YOUR ROOM

or, if you're Chinese,

THE WEST'S ANSWER TO FENG SHUI.

and by the same author

PSYCHIC ROOM READER

LIFE SKILLS & LESSON PLANS

ROOMIES' POEMS & SONGS

Hannah Jackson

Reviews

Marianne Gray - Author, teacher, former President of the British Critics' Circle, and Chairman of the London Film Awards:

"I really enjoyed this and would recommend it to anybody who's not 100 per cent content with the way they are living in their home."

George Dimitrov - Member of the Standard Committee of British Association of Behavioural and Cognitive Psychotherapies (BABCP), Member of the British Psychological Society (BPS), American Psychological Association (APA), speaker, author:

"There is an ongoing debate in socio/psychological circles: Does our environment affect our thinking or does our thinking affect our environment? Therefore, it was a great pleasure to come across so many stories of such clarity demonstrating how the answer is 'both'. In fact, Room Reader has inspired me to have my therapeutic sessions inside a client's property whenever I can. I am learning there is no point guiding someone in one direction if, for example, a picture or ornament they look at is constantly and silently guiding them in another. This allows me to try to help clients by suggesting psychological and environmental changes so one can support the other. And Hannah Jackson's enjoyable, jargon-free and evidence-based dramatisations of the stories of her own clients only serve to confirm my own very positive experiences with mind-reading rooms."

Zhena Muzyka - Publisher, Enliven Books, Simon & Schuster US:

"Room Reader is a book whose time has come."

Alan Swindell - Headmaster, Steiner Academy Exeter:

"Hannah `Room Reader` Jackson's insights into what our spaces say about us translate to schools as well as the home. I experienced Hannah working with a large group of Year 9 (14-year-olds) as they transformed their own space in response to her input. The ideas were their own, but the all-important `nudge` came from Hannah. The fascinating and often touching stories in Hannah's book found an echo in the youngsters I teach. Their response was immediate, active, and transformational. Hannah invited us all to reflect on and experience what some might see as blindingly obvious. That we were duly blinded by it, suggest that she was helping us to see what was already, tantalizingly, right under our noses."

Angie Quidim - Executive Producer at TME Productions:

"Hannah's book really proves the old expression that you are a product of your environment. Much of the content are examples from clients written into delightful, easy to read stories that will change your perspective about the world around you. I can't wait to get my personal analysis from Hannah to learn more about myself."

Matt Farr - Fitness and functional nutrition/medicine specialist:

"I recently had the opportunity to have a reading from Hannah to help with an important business decision. I found the advice and suggestions she gave following the reading to be challenging and have helped me to grow in new ways which I am sure I will benefit from a great deal over the years. to come. Thank you, Hannah."

Lanja Ali - Kurdish singing sensation (the subject of Chapter 12) says on YouTube:

"I was not experiencing the daily happiness of life. I didn't know how much the whole decoration, the furniture, the objects in the house was affecting me. So busy, don't realise how much is going on around you. Then I thought: she might be right, she might be right."

Claire Randall - Actress whose relationship was transformed by Hannah Jackson's mind-reading rooms also says on youtube:

"It's a wonderful book full of stories and sound advice and suggestions and just a wonderful way of finding out how everything around you affects your thinking and your life, and your happiness."

"Hannah Jackson, Room Reader - show"

Interval interviews of audience. Full video on YouTube. **Excerpts:**

"I love the intro...Hannah's childhood and what to expect...I didn't realise what an effect on your life small things in your house can have. Fascinating. I'll buy the book now." - **Interior designer**

"This is a real insight into how your surroundings change how you feel and how you act." - **Businesswoman**

There no emotional connection in house-building any more...Now this (mind-reading rooms), compared (to feng shui) is easier to digest. It's like common sense that isn't so common." - **Photographer**

"You can't just 'fix it'. He must go home and change his life as well because treatment on its own is of no value."- **Social worker**

"It's a powerful therapy."

- Iraqi theatre director and witness of five wars.

Acknowledgements

There are many people to acknowledge for their influence on how this book has evolved, especially those who were with me during challenging times. Like, a few years ago, I found myself amid a difficult separation and the process of moving my four young boys to London from Mauritius.

The person who has been there since a particularly soggy April afternoon, when even a wonderful park in Crouch End couldn't lift my spirits, was Anton Hicks. He splashed my stylish new trench coat while jogging. Right from that first rainy encounter, Anton gave me the confidence to put pen to paper, lent me his editorial support, championed my work when I lacked energy, and generously shared his contributions as a songwriter to this book and the mind-reading rooms Programme. Anton shaped Room Reader case studies into readable stories, capturing the colour of the very real characters that mind-reading rooms has helped.

I thank Barbara Connor, my high school English and drama teacher. Her gentle encouragement for performance boosted my fledgling self-esteem against a backdrop of upheaval at home and my general disillusionment with mainstream education.

The methodology of Sam Kogan's *The Science of Acting* course inspired me to pursue more insight into the political landscape and the world of policy and marketing manipulation. His approach aided my understanding of the influence of religion and culture; of furniture, ornaments, pictures, and of finding space in one's life, all of which helped me to develop mind-reading rooms.

My study in law enhanced my appreciation of context. Thanks to supportive lecturers, Dr. Caroline Derry and Anjana Bahl at London Metropolitan University who provided the intellectual space I yearned for, I developed a thesis which explored lesser-known positive aspects of gang culture. This foray into terrain so different from my own helped me to gain insight into another aspect of owning a space.

I owe a special mention to Helen Lawrenson for so many perceptive points and questions…
to Debbie Gregory (sadly missed) & Anthony Cullen for their early financial support…
to Marianne Gray, Debbie Brown, Mark Cotton & Claire Randall for their encouragement…
and to Naomi Ziewe Palmer for checking the final draft.

My four sons, Orlando, Jet, Darcy and Angel waited five years for my book to come to fruition; the book's the fifth child of the family. I'm so grateful to them that in spite of the times I said, 'Not now!' or, 'We're saving money at the moment', they cheerfully stayed integral influences in my own life, consolidating the book's messaging about building family, creating community and becoming more connected.

Contents

7. Mind-reading rooms outside-in

Mind-reading rooms for trains. House rules. Why organic?

8. The burning boy

What could've been done with a so-called "dangerous no-hoper."

9. The moth house

Oddly dressed girls, family dog that had to go, nervous mother and banker-father, all overcrowded with clothes, furniture and moths.

10. Photo-analysis for shorter case-histories

Description, analysis, then effective actions.

11. Torn (mind and body)

Post-natal depression. How therapy outside home wasn't enough. Scary furniture. Bad cesarean. (Song: *Clinically Spontaneous.)*

12. Gilded cage

Hannah helps a woman off painkillers by spotting a picture she mimicked. London-based, she is now a star in Kurdistan.

(Song: *Own Little Crown.)*

13. Making new spaces

A guide for when you are to share or create a new home.

14. Spotless Organic Ltd

An organic deep-cleaning company is created and sorely tested. Full exploration of the underbelly of the cleaning industry.

15. Keeping up with the Joneses

Hierarchies, social class, and buying-power.

16. The little mouse business

A defeated shopkeeper learns how her small things can mean a lot of happiness.

17. International mind-reading rooms (of a shanty house)

Hannah's Hindi ex-mother-in-law has mind-reading rooms. We see Mauritian life in all its natural splendour. (Song: *Motherhood.)*

18. The magpie

An idyllic household conceals an addiction. Hannah prefers pictures to reality and saves the marriage. (Song: *I Know A Guy.)*

19. A school's Room Plan.

Dupree Government School in Mauritius gets mind-reading rooms.

20. Sequins and MS

A Palladium dancer falls in love after her sequins and dancing days are done. How overuse of a body and a poor diet can be managed with a Room Plan. (Song: *Independently Dependent.)*

21. Twin-set and pearls

An immaculately presented, very successful lady lives disgustingly. Hannah offers help in vain.

22. Unplugging the Kardashians

We're now addicted to what Kim ate for breakfast or what knickers she's wearing. Isn't it time to laugh at ourselves? (Song: *Show-horse.)*

23. Mind-reading environments with an edge

Mauritian confidence with knives could help Western knife crime.

24. Life and death

Careless builders trash the family home. Dying grandmother's last wishes, referrals within the family, new arrivals, and her funeral.

25. Room Reader time-warp

A house stuck at different times reflects equally disjointed occupants. Mind-reading rooms moves things along.

(Song: *Light in the Gloom.)*

26. Desperate DJ

Bibi is a desperate DJ. She needs to turn around a dilapidated flat.

27. The Dog Woman

Reverse anthropomorphism: an aromatherapist smells, dresses, eats and chases cats like her six dogs. She just wants a two-legged lover. (Song: *Waterfall.)*

28. Steve Jobs – L.I.S.A.

Apple products are made for our homes, but Jobs had real problems allowing any furniture in his own homes. He objectified his emotional relationships in Apple designs. Room Reader spots what both Hollywood films missed. (Song: *When Evening Falls.)*

29. Jane Eyre and the sex box

Boy with too big a room (future trouble relating?); sister with poor self-image (future anorexic?); mother with no sex box keys (future patient?) and father with bad attitude. (Song: *Plastic Flower.)*

30. The Cookie Queen

Martha failed according to her family, her school, then the ever-changing media, and became a victim of her size. Hannah reduced her kitchen and cookie-craving without any dieting.

31. Elton John & David Furnish – my heart belongs to Daddy

Elton represents the angst of gay society. Breakthroughs have been made by some of his challenges. Soon, Westerners will drop the term 'gay parents', we'll have so many. (Song: *Amazing Greats.)*

32. The broken (door) knob

A wannabe actor seeking solace in porn has a broken (door) knob, a filthy flat and terrible habits. Hypnotherapy and mind-reading rooms get him connected. (Song: *Full of Theory.)*

33. The Priory Lady

Fat dog overprotects underfed lady in overlarge, underused house.

34. Tracey Emin – My Bed

From teddy bear, hangman's noose to bloody pants, Hannah applies mind-reading rooms to Emin's £2.54m My Bed and upturns all our views on England's so-called smoking, drinking 'slut'.

(Song: *Defiance.)*

35. Porcelain doll

A black woman doesn't know why she's agoraphobic. Hannah realises she's over-identifying with – deifying – white imagery and helps her back to her true colour and culture… freeing her.

(Song: *Never More Than Tonight.)*

36. The fish-man

A successful surveyor destroys his loves and potentially his existence with drink. After a meeting over fish, Hannah – through mind-reading rooms and his environment – starts to turn him round.

Epilogue

The *revolving door of treatment* is often cited as inadequate and leads to relapses. Mind-reading rooms helps us exit that door.

1. Room Reader: our world is our home

I grew up with my teenage parents and two sisters in a volatile, religious home on a council estate in the north west of England. Life wasn't always easy for any of us, and personal space in a maisonette was an issue. As a young child, I played a game to apply to my own space that helped me to secure a modest sense of self. These early techniques would become 'mind-reading rooms'.

I am now a master at reading the minds of humans or animals via the rooms they inhabit. I can mind-read individual items such as the interior of a wardrobe or drawer, a fridge mid-week, handbag, garden, or car. But, to get a consistent pattern of consciousness requires confirmation of those initial observations and that is why mind-reading rooms - including ornaments and pictures - is the most accurate source of information for me. What might take the average person months of analysis will take me minutes. In time, you will be able to do what I can do. We all have the capacity to intuitively read spaces. So, 10 or so years from now, I will seem quite ordinary.

We create little rooms wherever we go. For example, the moment we choose to enter a particular café, we begin to create... we choose a place to sit, arrange our table and chair, put our bag on the side near to the wall, our coat over the back of the chair and our latest book close to where we look forward to placing the coffee. Our office desk most likely has pictures of loved ones or paraphernalia that others overlook but holds a special memory for us. And even our picnics and sports areas are made into temporary personal home-bubbles ... that special bat, the wicker basket, the flowery fabric that becomes the table.

Any mechanic worth paying will arrange his work-tools, oils and rags just as a cook or dentist sets out their environment. And each one is created to make us feel specific things, whether it's a clinical or relaxed space, in- or outside. Our world is a home within a home! Parks and gardens are designed to exercise in, provide comfort or allow reflection. Castles and churches leave us in awe and help us connect with history and religion. But it is what we bring into the space rather than the space itself that creates and re-creates the environment. Each person entering or adding to a space changes the dynamic. Churches are still beautiful, but these days find use as converted apartments. Why?

I believe it is because many of us have stopped providing the vital component, our minds. The message of religion has been supplanted by a bigger brasher voice: the call of consumerism. I am not anti-religious but unless religious organisations can provide ordinary people with practical structures and support there will surely be more interest in apartment-conversions or, worse, extremism. Extreme religious ideas are active; they allow people to participate actively. Sadly, this is often for the wrong reasons.

Numbness creates extremism as people try to shake themselves out of passivity. Our minds are like water, ever-shifting. Therefore, the only thing we can reliably work with is our environments, and to do that requires the mind and the body working actively to perform tasks. When we lose physical engagement, our mind starts to shut down, it becomes less creative and prone to ill-health and depression. So, if your business, school or home isn't functioning in a balanced way, instead of being passive or seeking expensive solutions, you can re-balance the environment using mind-reading rooms.

Mind-reading rooms will allow you to exercise more control over buying and practically transform your environments. Know how to create a seductive or happy space with a few simple changes. Begin to understand how an object can hold immense power over us because we imbue it with memories and feelings; we make it live! By the end of the book, you'll be adept at practising mind-reading rooms. It's also a reflective process, so journals and scrapbooks are encouraged. Mindfulness in space attunes us to greater depths of connection with ourselves, our objects and others. This can only bring us greater understanding and peace of mind.

The business of living can be all-consuming, but it's important to acknowledge the reality of death too, which is not so much the opposite of life but a part of it. Many of us are lucky enough to have shelter, food to eat and our basic needs met. And yet, we often face challenges born of uncertainty. Facing death as some of us do - or all certainly will - can reinforce that sense of uncertainty. Anything can happen to anyone any time, and because we know this, we sometimes adopt patterns of behaviour or thinking in which to seek solace.

But what if we could do away with our craving for certainty? Imagine instead occupying both a literal and figurative space that is healthy and nourishing for yourself and your relationships. Homelife doesn't have to take place around the mundane, the big shop and juggling everyone's TV preferences. Instead, your home can be the place that facilitates the full expression of who you are. Getting to know yourself is the first step.

This is not a fanciful book about dusting ornaments and upcycling objects. Nor is it about Feng Shui or interior design. This is a practical book about the psychology of the home that will help you to engage with and transplant its principles into your own living space, helping you to bring about changes that you might never have predicted.

***

40 years after scrabbling for self-expression in the council house I grew up in, I'd like to pay homage to Mrs. Beeton and her classic *Book of Household Management.* Rather than a book of recipes, cooks, chambermaids and butlers, Room Reader is similar to Mrs Beeton's famous work in that there is a strong societal underpinning to the content. But the real Mrs Beeton had a backstory.

Married at 21, Mrs B did like to keep an immaculate home (although her servants helped a great deal). Brilliant though she was, she drank heavily, raced horses and died at 28 of venereal disease. All this couldn't be further from the matriarchal image that has stood the test of time. Read the iconic 150-year-old book with fresh eyes to observe her social commentary; her thoughts about land and property, her entrepreneurial and original philosophy – all formed against the backdrop of her marriage to a spouse who fraternised with prostitutes. Read between the lines and see that writing about maintaining a 'good' household was partly an effort to keep her husband in it.

Mrs Beeton's book couldn't possibly confront the taboo topics of her day like the syphilis she died from. But were today's on-hand psychological insights available, her book might have looked a little more like this one. Still practical, still concerned with the maintenance and enhancement of the domestic space, but with another dimension to it. Instead, she concealed her difficult reality behind her all-capable domestic image, her recipes for game pies and quivering puddings.

Room Reader uncovers and resolves stories hidden in a space and in the objects contained in that space. In a materially focused, consumption-obsessed climate, it's too easy to feel lost in the gulf between our aspirations for a home and the reality we experience within it. A certain Mrs B would likely have agreed.

The true stories - mainly my clients - collected here encourage a sense of exploration, curiosity and insight into the self through the space we occupy. And mind-reading rooms can be expanded onto our wider living spaces: into our communities, countries and beyond. As Kahil Gibran wrote in The Prophet, 'Your house shall be not an anchor but a mast.'

Mind-reading rooms is a starting point for a journey of personal transformation. It's about gaining a deeper appreciation of what we have and making the small adjustments to make a big difference. As our spaces are the outward projection of our minds, then we need to keep working on them, keep them hygienic and healthy to observe the positive differences that manifest in our everyday lives.

If you're struggling to accept 'the way things are', be that in the local context of the home, or indeed the wider picture of the political and social landscapes, and if you feel that the status quo is maintained by a seemingly immovable system of forces beyond your control, then we must focus on the immediate: the things we can influence and take ownership of through taking action.

Today we spend a lot of time living digitally through our social channels, we often see our spaces either as peripheral to our life or in the context of how many 'Likes' an aspect of it might achieve. But perhaps it's time to live less virtually and to get real again, to occupy the physical wholly, so it becomes somewhere our family and friends want to visit, cook, play, live and share.

We can achieve this by keeping it real, by disassociating ourselves from the pressures of the world that's marketed to us, making us spend on the wrong things for the right reasons: we want to feel better, more integrated, more connected. Too often though, we will make a pricey purchase to enhance a home that does little for it; and our consumer-focused world does a great job of encouraging us to do just that.

As consumerism keeps escalating so does depression and disconnection to ourselves and each other. We have become addicted to buying happiness. That seems to be our only commitment. We justify having enough - even more than enough - but after that, it's just passive consumerism inhibiting opportunities to make a difference to our fellow man and severing instinct to collectively thrive. For example, a woman goes into a fashion store. She sees a dress and thinks: 'Wow, I'd look great in that.' Then she looks at the price tag; it's £75 or £750 depending on the family's finances, and in either case (whilst she has more than enough), she still buys the dress.

She is part of the herd of not-that-happy shoppers lost in a spending spree - moved along with the promise of utopia - in the ever-bigger and more ubiquitous shopping malls. But when she returns from fantasy land with her purchase, the bright lights, the music, the colour, the helpful staff – all within one spectacular space like a modern church – and she rejoins the ordinary, she might not feel so great. Too often, she simply feels guilt and emptiness.

We all like buying nice things, so this book is designed to help you better gauge when you've stepped beyond happiness. Our greatest gift is empathy and, as such, we thrive on interactions not transactions.

Mind-reading rooms allows us to stop buying more than is useful to us. It's a practical approach to transforming our lives by better using our space and the objects within it. Through this, we can begin to understand how an object can hold immense power over us because of the memories and feelings we attribute to it, and how we can ensure we are not owned by the things we own.

***

Although I had the option and privilege to retreat from the capital to embrace a simpler semi-rural life with my partner and four boys, not all of us can up sticks from urban consumer playgrounds to live the good life. So, this book helps us to make the most of what we have, to give us the freedom we crave.

A gentle warning:

You will see from the case studies that big changes can take place for those who apply and respond to mind-reading rooms techniques. But be aware, even when you feel it's all falling into place, you are nevertheless going through a transition which can mean an aspect of yourself may try to hold on – fearful and uncertain of the unknown.

My own move to Devon from London was embraced by my children, but it also cast a light on the space within my relationship that had been consumed by identifications that were part of my 20 years in London: my favourite little Turkish café and the family who owns it, the local swimming pool, the friends I met, and coming back home to my flat surrounded by neighbours who knew me well. Now, my partner and I were fully involved in every aspect of the other's life, and aspects of ourselves we might have been distracted from before were amplified in the new-found peace we'd discovered.

If you experience the opportunity to engage with new aspects of yourself or those closest to you, be kind. Don't rush to force your new space to work; allow your new space to slowly and organically become your home. Grow into it, together if you can. Some changes come with things you cannot leave behind but have to evolve instead.

Maintain the dynamism as you and your family adjust together. Home is a process not a finished product. Get everyone involved in that process by joining in with the chores, the design choices, the decoration, the organisation. Invite nature into your home along with friends to make it a space you can fill with warmth rather than things, with happy memories rather than unspoken or unfelt feelings.

Another warning:

It's possible you don't yet know who you are. Mind-reading rooms can draw your attention to this sometimes-unnerving reality. After all, you have become this person over many years. But be reassured that this person you 'are' is not fixed. You can take the best aspects of yourself forward into new phases like those of the clients in these case studies.

One last warning:

When you undertake the process of mind-reading rooms and observe its impact, be prepared to feel differently about the wider world. As a parent, I am conscious of the involvement of the state in our home lives. Control systems exist that minimise individual decision-making, reducing our personal freedom about the best way to run our lives, a simple example being when to have a holiday during the school year. The threat of prison or a fine seems disproportionate in return for the modest wish to take charge of basic decisions, such as when to rest; and schools are being weaponised to enforce these arbitrary decisions.

This tip of the iceberg hints at a society that's disconnected and divided and lacking empathy and collaboration to accommodate the challenges of diverse home lives. We need a deeper communication. And, when the vast might of the state seems tone-deaf, that communication begins in our homes and moves outwards from there.

Our place in spaces:

Look into a shop window after closing, or step inside a lonely bar. Compare this with a packed-out gig and its buzzing atmosphere and remember that it's the collective that empowers the artist on stage. Alone they might be great, but it's the crowd that elevates them. The superstar disappears when we no longer give them our magic. On the other hand, we might wander amongst the graves in a churchyard, or climb a mountain solo and in those moments of quiet our consciousness - our mind - comes to those spaces, bringing the atmosphere to life.

There is a lady who has a kilim rug. The rug had been in her family a century and had witnessed wars in Sarajevo, loss, recovery and refuge in another country. The kilim rug contained the history of a whole family as well as that of a country. Now the rug lies on the floor of a London flat. Its owner regards it with deep emotion and, wherever she places it, that space becomes sacred.

A house in Mauritius has an old wooden larder filled with dry foods. The century-old darkened bark of the larder door has the energetic signature of a family imprinted on it. The newspaper sheets pasted on its shelves document its history, connecting the visitor with the family and time it was first there. The connection with the practicality of the space and the love for it is still palpable, poignant, precious, and will surely last another 100 years.

Mind-reading rooms prefers handmade furniture and homemade crafts because simplicity and high engagement with objects are preferable to poorly-made, easy-to-dispense-with items. You'll notice a bias towards 'natural cleaning' over the use of toxic chemicals, and mindful decluttering as opposed to ruthless and unsentimental clear-outs. Big purges leave emotional voids that feel as though they need to be immediately filled up with more acquisitions. So, we apply mindfulness and practicality in spaces designed by you and for you.

Room Reader will help you access stories that get you observing things in ways you hadn't before. It may encourage you to make the simple gesture of adding a sunflower to your office desk, or transform the first day back at school from misery Monday to merry Monday.

Britain's first astronaut on the International Space Station, Tim Peake, was asked on radio what advice he'd been given by other astronauts. They said: "Don't take pictures. Don't look at life through a lens. Enjoy the moments. Appreciate the incredible reality." You'll find the incredibleness of your own life through Room Reader stories.

You will soon be inviting your friends (Roomies) to help you deep-clean your room in exchange for helping them clean out their bike shed; creating good house rules at home, work or school that people want to follow; or saving money, not by being miserable or stingy, but by being a mindful advocate of better living standards. Room Reader comments on the wider social implications of environments because we must have the freedom to create our environments inside and out. I'll share my personal and professional experience. You'll decide what works.

A couple of Room Reader stories are combined cases but all are essentially true; some (not all) names have been changed to protect anonymity. Room Reader allows Roomies to ask questions and discuss at a 'safe distance' with the book utilising the concept of ornaments and furniture as a way of addressing discord or creating something new.

The album *Hannah's Roomies* - download on iTunes or Amazon - can accompany many Room Reader stories, augmenting your reading with aural stimulus from across genres. Music helps us engage with the intuitive aspects of the stories, and to be receptive to each subject's unique challenges. (Listen to this chapter's song *Commitment.)*

2. What is mind-reading rooms?

Mind-reading rooms is a new creative medium and holistic approach to make practical changes to your space that will shift imbalance in the mind of the individual and/or the whole family. Feng Shui (which originated in Chinese religion and culture), and Vastu Shastra (from India) are both based on magnetic fields and rituals. In contrast, Room Reader (and therefore mind-reading rooms) is English and created on a metaphysical basis. Room Reader examines the nature of our reality, including the relationship between mind and matter. Mind-reading rooms influences mind and matter to effect transformation of the overall consciousness. This means that moving people in their space (home, school or even public area) whilst adding or changing objects – a bed, a picture or even a person – has a collective benefit on everyone who lives there. Mind-reading rooms can be applied to any space as long as it has a metaphysical basis. In other words, the space must have two elements: mind and matter.

Mind-reading rooms evolves with time and culture. Unlike feng-shui or a specific religion, it is always up-to-the-minute because it is created and re-created by those who practise it. Nothing is fixed, everything is in process. This philosophy is based on the knowledge that transience is the truth. Humans like to fix and confirm right and wrong. But the reality is in the grey areas of history, knowledge and people. Transience makes it OK to make mistakes and try out new things. Mind-reading rooms accommodates the transient nature of things.

Your understanding will grow by engaging with the structures and stories in the book. Children and teens can develop new interests and life skills as a result of practising mind-reading rooms. My greatest wish is that all types of people practise for – and with – each other freely.

A Roomie group is formed by three people as a minimum. Anybody can set one up and you might even consider asking your community centre, library, school or health centre to support you. You don't need a home to join one. Introduce a Roomie group to an existing group like a Women's Institute or simply start your own.

Room Reader is also available for use in schools in the UK and Europe as well as similar programmes worldwide. So, you can support your teenagers by setting up a Roomie group for parents in your schools or at home. 'Life Skills' is a broad subject and we believe that parents can support teenagers – in tandem with a school programme – by mind-reading rooms. It can help parents and their kids to be on the same page.

You do not have to agree with everything in the book. I'd be amazed if you did. The aim is to create empathy for each other with or without agreement and with lots of activities that generate support networks. I have captured stories from people I have helped over the last 10 years. These stories will give you some understanding of how others are living and how their lives have translated into their homes. Start by discussing stories in your Roomie group. The book will increase your knowledge and level of expertise over time from the early chapters right through to gaining a high level of understanding and application by the end.

Room Reader can provide strong structures for you to apply mind-reading rooms in an adult or teenage group setting. Finally, a scrapbook 'n journal you make invites you to doodle and stick in what inspires you about your own home or setting.

You will have opportunities to practise mind-reading rooms individually and with your Roomies. Create a simple, inviting poster to put up around your community centre/library/doctor's practice and local area. Put on your contact details and set a start-date to encourage people to join your group.

If you have already read the book and begun to apply mind-reading rooms, you may want to invite me to lead an advanced programme in mind-reading rooms. You may have a specific group of people you want to aim your Room Reading group at, like young families or LGBT parents, teenagers, or families dealing with addiction. I can work with practitioners making mind-reading rooms fun and life-changing for those in it. And, of course, you will find scrapbooking an easy way of putting your ideas to paper. Transforming your own space is the start, then your Room Reading group will help to transform a disused piece of land or an estate that has a poor social record because you and your group will see possibilities in everything around you. When you do, share your ongoing stories/pictures with me on

info at roomreader dot com (Put 'STORY' in the Subject line.)

The original pop album **Hannah's Roomies** provides a song for many of the stories. You should play the song at the end of the chapter as a reflective or complementary process. When a chapter does not specify a song, choose your own.

The **scrapbook 'n journal** is bought or made by you to use to describe or share emotions and ideas for your spaces. You can easily note Room Plans and House Rules inside, too. Fill it with inspiring thoughts and images. This is helped by collecting memories and writing about or drawing them to bridge the gap between the past, present or future. Journals can also assist in manifesting work or relationships. Collect images of your ideal partner or workplace and create activities to make your life and love happen in your space. Create your space to encourage the changes you want, sooner rather than later.

A **Room Plan** is a plan of action created by three people who each take on a role: one person is the home-dweller (the client), the second either takes a photo or sketches each room to be transformed; the third will apply the principles of mind-reading rooms, i.e. the subtle process of utilising the space and objects to deal with or re-balance the mind. Roles can be shared. At the end of gathering the evidence from the client and the space, a Room Plan for each space is written-up ready to action. The Room Plan can be framed within - can take - a single week or a whole year of light- and deep-cleaning. The Roomies decide the breadth and depth of the Room Plan. Room Plans can also be created for schools or estates, any place you're ready to transform.

Key Themes are located at the start of most of the stories. These are designed so you can find stories in the book that specifically relate, or are similar, to your issues.

Key Actions are noted at the end of most stories to provide a simplified list of activities transform that (or a similar) environment.

The Housekeeper is an age-old name that lends itself to the application of a Room Plan. It allows for both non-experts and experts to manage domestic cleaning duties, along with defining the deep-cleaning needs advised within the Room Plan.

A **Roomie** is a person who practises mind-reading rooms as an individual.

A **Roomie group** is a minimum of three friends or family Roomies who help each other mind-read and plan to make changes to each other's homes.

A **Room Reading group** is a larger group of Roomies that discusses - in a more formal setting - the book's mind-reading themes, and create action plans.

All three of the above practise mind-reading rooms. It's just that the more people involved the more interesting it gets!

House Rules must be created by those living or working in shared spaces, or alone. Such rules will keep you to keep on top of simple cleaning duties and enable you to keep an order that will help you lead a healthier, calmer lifestyle.

Deep-Cleaning is a step-by-step plan to help you. The plan can be used to deep-clean any space in the home.

Our homes are largely stuffed with dusty unworn items, sticky coated ornaments, dusty paintwork, moths and more! I felt helpless tackling this work on my own! Even knowing the health issues described above, frankly, I didn't want to do all that hard graft. I'd rather go to the gym for a work-out than sweat-it-out at home. I Googled specialists in proper cleaning but only found thousands of domestic services, toxic moth-removal services and a few professing to do more detailed work who – when I questioned them – were not that convincing.

I had to do this myself. I needed to spend much more time, use fewer or non-toxic cleaning products and ideally create a team and a detailed system. For my first Room Plan, I roped in a few reluctant individuals on the promise that the activity would provide them with a systematic deep-clean of any room in their home in exchange for help with my kitchen. What would have taken me more than a day on my own, took three people just four hours each. The results were amazing, which they would not have been had only one person attempted the task. We cleared a moth-infestation by emptying every single cupboard and drawer, discarding out-of-date or open products, cleaning in detail and later – to ensure no further infestations – I put pheromone stickers in cupboards to catch male moths and stop them breeding.

The deep-cleaning system I have created has been tried and tested a thousand times, so you can be sure it works! Once we had tackled the kitchen, my Roomies did one of the other's bedrooms. It took around three months of scheduling Room Plans with each other. The results were that three homes had a thorough deep-clean, we all had fun, and we used organic or natural homemade cleaning products, which we know is better for our immediate and long-term health and our children's health as organic or natural products will not damage the seas, rivers, land or atmosphere. It cost us only the time taken to implement the deep-clean in each space.

You can adapt the following structure to any room. Now look around you and start enrolling two friends into a systematic deep-cleaning swap of each other's homes. You'll create Roomies for life!

Deep Cleaning Structure:

Three Roomies

A magnifying glass

A large broom

A bin bag full of lint-free cloth

A bowl or bucket of hot water

Gloves and aprons

At least one stepladder

A disposable paper mop & bucket for wooden or tiled floors

A rented carpet shampoo machine if carpets need shampooing.

LDC super degreaser (used to clean oil from 25,000 penguins in South Africa) an all-purpose soap for damp-cleaning – or another mild soap.

Dry cloth

Glass cleaner

A creamy non-toxic polish for wood

Two lambs-wool sticks for cleaning high, low & behind furniture

Two vacuum cleaners with HEPA filters

A range of lavender or cedarwood sachets

Scented anti-moth drawer-liners

Clean bedding

Big plastic bags to take unwanted items to charity

One recycle bag for each drawer and one per wardrobe

How to do it -- Preparation:

Open windows to let in fresh air and sunlight.

Remove existing bedding, curtains and nets if laundering.

Open drawers one by one and remove any worn, small or no longer required items to a recycle bag.

Open the wardrobes and remove any item not worn for more than a year (it's a dust hazard and becomes a moth- and/or beetle-home).

Bag wanted items to return after the clean (one bag per drawer or wardrobe).

Roll up rugs and take them outside if you have outside space. If not, put to one side.

Move the mattress. You will need two people to take it off the bed and outside, or if not, prop it up in the middle of the bed or against a wall near an open window for at least one hour in the sun.

Move the bed if it is against a wall.

Carry out bedbug and moth-lava inspections using the magnifying glass around the edges of the base of the bed, inside corners of drawers and the tops of cupboards.

Inspect clothes not recently cleaned as they are attracted to proteins in sweat, and lava may be found there.

Any infested items will need to be put in the freezer and/or washed in very hot or very cold temperatures, or dry-cleaned.

Healthy mattresses require regular turning and careful vacuuming.

Top-down cleaning:

Two people vacuum all edges and inside of the room and inside empty drawers and wardrobes.

Each person then cleans inside and out from the highest point.

Only use a damp cloth for wiping wardrobes and drawers, leave them open to dry.

One person cleans the light-fitting and then the smaller walls and everything on them and inside such as drawers and shelves.

Another person cleans wardrobes from the top and if possible pull out to clean behind.

Hold the spine of books open to the centre and gently knock – tap on sill – near an open window.

A third person will usually clean all the paintwork with a damp cloth and light soapy water, then the window frames and the glass with a clean dry cloth and glass cleaner.

Don't forget light-switches, especially around the actual switch and the sockets, but handle with care - no damp cloth, only a light spray onto a dry clean cloth.

Bed frame to be damp-cleaned, include legs, base & headboard.

Once all paintwork, windows and furniture have been damp-cleaned, vacuum around the whole edge of room before the centre.

If you do not want to clean curtains, vacuum down the sides, the tops of the hems insides and front and backs.

Do not shampoo carpets until the end of the cleaning.

Mirrors and picture frames must be held in place for careful cleaning, gently clean backs and sides with the lambs-wool stick.

Only use a completely clean dry cloth when polishing glass.

Frequently replace dirty cloths; put used ones in a cloth bag.

Never shake your cloth!

Rugs ideally can be beaten over a garden line and left to rest.

Once the furniture is fully dry, polish with a clean dry cloth.

Use aromatherapy oil-infused drawer liners to repel moths.

Polish or shampoo the floors depending on the surface type.

Do not wet-clean under beds with less than three inches above the floor as this will result in mould problems.

Always clean around the edges of furniture so there are no marks.

If moving items, ensure carpet is fully dry before returning them.

Polish wooden floors by hand using a circular motion or, if you have a floor polish machine, use this.

If you have only one set of nets and/or curtains, plan to drop and pick up from a dry cleaner in one day.

Afterwards: when everything is back in place and the bed made up, put scented drawer liners and lavender or cedar-wood sachets in drawers, scented hangers in wardrobes, and – after a gentle shake at an open window to ensure pest-free – return clothes into drawers and wardrobes.

3. Room Plans

You may now be forming your own Room Plan. This could start via other existing groups such as book-reading clubs or social networks. A Roomie group can evolve into bigger groups. The underlying theme for all Room Plans is 'movement of space' delivered with generosity. Generosity is an artform that creates a powerful energy within your space. The level of sharing and give and take, kindness and acceptance, between Roomies will grow. And if anything falls off track, generosity will return you or your friend back to the Plan. Movement of space need not be more than the removal of dust from the space, it can be that subtle! It's still mind-reading rooms; the results of your endeavours must not be underestimated.

Share the stories and themes in this book, discuss the themes with each other and how you could relate it to your home. Learn from other people's home management tips, especially the use of natural cleaning products. That is always a good starting point for a Room Plan.

Discuss buying habits and products, how you currently manage the cleaning of your home and whether it's enough. You can talk about making things for your home and creating cleaning schedules for yourself or your domestic cleaner. Women are often expected to know exactly how to manage their homes, but few of us are born with the skills required to run our homes efficiently.

Inviting Roomies to create a Room Plan is a step towards enjoying the benefits of mind-reading rooms. Once you understand the key themes and key actions in our stories, you are ready to have a go with your own and others' homes.

At the most basic level, all three of you provide each other with deep-cleaning (remember, you can adapt this to any room or space in the house). Once you have each done three deep-cleans – one for each other – you can easily move on to decluttering, moth-proofing and, at the highest level, changing or moving items and rooms. It can also evolve into a furniture-swapping system; a buying-group for quality items identified by the Roomies – and more! If you work with others, you can help transform your spaces to tackle emotional imbalance. No-one has the perfect life but, armed with mind-reading rooms, you can make informed choices and assist others in doing the same. Write-up your three case histories and share the information with your Roomies.

Setting up a Room Plan:

You will need to take photographs or roughly sketch the room, so don't forget your camera. You will also need to bring a small stepladder, a pen, pencil and notebook, a magnifying glass if your 'client' has indicated a moth problem, small stickers to identify drawers that need decluttering, and one pair of white cotton gloves for checking dust levels with a light-fingered touch. One of you will be the client, the other two will be creating the Room Plan. The Room Plan lists the recommended actions for each room and communal space in the client's home.

You must all agree in advance how you will manage the information you gather. You may decide to keep your Room Plans confidential between the three Roomies; this would include any conversations and disclosures that may be sensitive to your client. Also, decide in advance who can access the photos and for how long. You can take photos at the end of your completed Room Plan and make a project album for your client to keep online. Make it non-downloadable with access via a password known only to your Roomies. Also, decide whether you're going to do the deep-cleaning, declutter and changes yourselves or hire a team of three cleaners. If you do hire cleaners, you will need to give them careful direction otherwise you'll not get the results you want. Agree how many rooms you're going to transform. Each of you choose one room – a room that really needs a movement of space – then see how you all get on. You'll need around three sessions; one to gather your evidence, a second to review and make a Room Plan for that room, and a third session of three to five hours to transform that space. Don't ever rush. If you break for lunch, it's a day's work for three people in each room. And seek expert advice on any medical issues.

Use eBay to sell unwanted items and work together to identify alternatives to those needing replacement. When replacing items, you need to be clear on what the replaced item is going to look and feel like. You also want to have a good idea of the size of the new item, 'beautiful but too big' won't work! Anyway, mind-reading rooms isn't about how things look to you, but how they impact the 'client' and others in that space. Always prioritise your 'client' and the people who live there: Does this object work for them?

I was once invited to do a photo-analysis of a fellow guest's bathroom live on Soho Radio. The owner had a bedside cabinet under his sink. His friends said it should go because it didn't look right.

However, it allowed him to put books on top just next to the loo for him to read, and the bedside cabinet (neatly under the sink, remember) did not obstruct the sink. To his delight, I disagreed with his friends because it's his home and it makes his life more enjoyable. Overall the item was in balance with that client. So, who would I be to come along and tell him he was wrong!

Ask people to post unwanted items or swap in your Roomie group. Because mind-reading rooms is a transformational medium, encourage people to give and take items free of charge within your group. Find Roomies who will move the item from giver to given. Your generosity will create an awesome Roomie group and many Room Plans.

Who can join your Roomie group? Anyone who wants a transformed space! Children can be involved as long as parents agree. In fact, I can see children forming their own team for a Room Plan. They will need a parent to assist them with agreeing on replacing or helping to move objects and making requests of Roomie participants. If you're buying new items, allow delivery time as you decide dates for your Room Plan.

When you take your photo/sketch of each room, start from the entrance – the threshold – of the space. Try to capture the whole space. Stop here for a few minutes. Observe the feel of the space. Write your first impression of the space as a whole before entering and defining individual objects and potential issues. Upon entering you can now inspect individual or group items such as a three-piece suite or a cabinet filled with items, pictures, beds and so on. Always ask your client if you can open every drawer and cupboard so you may inspect them. If you don't want to take pictures, sketch items and note issues found in each room between you both.

At this stage, the client usually chats with us as we go about our business. All this time I will (and so should you) be listening carefully to what they say is the problem. What is missing or needs moving? Who else lives in the space and how may they be affected by the presentation of both the home's communal areas and their own space? Remember to include pets in assessments.

Identify clutter-problems by:

Checking if the drawers open with ease or whether they are crammed. Kitchens might be packed out with cutlery or foodstuff. Do they have items squashed under beds? What are these items? Make notes and take photos.

You do not have to give an analysis whilst in the home. Simply ask questions, listen and observe the current use of the space. Does the space flow around and under objects? Is furniture well-made and useful (neither too big nor too small for its purpose)? You might make suggestions or observations to see how the client reacts. Most clients will know what is required and having two people assist empowers them to take action.

Is the room overall in or out of balance? For example, a room with a sofa that is too big to allow comfortable access to the space is clearly out of balance. Or, if your client has a dust-mite allergy and the room is filled with clothes, this is an imbalance that can be rectified by reducing and ordering the items in the space.

Have you identified any overbearing beds, rickety cupboards, doors that don't shut, strong pictures or ornaments encouraging a particular state of mind or physical reaction, cupboards with out-of-date items, fridges with filthy seals, kitchen knives that don't cut, or lots of irritant products that may be linked with skin conditions? Identify the service levels in each room: deep-clean alone or deep-clean and mindfully declutter. Count how many drawers or rails or shelves you want decluttering and put the number next to the room. You can put a little sticker on those drawers/shelves/rails that need sorting or ordering.

When you're organising clothes, repair and clean them before folding or hanging them carefully. You may find a Roomie who can lead workshops on mending clothes. Put them into colours and seasons, storing items if they are not needed. For example, summer clothes can be packed away during the winter season. Place these clothes in sealed containers, with some lovely anti-moth aromatherapy cards. This helps you enjoy your clothes for more years. When it's time to get them out, you won't have seen them for months. Limit how many of your stored gifts you open to one per week. As you hold the container, it will be like you have just purchased a wonderful fragrant gift with a bonus sweet sense of anticipation at each personal mini-opening-ceremony! The longer-term satisfaction you will get from these practices is self-confidence, and money in the bank for bigger dreams.

Antiques or vintage items of clothes and furniture may need to be expertly valued if you're not giving them away for free. Contact an auction house.

Here is an example of an image that impacted a communal space: As I walked down the stairs through a communal hallway where I lived, a matchstick-man painting by L.S. Lowry in the hallway was the first image I saw each morning. The painting showed an overcast day enveloping people huddled over walking towards the factory with smog rising from chimneys in the background. What a depressing start to the day. I soon persuaded my neighbours to replace it with a beautiful sunflower. I assure you the energy in the hallway shifted. The people living in that space became friendlier and I looked forward to seeing the big yellow sunflower instead of the depressed factory workers.

I have seen some desperately negative paintings, prints and ornaments that have impacted whole families in the home. I recommend images of real animals or people, beautiful or inspiring buildings, outdoor or indoor scenes that depict calm, joy, nostalgia and togetherness; colourful flowers, seas or nature and images that inspire you to action.

After all the evidence is gathered, we start to research any particular issues the people in the home may be facing, then we create a Room Plan. The Room Plan is exactly what it says: a detailed recommendation for every room in the house. It may also contain specific advice on health issues with recommendations of particular therapists or treatments. It sets out in detail what we think is required to shift the space and all those who live there. You will see I often recommend activities at the end of the Room Plan. Activities are designed to move the person or persons to take account of current health and well-being tips. Always seek medical advice if the person is in any doubt before embarking on any activity.

I recall running around the top of a high hill, testing myself physically and mentally. For you, this could be doing less or doing more, or doing something new. It often involves activity with a partner, too.

The Room Plan is empowering. It provides choice, breaks down issues and allows the customer to tackle the issues themselves or bring in experts to tackle them on their behalf. No two Room Plans are the same. The advice may vary a lot depending on the needs of that individual or family. To give you an idea of what we might suggest, I am setting out some real Room Plans for you. You will see some oft-repeated advice and some unique advice only once.

The level of involvement can be simplistic (reading and relating to the story), active (applying principles from the stories), or interactive (setting up a Roomie group). From there, it will depend on the group. They might take on the prescribed roles within a Room of three: the first analyses the space, a second photographs or sketches the space, and a third is the client. All three then create a Room Plan. The Room Plan can be as detailed as the mind-reading rooms procedures set out in the book, or the plan might simply involve transforming one's space with a few objects being added or removed. A Room Plan can be simplified or partially actioned by the group. A Roomie may want to swap daily chores with another Roomie.

If budget allows, some of the Room Plan can be managed by paid staff and the Roomies will simply create and oversee parts of it. In this initial Room Plan, we are not so concerned with the case-analysis (as we are in the main stories), but in a more practical application of mind-reading rooms to create a year-long plan of deep and lighter cleaning with staff, by yourself, or ideally with Roomies and family.

Cecily and Matt are art collectors and dealers with galleries in the UK and USA. They live in a fantastic flat in south London with their two daughters. Their home needed deep-cleaning and ordering, especially around clothes-management, with some moth-removal and advice on housekeeping schedules. This was their Room Plan:

Dear Cecily and Matt,

The 'dream housekeeper' you mentioned, well, I recommend she comes three times a week, each for three or four-hour sessions. Plus, you should have one session extra a month to re-stock your household items and to do any online shopping such as for underwear, towels or bedding.

I suggest the hours are 8.30 am to 11.30am Mon, Wed, Thurs plus one Sat or Sun a month 9am -12am.

Housekeeper Schedule:

The housekeeper must be given a run-through of the expected service.

Mon: Collect all rubbish and replace bin bags or vacuum bags, vacuum throughout, emphasise washing clothes with checking of labels to ensure temperature and cycle are correct. The bathrooms and cat litter will also be cleaned. We can identify a hair-remover tool for your plugholes.

Wed: Collect all rubbish and replace bin bags, vacuum throughout. Prioritise ironing clothes and cleaning living room and kitchen.

Thurs: Collect all rubbish and replace bin bags. Vacuum throughout, prioritise changing bedding, cleaning bedrooms, office and cat litter.

1 weekend a month – Sat or Sun 9.15am to 12.15am – clean hallway and windows inside, place orders for shopping basics and other items like vacuum bags, dishwasher filters, light bulbs etc.

Cecily & husband:

Meditation and life-coaching for the kids.

The children to go to bed at allocated times whenever possible.

Other childcare… I would have a qualified babysitter at nights so that you and your husband can go out. Or a housekeeper that can babysit and prepare a simple meal when needed.

Deep-cleaning and declutter. We recommend a 3 - 6 monthly deep-clean of one or two rooms all the year when you're away or around.

Living room/dining room and kitchen deep-clean and declutter x 15 shelves x 25 drawers. Paintings can be taken down by two people and cleaned behind.

The piano needs cleaning inside twice a year by your piano cleaner. We will polish all areas of the outside.

Rafters and lights: we will clean as high as we can with a long ladder and lambs-wool sticks plus your telescopic poles (throughout the flat).

Office deep-clean and declutter x 3 shelves, x 2 drawers.

A Bathroom deep-clean and declutter x 6 shelves, x 6 drawers.

Other Bathroom deep-clean and declutter x 4 shelves, x 2 drawers.

A Bedroom deep-clean and declutter x 5 drawers, x 10 shelves.

A Bedroom deep-clean add declutter x 4 shelves, x 6 drawers.

Hallways deep-clean includes side hallway next to Jemma and Mace's room.

Rugs/carpets each deep-clean using organic compounds x 3.

Deep-cleaning is a meticulous clean of all areas we can see and reach, inside and out. This includes paintwork, doors, upholstery, floors and windows inside.

Mattresses can be turned, vacuumed and bed linen changed if needed.

Declutter of any drawers or wardrobe: this service can include simply folding or sorting out what you do and don't want or ordering to manage clothes by colour, style or season.

Identify the service levels in each room: deep-clean alone or deep-clean and declutter. Count how many drawers or rails or shelves you want decluttering and put the number next to the room. You can put a little sticker on those drawers/shelves/rails that need sorting or ordering.

The moth-pack includes scented drawer-liners fitted by us for the whole flat, a spray you can keep to refresh upholstery, little cards infused with oils, and cards with ribbon ties that can be added to hangers. All these smell horrible to moths but great to us and can be purchased online.

Use water filters for proper hydration (oxygenated water filters fitted for the whole flat) then you can simply fill a bottle. For a small fee, they can change cartridges and ensure the system is kept in good order. (I can arrange this or you can go direct.)

Organic Juicer. Twin gear juicers are excellent. Juice organic carrots and apples daily for the whole family or get the housekeeper to do it every other day.

Juicing with a cold-press juicer will help your family get a fresh supply of vitamins. Twin- or single-gear juicers beat masticating juicers; masticaters have bigger engines which heat the elements & destroy vitamin content.

You asked me whether organic food is better for you. I remember saying 'yes' simply because I know it doesn't have the carcinogenic pesticides and – in meat – steroids that non-organic foods do. (You inspired me to learn that it's not only kinder on the soil or on animals. Organic is kinder to us at the top of the food chain, where toxic deposits remain - have nowhere to go - causing cancer and other degenerative problems.) Interestingly, soilassociation dot org quotes Nottingham University's 2013 study – the biggest of its kind – which proves beyond doubt that organic is not just less dangerous, but far more nutritious than non-organic.

So, eat less meat and make it organic or locally farmed produce where methods are less intensive (reliant on chemicals). Eat salads, sprouting vegetables, soups and gluten / wheat-free bread whenever you can.

Family to have at least one planned outing a month.

Parents to have allocated time with the children according to a written timetable. Time allocated must be on at least four occasions a week 1- 2 hrs for each child or both together. This can include painting, messy play, reading, bath time, dressing or cooking.

One of these sessions must be outdoors at a local park or soft-play area. Parents to have at least one class a week outside the home, e.g. life drawing, yoga, group meditation, cooking, etc (these kinds of arrangements may already be in place).

Family coaching session once a month: I think it would be great to have someone popping in for an hour to review the month with you all.

Clothing/Storage/Repairs:

I noted the family likes clothes! OK, just note though that more clothes increase the likelihood of moths. We recommend each family member has around 8-10 base items; these can include trousers, dresses, skirts, suits, jackets. Two coats, one winter and one raincoat per person. 6 pairs of shoes, includes one pair of trainers, one pair of boots, slippers or flats, smart shoes x3; 8-10 underwear, vests or bras. One tracksuit, one swimsuit or bikini.

Buy seasonal packaging or arrange help to store clothes not in regular use, outside of the home. (You can also have an online wardrobe storage service for the whole family from Total Wardrobe). They also repair items by hand and can deliver selected items as and when you require them.

I hope that all this helps. If you need anything further, I'm here. And once I know exactly, I will split the job up with some dates for each bit.

Yours, Hannah

A Room Plan for another family of entrepreneurs with a challenging health issue was for Janice who lives in north London with her two children and DJ husband. Remember, if budget allows, some of the

Room Plan will be managed by paid staff and/or the Roomies will create and oversee it.

Janice wanted help to sound and draught-proof the dusty converted church that her family loved to live and work in. They spend half a year in Australia and are thinking about moving for the health of their eldest child, Clarissa.

You will see some advice is the same, but many parts of this Room Plan are specific to our client. Don't be fooled into thinking 'one size fits all' but see that we have some general principles that you can adapt for your Room Plans.

Dear Janice,

I recommend you have a housekeeper three times a week, each time for three hours. Plus, you should have one session extra a month to re-stock your household items and any other online shopping such as underwear, towels or bedding; this will allow more time for you and baby on weekdays.

I suggest the hours are 7.30 am to 10.30am Mon, Wed, Fri plus one Sat or Sun a month 9am -12am.

Housekeeper Schedule:

The housekeeper must be given a run-through of the expected service.

Mon: Collect all rubbish and replace bin bags or vacuum bags, vacuum throughout, prioritise washing clothes with careful checking of labels to ensure temperature and cycle is correct. The bathrooms will also be cleaned.

Wed: Collect all rubbish, replace bin bags, vacuum throughout, emphasise ironing dry clothes and cleaning the living room.

Fri: Collect all rubbish and replace bin bags. Vacuum throughout, emphasise changing bedding and cleaning bedrooms and music studio.

1 weekend a month – Sat or Sun 9.15am to 12.15am – clean prams and hallway, place orders for home-delivery services and

other requested items. Vaccum bags, dishwasher filters, light bulbs etc.

The bathroom in Clarissa's room needs to be changed into a utility space. I choose this room because its outside window ensures air for drying hanging clothes. The dryer, washing machine, ironing board and iron can all go in.

You can buy some hanging lines, install a linen cupboard for towels, bedding and retain the bulk of medicines in this room. The room can be locked to ensure child safety. Ironing can be done in this room. Put in a large sink for scrubbing dirty items and retain the loo.

Respite care for Clarissa and Janice:

Even though Clarissa is now at school you could both do with a week every three months when you're off duty. Have you ever had this? Could you get it from the council? The Children's Respite Trust provide help with building a case for you to get this care and may also provide the actual care. I found many providers of short-term respite (e.g. a week) and, depending on your finances, I think it's essential that you put this in place within four weeks.

Janice:

Meditation - home visit. And life-coaching.

Living room of a converted church.

Fill in the remaining gaps to the ceiling with soundproofed insulation. You won't lose any of the character and it will reduce the dust levels and decrease the disturbing noise. And then you can add some warmth with wallpaper or paints.

The white units stretching along the far back wall should be re-used for the sidewall and to extend the kitchen. A new sink needs to be fitted at the window. More cupboards for more food stocks will make life easier. I would move the table to where the white cupboards are now (along the back wall but with some space). Display fresh flowers weekly on this table with lots of bright fun colours (fire-colours: orange, yellow and red).

Does Milo cook? I'd like to see him cooking for you and friends at least once every six weeks and you sitting back with a dress you don't normally wear and a glass of wine. Milo and you arrange at least two dates a month where you both go out alone.

Clarissa – medical history:

Write a dated history of Clarissa. Do five copies, hand over as and when asked to recount by medical experts. Review monthly, update when necessary.

Music studio - enclose this space fully I would like this space to be boarded from the front (when the new window is put in). I don't think it will work as a bedroom as you're both too far away from the bathroom and kids.

Does Milo have a work schedule? If not, he could create a rough one so he's left undisturbed then, at allocated times, he can assist with Sam or make lunch.

The timetable can be displayed (with space to add your requests).

A door to the music studio needs to be added, whether it's sliding, fabric or even fine beads.

Allocate a time for you and Milo to discuss and create the next week's schedule, even if you're going to most of the medical appointments. Knowing Milo is with you to discuss is always nice.

Future homes to explore: Australia – since you go there anyway – is good, or any location where Clarissa can receive a high level of care that supports her development and that of the family.

A natural environment will help take the pressure of the airborne toxicity of city living. One day you may find a balance between even "Clarissa's great school" and other needs such as warm clean air and beaches. It may not work now, but in the future, it may be perfect, so keep exploring options and share with others, go and look at some bungalows near the seaside not far from London (have you ever been to Margate?) or visit Australia soon. You don't have to move but you must identify all your choices.

The two children have a great relationship, but Clarissa can get jealous of Sam. I'd like to see Sam sharing a room with his sister, it gets him out of mummy and daddy's room and Clarissa will be less anxious knowing Sam gets to sleep with her (rather than you two while she is on her own).

Neither of the children should be encouraged to sleep with mummy and daddy. You two are great and you both need an intimate space for love. You do more than most other parents already, so ensure your time is sacred.

Only if one or the other is sick over and above the normal should you be sharing a bed or letting them share with you.

Your bedroom and the family bathroom. If you take my advice on sleeping arrangements, keep the en-suite family bathroom (it is the biggest). But what if you and Milo moved into Clarissa's room and the kids went into your room with the en-suite?

Bathroom in the hallway:

Keep it, it maintains your privacy, it's handy for the many necessary visitors to see Clarissa and has them in identified spaces.

Grandparents and Janice's Mother monthly rota:

I suggest that the three of them stay at the flat together at least one weekend a month so you can join Milo for the whole weekend DJing. The three of them can manage the two children. Ensure they create a rota so that they know who is doing what and when, who is cooking, shopping and so on.

The second weekend just you and your mum. Third weekend, just you and Milo's parents. Your fourth weekend you will have the housekeeper and if needed other outside help. Please talk to them about my proposal, you have been doing it all for far too long and it's time to put in some structures to help all the family.

The children to go to bed at allocated times whenever possible.

Other childcare:

If Clarissa is at school weekdays I would have a babysitter at nights so that you and Milo can go out and have some exercise classes or social life. The housekeeper can also babysit and prepare a simple meal. Long haul trips (holidays) may require extra help that could be provided by the babysitter or a close relative (your mum).

Deep-cleaning and declutter:

We would recommend three-six monthly deep-clean of one or two rooms all year round.

Living room and kitchen deep-clean:

Rafters we will clean as high as we can with a long ladder and lambs-wool sticks or telescopic poles (throughout the flat).

Music studio deep-clean; bathroom deep-clean; bedroom deep-clean; hallway deep-clean; rugs organic cleaning.

Carpets in each room need organic compound cleaning. This system is a dry product and is excellent at lifting dirt from the bottom of the pile.

If you want us to help swap rooms over, allow extra time for lugging furniture!

Declutter of any drawers or wardrobe per rail and per drawer, or kitchen cupboard or medicine cabinet. Deep-cleaning is a meticulous clean of all areas we can see and reach inside and out. This includes paintwork, doors, light-fittings and windows inside. Mattresses can be turned and bed linen changed. A moth pack and scented drawer liners from Total Wardrobe (Julia also has lovely boxes and clothes covers. Have a look at her website to order).

Proper hydration from freshly filtered water (oxygenated water filters fitted for the whole flat) then you can simply fill a bottle.

Organic Juicer.

Organic meat has fewer chemicals, eat more of that. Vegetables and fruits the same, eat as much as you can with every meal. Salads and sprouting vegetables. Soups and gluten wheat-free bread. Lactose reduced or soya milk.

Family to have at least one planned outing a month (parents & kids).

Janice to take Sam to at least one stay-and-play per week, baby swim classes or baby massage weekly.

Milo to have allocated time with the children according to his written timetable. Must be on at least 4 x week 1- 2 hrs for each child or both together. This can include painting, messy play, reading, bath-time, dressing or cooking.

One of these sessions must be outdoors at a local park or softplay.

Janice to have at least one class a week outside the home (life drawing, yoga, group meditation). Janice not to do any more than tidy beds and light washing up or cooking during the week and not more than one weekend a month, as that's when Milo and grandparents are not around.

These arrangements may well already be in place, but there is an obvious overload on Janice. This imbalance can be corrected with Milo's input. Whatever has happened until now has passed. I am only interested in assisting you both to create a future that works.

Rapid-eye teaching for Clarissa.

You asked me to identify an area in the house for this. The lounge area is working. Unless you need to do much more, stay where you are.

Invest in three beautiful silk screens to close down any part of the main living areas as and when you want to, or get a curtain maker to frame out the living room and split it with internal calico coloured cotton curtains that open or shut the space. This could be fun for the kids. I can instruct a suitable contractor.

Family coaching session once a month. I think this would be great to have someone popping in for an hour to review the month with you all.

Stylist: I have seen your clothes. You have great style. You need some time to play with your clothes. Indulge in manicures, hair salons, and saunas.

Nanny for holidays? If you are going to have help with the children, I recommend limiting it to term-time breaks. You could even arrange term-time help abroad. Or you could have the housekeeper work daily during term-time breaks so you can look after the children yourself and have the flat looking great.

I hope all this helps you, please come back for anything further.

Yours, Hannah

These two examples should give you an idea of setting out a Room Plan on paper. Share in each other's space, one room at a time, creating your bespoke Room Plans and have fun helping to deliver the service! It doesn't have to cost you anything, and time normally spent shopping can be allocated to transforming what you have.

So instead of going out with your kids or friends for lunches and shopping sprees, bring your friends and kids home; eat at home and have fun re-arranging spaces, sharing knowledge and involving your children. When experienced, you can help Room Plan a whole house, your own home will cost you less and give you so much more. People will value you for valuing your home, and even more when you show them how to value theirs. (Listen to the song *Homes)*

4. Mind-reading rooms used in partnership

Mind-reading rooms can facilitate experts in a clinical or non-clinical setting to empower the client to adjust at home and beyond whenever there is an imbalance. Setting up a Room Reading group using the book or my extended programme within your practice will add to your expert interventions. As **George Dimitrov** explains:

For more than 12 years I have been a practising psychologist and hypnotherapist. I encounter a variety of human issues from clear or obvious symptoms such as stuttering, smoking, weight-loss, to the less evident such as psychosomatic pain, phobias, fears and post-traumatic stress disorders. Some will be short-term (or acute) problems and others long-term (or chronic).

At the preliminary session, I take a full picture of the client's issue and estimate how powerful their personal resources and motivation are. I also like to be sure they are informed about the format of further sessions and how we are going to proceed.

One of the factors enhancing the therapeutic effect of each session is the environment. The environment around us – even more than the one in which we have grown up – is really important as everyone is widely and deeply connected to it. Many times in my job I have realised that issues have been caused by obstacles in the space around us.

Sometimes there are small but significant factors which can be easily changed to improve the manner of living and affect the continual wellness of somebody's emotional state. Here, for example, would be the choice or amount of furniture; one of the focuses of mind-reading rooms. This was crudely highlighted when I worked with a lady whose partner's choices were tempting her to get divorced. They lived in his house in South London. He was obviously a big fan of Nazism; several walls were covered by swastikas and pictures of Hitler. On the other hand, she was Russian and very distant, closed and frightened of everything personal. Within moments, I suggested to them (actually him) to change this environment if he wanted to help her.

He was not happy about my advice but complied for the sake of the relationship. When I saw them weeks later, I realised that her mood was improved not just for a moment but followed a new tendency to smile and be easy-going in her home and workplace, and between friends as well. From my perspective, it was not just because she knew he did something because of her, but unconsciously she became more relaxed living and sleeping among peaceful images, and pictures of nature. But the most interesting aspect of this simple case was that man himself became less authoritarian in his kinder environment.

Another case I worked on recently was a woman who had social phobia. This phobia (also known as Social Anxiety Disorder) is the state in which the person suffers from a strong fear of being the point of direct interest. Eventually, the person won't go out to public spaces in case he or she is spoken to. This, of course, affects their everyday living and requires treatment. At the initial session, I estimated her condition as appropriate for a course of hypnotherapy. However, bearing in my hypno-psycho-therapeutic mind the particular problem with which that person was suffering, I again decided to work in her house. This meant she could be relaxed during our sessions as there was no need for her to be nervous of how to get to my therapeutic studio, or to have any tension when she arrived at the – for her – strange place.

The improvement was little by little but visible with each session. I began with the systematic desensitisation developed by a behavioural therapist during the 1950s. Somewhere later she started to go out, first in short distances, and later, longer ones. At the end, after six sessions of her home-based hypnotherapy, she was already able to go out and to spend some time without any scary feelings or tension.

The Ericksonian hypnotherapeutic approach is one of the most highly effective therapies nowadays. It achieves overcoming of deep issues and stable healing. As a hypnotherapist, I am sensitive about each factor in a client's story which may become helpful – or, indeed, a hindrance – to a long-term successful outcome. That is why for some cases I prefer to provide my hypnotherapeutic sessions where the person spends most of the time. The usual places are the work environment (if the reported problems are mostly manifested there – a bad relationship with the line manager, with colleagues, lack of motivation) or in their houses. One of my recent cases was a man with erectile dysfunction. He had a really valuable relationship with a woman he loved. The complaint was focused on his sexual performance so that was the issue we started on. After a few sessions, a real effect was achieved. As I had realised his conscious mind was deeply connected with his room and stuff in it, each of those sessions was provided in his house, working in tandem with mind-reading rooms.

Being a clinical hypnotherapist, following the Ericksonian approach for me is important; my clients must feel comfortable during the sessions. Thus, the hypno-inductions I provide are shorter and less visible, which means more effective. For non-professional readers, I must clarify that this kind of hypnotherapeutic approach is based on calmness and light, a medium or deep level of relaxation (depending on the particular case). The contemporary hypnotherapy is an eclectic one – it can accompany other psychotherapeutic approaches, alongside Room Reader, and the results are really remarkable.

George Dimitrov.

I've always been fascinated by the dynamics of people and space. As a child, I'd spend hours in my room re-organising my toys. How would I feel if my doll, rather than sitting in the window, was standing facing the sun? I moved the doll and other toys, finding that just by these small changes I'd change my state of mind. These transformations affected other family members, too. My younger sister had left our shared room, upset over something. Minutes later she returned, still sulking, but to a different room... the curtains were pulled right back allowing sunshine to energise the space.

She saw my doll and teddy now upright with outstretched arms on the window sill; my swan cuddly toy that moments before had lain flat on the floor was now 'gliding' across the bottom of my bed. My young sister's eyes flitted around the room and the changes changed her sulk into a smile. This, in turn, gave me a sense of joy. By moving objects and increasing the sunlight, I had changed the energy of the room and thus transformed my playmate.

"Energy cannot be created or destroyed, it can only be changed from one form to another." (Einstein)

You already know how a friend's energy can uplift or drain you. Similarly, your sofa can relax or irritate you. A freshly prepared salad has a vibration you won't find in a typical burger. There are energetic subtleties in our lives. Mind-reading rooms stimulates and generates new frequencies, shifting energy in and around inanimate and animate objects. We call this 'movement of space' in the home.

We'll start to identify quality furniture. It's something that's well made, usually of solid materials, such as wood – and highly practical. It ought to be used with the minimum of fuss or strain on the body, so I don't recommend low-slung sofas that once you get on are not get-off-able. Heavy chairs requiring a forklift truck to move are not going to help your little ones get comfortable at the dining table. Light, well-made chairs and practical multi-use surfaces are ideal. Drawers that open smoothly and wardrobes with working keys are all good. Or easy-sliding wardrobes that open fully with plenty of shelves and rails, but not so much space that you keep filling it with more superfluous stuff. Beds are a key item in the home and I've seen hundreds that are rickety, cheaply made, poorly structured with mattresses that will ensure restless sleep. I will teach you how to make more informed choices. This will save money and improve your life.

If you've recently experienced any kind of trauma – direct or indirect – do not start changing furniture or colours until you have returned to a more stable state of mind when life is plodding along. On the other hand, if you're amid trauma and life feels stuck in negative patterns, mindful de-cluttering and deep-cleaning will certainly help. Roomie groups may exist near where you live. If there isn't one, start your own and invite others along.

Mind-reading rooms brings the happiness into your home which, naturally, helps bring the fullness out of your family.

Back in Widnes as my younger self, my elder sister was proving a more complicated case. She was always given precedence over me. I resented that because I wasn't given the same precedence over my younger siblings. So, I could not understand why she always had her own room. She bullied me and treated me roughly at school. Around 10, I wondered what would've happened if I swapped rooms with her... would the relationship have changed long before we grew up? (We had a loving relationship as adults.) She should've been made to share – at least sometimes – so that she didn't think she was better than me. (I wish my mother had had this book). You know what the relationships are in your family, now you can start to transform and rebalance these just by room changes and furniture rearranging.

Do you have some sibling-competition going on? Consider swapping or sharing rooms as a mechanism for transforming the rivalry. I was a sensitive kid living in a family of insensitive people. Do you have a child like that? Often this type of child is not given the space to be sensitive. The impact of such emotional blunting is likely to lead to problems later on. I was crushed by my family and it has taken years to recover myself. I am not saying they acted in this way intentionally, but every child is different, and the job of parents and state is to ensure that the child is supported to avoid a harsh and disconnected society, thus world. Mind-reading rooms will help you identify aspects of your children or other family members that until now you were not aware of or insensitive to. This will help understanding and connecting with yourself and others. Use your Roomies to check and develop skills. Three heads are better than one. Adults may feel they were misunderstood as children; now is the time to start to clarify who you are; now is the time to heal the past hurt and create the life you want in your personal and wider space.

Sharing space is also a way of developing cooperation and communication between roommates, especially if the room isn't ideal for sharing. Then both parties have to work together to make something unworkable work. We often make choices based on 'norms' but you're the expert here. See your family becoming the best it can be through mind-reading rooms. No religion, superstition, styling or interior designer needed.

Given that an older child often gets his/her own room, why should my sister have shared? Mind-reading rooms looks at the whole picture. The impact on me was that I felt bullied by her and overlooked by my parents. The impact on her (of always having her own room) was self-justification of her unfairness towards me. I doubt any amount of discussion could have changed that. Why? Because even if talking things through improved her behaviour, while the status quo remained she would have resisted being nice for long.

You can see from this story that the impact of not learning to share, inflates the ego. It can allow us to denigrate those who have less than us, and give us a sense of power in ownership of space to the extent that we covet space over and above relationships into adulthood. It also teaches us to steamroller sensitive people. And this attitude leads to other discriminatory behaviours.

In my room-transformations, you will identify aspects of yourself and others. Discuss the themes and stories with your friends, family, teacher, doctor or therapist. Use the home and the objects in it when you want to transform relationships, build trust, understanding and co-operation. Analyse your, or a friend's, space and create your Room Plan. This is the final structure for each room in the home. It's created through gathering evidence, taking photos/sketches of rooms and identifying issues, whether they concern a lovelorn painting or a scary sofa. The scrapbook 'n' journal is a good medium of inspiration. It can be used to inspire ideas for your Room Plan.

Crafting/up-cycling/swapping/growing/cooking/foraging are all great complementary activities for a Room Reading group as you can make simple changes and share times together with your Roomies.

5. An uncomfortable place

I have always been intrigued by room-dynamics. Any room I spent time in became my experimental space. I am very present to what happens in rooms. In fact, we are all present to the influence of objects such as furniture, books, ornaments, pictures and the windows in a room. But until now we did not really consider that by moving these elements or adding here and there we could affect our family's and our own health. This is why my journey will empower yours.

In my family home, we had a room where I was confronted by my parents. At the age of 12, I wrote an explicit letter to a boy I had a schoolgirl-crush on. I described him fondling my at-the-time non-existent breasts and kissing me on the mouth. My mother came across the love letter when she was putting away my clothes. Mum and dad were convinced that I had been up to no good with this boy, and they called me into a small utility space. It was an unfriendly room, full of square, hard objects like a barely-used table with a lonely, cushion-less, hard-backed chair finished in a dull brown stain; an old fireplace with an electric heater and a large, solid iron. I remember feeling the pressure of the room and was desperate to get out to anywhere else in the house. The room's sparsity and lack of warmth confronted my delicate senses and confirmed my guilt. Actually, the letter had just been a girlish fantasy but that didn't stop the room affecting me.

Have you ever found yourself in a room like this? Do you have one like this? Now you can start to observe the impact of the space on interactions and re-create the space by simply adding some colour with flowers or water-based paints, and a cushion. Such actions would soften and add warmth to a space like this. This, in turn, would aid communication and encourage the presence of empathy, even in challenging circumstances.

I had a mixed childhood with volatile teenage parents, and grandparents who kept things in balance. My very young, working-class parents resented the responsibility of being shackled with kids. My mum had a birthday, a wedding and gave birth practically all at the same time. We have a picture of her in slippers on her wedding day when she'd only just turned 16, and within months she gave birth to my sister, Jill. A year later, I arrived. As Catholics, the pill was not an option, so mum had three (of the final four) of us by the age of 21. Still, my parents did knuckle down and owned the responsibilities they created but often had tantrums ending in violence, dramas and make-up sex.

Widnes - in the North West England borough of Halton - is my hometown. It was created around a large chemical plant. The small town seemed big when I was a kid. Only recently has it experienced expansion, now extending from the Lancashire border to Cheshire. My parents worked hard; dad in an industrial plant, a chemical factory. Even back then, I was acutely sensitive to the twin turrets and the dangerous puff exuding from our very own twin towers that engulfed the town. I'd stand in our house's backyard and look up at it making shapes of lambs, horses and giants. The poisonous chemical smog then became interesting. My mother worked in the Golden Wonder crisp factory. The great thing about mum's job was she used to bring home bags and bags of crisps. My sisters and I loved making crisp butties (thickly buttered white bread sandwiches filled with our favourite crisps). Yummy!

I was raised partly by Granny Connolly – my mother's mother – a professional housekeeper. Granny Connolly always had her copy of Mrs Beeton's Household Management. It was her bible. Granny Connolly couldn't have used anything else. The house, filled with the aroma of homemade cooking, was always in order; everything had a place. I was the second of four females, but despite the ratio of women in the house being five to one, my father was very much in charge.

The first thing you see when you enter the town is the chemical plant's twin towers. They still billow out the chemical spew created from the manufacturer of the many household cleaning products that line our supermarket shelves. One in three people in the expanding radius of these toxins will die early of cancer. My sister had bowel and liver cancer at 48. She did not see 50. And (according to the Halton Cancer Profile 2016) "Halton has a much higher rate of lung cancer incidence and mortality than England." Every time I see this smoke, my mind is crystal clear that we in the UK are chemicalised. We have too many supermarkets cheerfully selling 2-for-1 poisons with which to clean and polish our homes. This is unlike in the US where many states have banned these products. But it seems too few politicians or manufactures give the long-term impact on human health much thought. For my parents, health gave way to short-term security. Cash cotton-wooled cancer.

My sisters and I formed a useful team for my grandmother's cleaning and managing our home every other month. Granny Connolly was the family's rock, holding my hard-working yet volatile parents together for 14 years; none of us could have managed without her. She delegated tasks between my sisters and me: one would manage the stairs with a brush and pan holder; another would clean and polish every crevice of our decent but worn furniture. When we were cooking, one would stir; another would break the eggs and the third, bind delicious combinations we'd all later enjoy around the family's kitchen table.

A designer kitchen or bathroom that has a sink so tiny you can barely fit in a few items, and so shallow your clothes get soaked, is hardly workable. Kitchen and bathroom fittings must be made of the best quality materials designed to last at least 10 years. When fitting out these rooms, go into the details of the small parts that help make up the whole. We tend to spend money on making things look good at the expense of workability. Workability comes down to strong clear functions that allow our lives to work better. So, spend the money on a well-made tap over a glossy drawer finish.

The activities my family worked at to achieve a collective positive outcome can be developed on your own so that you become better equipped at home management. This can be done by allocating specific tasks on a day when family members have agreed to be around. The first step is to invite them to cook a meal or clean out a cupboard that everyone uses or would benefit from (if it was cleaned and ordered).

Even small children ought to join in as it helps them learn to look after themselves by managing bite-size tasks, whether it is sweeping a bedroom floor, putting some toys away or helping sort out socks. Children of all ages love to have a Room Plan. They learn that the benefits of keeping their bedroom tidy go way beyond pleasing mum and dad. They develop an awareness of the impact of chaotic space over-ordered working space. Your children will also become choosier over how much stuff they have in their rooms. They'll be less consumer-led when they see they are constantly being sold to by marketers. Room Reading groups are ideal places to explore such issues and put the brakes on unnecessary consumption earlier rather than later. You will be able to reason with your children so the whole family makes better choices and enjoys life more whilst spending less.

My mother struggled with her weight. Often pregnant for nine months (a lifetime to a child of three) she would indulge with abandonment, scoffing on jam and cream sponges, apple pies, hot heavy stews and potatoes. She was enormous before the birth then we all suffered the loss of 'the goodies' afterwards with her slimming club diets. The nine months of heaven led to six months of enforced leafy salads and diet chocolates.

When a mother doesn't want to be tempted with 'goodies' in the house, children ought not to be impacted by strict adult diets. We do, however, advocate a healthy balance where everyone is within BMI (Body Mass Index) guidelines. This can easily be achieved with fruits, salads and vegetables. When you do eat out with children, insist on salad or vegetables as part of their meal. Many cafes these days do not serve these necessaries. Stop eating in such places if they do not start including veg or salad.

Our children are being conditioned to think it's fine to eat a large portion of fried chicken or a burger without salad. Fried food is bad enough but when – as one of my boys did – they start arguing that all they need is a portion of chips as their daily portion of veg, then you know something needs to change. This also happens in the home.

Children are being served up beige meals of meat and waffles or chips with nothing else. Better to give them beans on wholemeal full-fat buttered toast or an egg with loads of fresh tomato.

Dr Aseem Malhotra was an overweight cardiologist seeing a range of other obese or unhealthily thin clients. After enjoying the eating habits of Pioppi, a village in Southern Italy, he discovered that we do not (nor do most of Italy) follow the true Italian diet; we over-consume white flour pizza and pasta. Pioppians only have small pasta starters, and pizza is a monthly treat.

Stop eating low-fat foods and white pasta/pizza; reduce – better, reject – refined sugars and factory-farmed processed meat; introduce a modest but full-fat, non-genetically-modified diet, including grass-fed butter and olive oils along with five vegetable portions a day and oily fish. So, don't bother counting calories anymore; focus on their quality. Have a heart and new waistline as healthy as Dr Malhotra's.

I suggest you reduce meat consumption to a maximum of 10% of your diet, especially if you have health issues. Meat must be broken down and creates a lot of uric acid in the body. This uric acid causes arthritic problems, cancer and weight problems as well as the milder issues such as constipation, bloating and hormone imbalances.

Despite the interest in baking and cooking shows or books, we are not participating in home-baking and cooking much. We are living in a period of mass passivity where watching a programme or buying the book is thought enough. Our solution to every problem is to buy something and live vicariously. I am here to help you engage. Really engage. Mind-reading rooms isn't some fluffy notion. It's a hands-on activity that demands interaction. And it is accessible – bite-sized – to assist your development from passivity to activity.

In my Widnes home, there was a lot of activity, and life would be pleasant if only my dad could manage his anger and my mum her interminable screaming rants. I didn't understand what was happening; I just sort of knew I had to become the family scapegoat. I had to take the pressure off them (namely, from the family home). With a suitcase full of jam and cream-filled sultana scones, I'd run away to act as a diversion from my parents' constant arguing that would occasionally end in domestic violence.

As an adult, it has taken a lot of mental effort to deal with my past, to understand that my actions in creating calm from chaos and my running away were the actions of a responsible individual. Did you run away from home? If you did, please forgive and thank yourself for being wiser than those who were in charge. I carried the guilt of being a bad child for more than half my life. Now I can replace that guilt with self-love and gratitude. I was wise beyond my years! I faced less danger and stress outside of my home. Each time I ran away, I was taken back by 'experts' and made to feel guilty by them and later my parents. Children can teach us more than you might think. Listen to your children as the enlightened souls that they are.

During WWII, Granny Connolly had been a professional housekeeper. I think her first husband and three of her brothers only survived a few months in the war, so she was left alone with my mother's half-sister. My grandad – by whom she was initially employed – was a good catch. Surviving the war, he'd been to India. There he had covered his body with intricate tattoo-art. (In his case, it was real art.) I imagine such detail performed with just a sharp pin and

Indian ink (no anaesthetic in those days) was to both celebrate his survival and – considering the painful application – numb the guilt.

Grandad returned home to England on special leave. His wife was dangerously ill and died in childbirth. My Granny Connolly looked after the baby girl and his home. He was so taken by her skills that he married her when she became pregnant with my mother.

Granny Connolly, brought up on Mrs Beeton's Household Management, was essential to grandad; she applied natural remedies and ordered the home so that every penny was accounted for, she would arrange his clothes, cook, and look after his daughter's shopping. He did the gardening and bought and sold shares. Apart from the occasional boiling point between them, considering it was the late 1950s, this was a good relationship.

These skills are even more important today as the cost of living escalates and property eats up our incomes. But what if you and your family could become experts in mind-reading rooms? What if you could learn to be less impulsive when buying clothes or other items? If you could re-balance the constant pressure to spend your money through commercials and social pressure?

People in Cunningham Road were still using mangles to wring-out clothes and the washing lines were always full. Washing was put out in a very particular way; shirts, dresses and t-shirts had to be pegged under the arms, or trousers and skirts around the waistband to avoid peg marks. My mother and Granny Connolly had all our clothes handmade but we still had no more than the basics. Each of us owned around eight items of clothing and, once outgrown, would be passed down the line for re-use. Nothing was wasted. The clothes-maker lived in the next street. She made delicately beautiful, frilly dresses and flouncy skirts. But because I wanted to be in dungarees and t-shirts, I took great care to ruin them by climbing and rolling in the cornfields with my friends and terrier.

Locals deep-cleaned every three to six months with the older generation bringing out beds and furniture to get the sun deterring small pests such as moths. As for cupboards, every item inside them was removed and cleaned. All cupboard parts, such as shelves, hinges, tops and sides - inside and out - were also cleaned. So, furniture lasted a generation and is still used today. I'm often surprised to hear the criticism levelled at domestic cleaners... when a cobweb or filthy item is noted by a customer or expert, they blame 'poor cleaning' but no single domestic clean can be compared with a meticulous deep-clean.

There's a deep-cleaning plan at the end of Chapter 2 you can adapt to any room. With a three-to-six monthly deep-clean rota, you could save thousands on replacing kitchens and furniture, and improve air quality in your home.

Granny Connolly, my sisters and I managed the changing and turning of mattresses, cooking delicious English stews, soups and puddings, ensuring clutter was minimised and clothing, bed linen and towels were moth-proofed with lavender, cedarwood and sunlight. You see, I was already present to the feeling I had to 'hold' a space – be attuned to the atmosphere – and the people in it. I hoped I would be able to do something to deflect the anger and physical blows between my parents. But, being eight, I was ill-equipped, too stressed, and it would take time before I became skilled in recognising symptoms of imbalance and so make changes in my personal space. This doesn't mean children are not able to participate in making better choices for themselves and their siblings. Just keep their involvement to the level of understanding they display. For example, Mother asked Rosie aged 6 and Grace aged 4: 'Do you think you have too many toys?'

Rosie & Grace: 'Yes.'

Mother: 'Ok, what shall we do about that?'

Rosie: 'Let's give them to the girl and boy who live down the road. They don't have many toys'. Grace nods and smiles in agreement.

The mother empowered the girls to share not only toys but clothes and books with children they identified as wanting to share with. These children were not friends of the two girls; they were locals the girls saw as having less than them. The items were packed into a box, taken to where the girls knew these kids played and offered to them. Initially cautious at the generosity, soon the kids were rushing to their mother with new treasures.

My own childhood reminds me that children can so easily become hostile targets in the family home. My teenage parents sought to reduce my sexual expression because they thought it was real and probably because they feared I'd replicate them, pregnant at 16. If they had had maturity themselves, or around them, they'd have understood my letter was a fantasy safely played out with a pen and paper at home (a great start to my writing career!). We are often torn – even lost – between right and wrong. That is why community and communication are crucial.

I was angry that they misunderstood my expression; they were angry that I 'did it'. The real harm caused was the hostility created by them in that space because it made it impossible for me to speak!

We need to utilise other people's experience so we can make more informed choices at home. Get off the not-so-merry-go-round of buying happiness for yourself and your children. Happiness is created through balancing and simplifying aspects of life. Look out of your window and see the birds flying freely in the open sky. They build homes to accommodate their needs (no more, no less), they search for food (nutrition is the priority) to raise the family until strong enough to fly the nest. Animals live and die with a flow humanity seems to have lost. We're sidetracked to the point of isolation and confusion.

When you walk into that department store you will be made to feel that you need that over-priced perfume or designer dress. The inauthentic way in which we are taken over by the consumerist propaganda may not seem hostile at the time. But it is surely hostile when it disrupts and corrupts your real needs. Still, this inauthentic gift will be beautifully wrapped.

We think we are doing the right thing by buying ourselves or our children designer labels or allowing them to watch TV shows and play online war games. We think taking them to McDonalds or KFC is OK sometimes. Sure, you cannot deny your kids everything with which they are being bombarded. Be a stand for your children and family by having space to think more about what is right for you and them. Create space in your home that lasts beyond another take-away or pricey pair of trainers. Mind-reading rooms shows us how being responsible for our relationships and choices helps shift society from hostility to peace. (Listen to the song *Hostile Target).*

6. The light diagram

Key Themes: light-needs graphs; impact of violence on children and relationships; marriage breakdowns; created families; social activities that bind us; managing money; transforming old furniture.

If our light-needs are imbalanced, mood swings, frustration, anxiety and illness prevail. Post-partum women require night-time support and sleep. Shift work needs to include some sleep-time or sunlight. An experiment on mice, within just three months of light-deprivation, resulted in them not lactating or running around their wheel. This escalated to produce confusion, fights and cancer. On re-introducing normal 24-hour light-synthesis, it took a further month for the mice to recover (although for many it was too late).

This diagram sets out the perfect lifecycle for our circadian rhythm

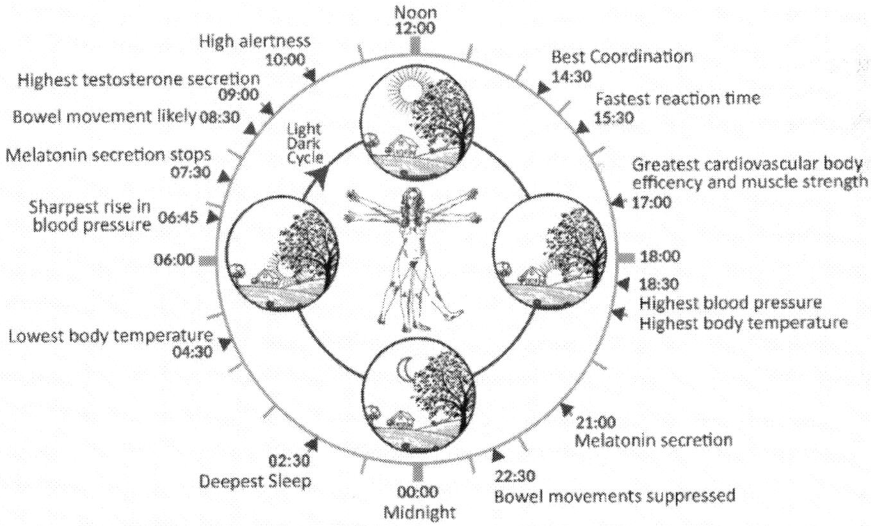

and – as seen in my parent's story – what can happen if you fail to follow your body-clock's natural flow. Yet we and big corporations are ignoring our basic needs. The modern world is full of alarming statistics relating to social issues from addiction to domestic violence. It's time to address this. A Roomie group provides a nurturing, non-judgemental environment for people to grow and learn.

With so many of us confined to working in office spaces it can feel as though our practical skills have become redundant. Often, we so lack confidence in our abilities to undertake what might be straightforward practical tasks that we outsource them. We are mostly brain workers, but even this is button-based. Activity has become the realm of the specialist or expert. It wasn't always like that. And in wartime, society becomes much more active; chaos creates action. I believe we can be active without being at war, without the associated chaos and devastation. We can then experience connection and transformation without fear. We must recover our control before we become nothing more than passive purchasing robots controlled by systems designed to reduce our engagement with each other. This consumer- and media-led system isolates us and has us thinking that life is a certain way and we are not getting it right. As things are now, we can never get it right.

Most systems are designed to maintain the status quo. Mind-reading rooms has the effect of challenging the status quo, leading people from a passive state into an active one. It begins at home. Each time you brush the floor, think of all the people around the world also brushing a floor; each time you fold, clean and order, remember, you are not alone. Simple acts done with awareness create a connection, generate peace and allow you to start to experience life fully.

These simple applications of mind-reading rooms will grow your capacity to play and your desire to play an active role in the wider community, reducing your longing to spend. You'll develop your capacity to empathise and reflect with your family and others. You don't even have to agree with others to generate active, peaceful communities around you. So, you'll be healthier and happier.

Roomie groups provide a new mechanism that connects us with real people and real life, instead of the one manufactured for us. This disconnection from the media and consumer influence on our minds will allow us to breathe and begin to take back control.

I say connecting with 'real people' and 'real life' because I believe we have not connected with our community and families for the last 100 years, unless in wartime, or through the brief triumphs of the unions which have over a decade been demonised and broken down.

We should take the positive elements of wartime-communities, and of unionism and family. We should take all those things that have been eradicated by fear, isolating us and leaving us with narrow choices in leadership. In wartime, the systems designed to control us must release the hold on us because an elite – an oligarchy – does not have the power to take the actions they want us to take following the decision they already took on our behalf. So, what might those actions be? Firstly, they will need to get our agreement by stirring up a particular position and evidencing it in the media. This happened in Iraq for the British and American people. Then they will want our young men to risk their lives; they will want us to believe they and all actions including death are the right and only actions to take.

But, if we could just make more collective mass decisions, the government would be less likely to get it wrong. Those decisions would rely on direct communications with other people from or in those countries rather than the mainstream media that can easily be manipulated by those in power. After our European Union Brexit referendum and then the Trump presidency, surely – when talking about going to war – it ought to be the masses deciding what action if any should be taken in a similar referendum? Alas, not.

In a world polarised by wealth disparity, the Trump phenomenon was not a surprise to me. It makes perfect sense that a billionaire reality TV star would be the next president, despite having no political credentials. But, as far as mind-reading rooms is concerned, Trump was - at the time - a better choice than same old, same old Hillary Clinton. Trump was supposed to provide business acumen and huge entertainment value. He was voted in because of his obvious faults, because he tears up the rule book. Trump was our dirty secret. Now in all his glory, we may live to regret our own behaviour, which we can observe through his actions and inactions in power (just as the UK may regret Brexit which, in turn, emboldened Trump and his supporters). He has proven that anyone with money can have a go at ruling America, and anyone can fail. Clinton was the politically correct choice, so she became a scapegoat for collective frustration. We are frustrated because it doesn't matter who is leading, we never have a voice beyond a couple of tick-box choices referencing why the latest leader appeals to us. Things will only change when we realise that agreeing on a few issues isn't enough to put someone or even a team in charge.

Mind-reading rooms is designed as a wake-up call to generate authentic communication amongst the masses, so when we realise that no individual – regardless of qualification, gender, colour or intentions – can rule the most powerful nation in the world, the whole political infrastructure will finally break down. Transformation can only occur when the collective communicates from within our societies, face to face, talking with as many other people as possible. I don't know what a future would be when millions collectively and actively make positive day-to-day decisions about our planet's wealth and health; I just know the outcomes for our children would be amazing.

Wars waged on countries have an impact on our minds. We feel sickened and helpless when we see innocent children being bombed in faraway lands, and many of us do not vote in political party elections anymore because we don't want blood on our hands. We know the political system no longer works, maybe it never did! We created our social and political structures and we can change them. Millions of us are voting online and across borders. Let's take this model further and make us all collectively responsible for major decisions. Think how quickly we collectively vote on a televised song contest or fill out our lottery cards. Wouldn't we feel more responsible if we were voting to prevent deaths of innocent children and families whilst saving our own sons and daughters from wars?

I did not engage in my formal education until adulthood. I was often bored in the classroom asking myself why it was I had to learn about kings and queens yet not why my country arms another. That that very country might one day retaliate, bothered me. Reading broadly or trying to research more broadly using the internet are ways to empower ourselves and ensure we grasp what is actually going on at home and beyond. As I write, the UK is not officially at war. Our children can walk to school without being bombed. But we had a major war in this country as recently as 1945 and the many threats are ever greater as politicians use us to gain advantages over other countries by claiming the moral high ground.

The recent wars in Eastern Europe had long-time neighbours killing each other over territory. In Zimbabwe, white farmers are being thrown off the land as it's reclaimed by blacks. We cannot say who is right. What if they had shared the land and shared the skills? Surely that would have shown all people to be incredibly generous and willing to forget past hurts rather than re-balance the status quo with a similar kind of one-upmanship. We see how Hitler rose to power in Germany, when (initially, parts of) the media and Hitler's party demonised the Jewish population or how Trump has spoken of Muslims and Mexicans. Demagogues thrive when they popularise a prejudice to divide communities and disconnect those who rely on them and the media for information, and who are trained to take up divisive ideas as if they are their own. How can we work towards everyone having a say in what's going on?

Connect with those around you so that communication prevents war. Get children interested in learning about global as well as local politics so that they become connected and interested in the child they sit next to every day. My son Orlando, now in secondary school, tells me that children born outside the UK tend to be in lower sets than black, Asian or white kids born in the UK and raised by at least one English speaking parent. Perhaps if greater interest was shown in current world history that reflects the real mix of learners in the classrooms, children and parents born outside the UK, but living here, would do better.

Here in the UK people from afar seek refuge. But where do we all go if we too need refuge one day? On the ground, we can be empowered through our Roomies to learn from and with each other. Share books and skills; arrange for people to come in and give talks on subjects unknown to us. What's our neighbour's story? Why did they come to this country? What is it like to be in the midst of a war? Why read (possibly a biased) newspaper when there will be many people around you that have first-hand experience and give you a wonderful insight into how to avoid ever having to have that first-hand experience. Our children in the classroom from Zimbabwe, China, Poland, Syria, Romania, India, to name a few, can offer the majority an opportunity to embrace world history, culture and religion to developing a genuinely global community. But we, the parents and educators, must nurture this opportunity beginning in the home and the classroom.

One of my clients, whom you will read about, came here from Iraq/Kurdistan as a child refugee. She and her siblings sat through an education system that focused only on British wars and times long-past. How frustrating for her and her siblings to have first-hand experience of British involvement in that war, and yet no opportunity or outlet to be involved in or involve her classmates! Repression of expression can lead to extreme views and behaviours later on. I should think it would be deeply hurtful and invite a lack of empathy and ingratitude for your safe haven in exchange for selling out on your own history and culture, and being unable to share modern British wars through your first-hand experience. Education ought to reflect the children it serves.

I spoke to my client, Lanja, today. Sadly, her 27-year-old sister died of a heart attack brought on by use of prescription drugs, being overweight and a heavy smoker. When I knew this beautiful intelligent woman in her early teens and twenties, she was taking advantage of her Western lifestyle. She lived-it-up with fast foods and drinks, but on the other hand, she was determined to keep her virginity (as is the custom in her country) for "the one". She was doing a science degree at a top London University, but I saw amongst the family, even then, difficulty in maintaining traditions and values as well as fitting in. The result was some excessive lifestyle choices at odds with their own culture.

Her young brother is just coming out of a UK prison for the second time. I knew him as a young teenager, a quiet boy built like a house but with some low-level autistic behaviour. This made him vulnerable whilst he appeared strong. His first 'offence' was when a group of modern teenage girls bullied him on the underground. Unused to such shows of crude contempt from his young sisters or women from his own culture, he retaliated. He was charged with assault. After this first confinement, he struggled to get a job, and so was soon drawn into other low-level crime. Lanja said if Britain/America had not been bombing Iraq, forcing them to leave Kurdistan and seek refuge here, neither of her siblings would have ended up where they are.

She explained that they came here indoctrinated by one culture, one religion, one history thus one narrow view. And then were forced into another culture, history and view and given no counterbalance. With no voice for her family, confusion, chaos and destruction reigned. Lanja said this has happened to many thousands of refugees here or elsewhere expected to only adopt the 'saviour' country's history and views. Thus, we see the need to communicate and share is essential to resolving inner conflicts and generating balanced communities. Empathy is such an underused and underrated skill.

This is how we develop shared values in the face of opposing views. It's possible in most cases, except of course when the views are extreme or discriminatory. Common values can be explored in your group with sharing skills like cooking and crafting.

Conversely, those communities who we ignore may group together to support only their own. This isolation and non-integrated position can be tackled by direct interest in other people especially if they are from other countries or refugees. It's not about knowing all the details; it's about being open to 'understanding'.

Then we have geopolitics where leaders try to edge out of their borders or control disputed territories. The masses are used by elites to flood out territory with their people. To learn more about how our wider environment creates or prevent wars check out Tim Marshall's book 'Prisoners of Geography' wherein ten maps tell us all we need to know about global politics. Mind-reading rooms is about the collective leading from within rather than led by those who think they have 'legitimate' access to lands or resources. Mind-reading rooms recognises that politics as it is today simply doesn't work for the majority. So, start thinking about how you can transform your environment and help create a world that better reflects the world you would like to live in.

I lived in a small block of flats with people from many countries and cultures. Over time, we recognised (especially the women) that we all hang our washing in the yard to dry, we all go shopping to feed our families, we clean, we cook and our husbands, ourselves or partners work to earn money, fix things (sometimes), and all of us direct our children to be responsible, socialised people.

In other words, the nuts and bolts of life are very evident, so let's not take these often unpaid and therefore underrated activities for granted anymore. Let's be thankful and acknowledge that these simple skills form the backbone of a successful life. While some search fruitlessly for 'The Secret,' there is mainly just more of the basics which are 'safe shelter' some 'whole foods' and 'clean clothes'. Sam Kogan, a great teacher of mine, said money was overrated because once you have the basics you can only get more, bigger or better of the same, and then you will have more to manage.

The UK's Thatcher era and boom of the computer industry along with the erosion of blue-collar work in favour of white-collar made craft, domestic science and woodwork classes fade from school curriculums in favour of computer screens and button pressing (passive activity). We must talk face to face. We must gather together physically for, and with, each other to understand what our real needs are and to assert ourselves like never before.

With the fractured family structures we have now, it's a shame that the older generation has been largely discarded as they are such an important part of a well-balanced family. This rejection of old people is yet another symptom of passivity: treating human beings as throwaway items. And look at older people in your community: they socialise much more with their dog or cat than with other humans.

Older people hold a wealth of knowledge and experience, yet they are alone, they must watch the single mother – also alone – struggling with her children and grappling with the system for survival. Unburden yourselves and invite people in.

I encourage the reinstatement of the older generation as an invaluable resource for raising children. It's not important that people are connected by blood; I recall the old line: God chose our relatives, so thank God we can choose our friends. What's important is consistency and social integration of groups that form modern families. For example, when two gay parents have one or more children (biological or not), they form a connection with older people in their community (Mrs Smith, now widowed, and Mr Patel, divorced). Collectively, they create a modern family that supports the grandparents, parents and kids through becoming Roomies or joining a Room Reading group.

Male role models that promote and empower women and men as different but equal are vital to growth and control of self. Since women have started working and outsourcing childcare to men, men and women are working better than they ever have. I also think that men are great when allowed to parent. A lot has changed in the last 30 years since my Granny Connolly's time: women mostly used to look after the home and children. However, with work (nearing) equality, female cancer and infertility are on the increase. Women need to empower men even more to take on care and management so that both parents have equal work and familial roles.

Women also need the freedom to express themselves and to socialise. It's crucial that this role-rebalancing happens; the way ahead is for women to stop playing the heroine and doing it all as a single parent. One parent is rarely as good as two, whatever the gender or sexual orientation. I would encourage single parents to set up or join a Room Reading group. They will find solace and companionship as well as much needed practical help and maybe, one day, a partner with whom to continue to build a home and life.

Do try to manage breakdowns effectively when they happen. You can see that ultimately money must not take precedence over contact with the children. Keep your feelings of anger and hurt separate from your ex-partner and your children. Such advice may seem unimportant when everything is falling apart. But nastiness can pass. Thank yourself for ensuring your children don't lose a parent forever.

One way of managing a marriage breakdown is to ensure pick-up and drop-off, of children are done outside of the marital home. Meet at a neutral location. I suggest this because whoever is standing at the front door of what used to be the marital home is holding the past (it's usually the mother) and the impact is overwhelming regret or anger. If you can meet in a place where there isn't that strong connection to the past it helps both parties manage emotions. And, given the venue is probably not that convenient, it encourages you to get on with simply handing over or dropping off the children.

Also, arrangements for child access ought to be discussed away from the family home and ideally with a neutral person (not new partners). Take your diary and invite your ex to do the same. Treat it like any other important meeting where it's simply working with your ex to agree dates and times. New partners, maybe with the best will in the world, can cause emotions to surface on both sides, especially early on in marriage breakdowns. To keep yourself focused, agree to discuss only access arrangements and frame it within specified times.

Looking back, I have compassion for both of my parents. My mother hadn't got over one pregnancy before she was into the next; my father wasn't around; he did shift work. Both struggled with the 'night shifts' – her feeding babies and his packing-up chemicals in the factory.

My parents needed nurture in their life with some flowers, colour, the introduction of more light and more quality time together. A Room Reading group would have supported them and encouraged them to share knowledge with peers. This could have helped them to mature, and to value being parents. Whether that would've been enough to stop the huge rows and occasional spill-over into domestic violence, who knows? I only know it would've helped. They found little joy in managing the needs of four young children and daily shiftwork; they felt trapped and exhausted. Being so young, lacking experience, it all – we all – became a chore. It was hard for them to appreciate the beauty of having children, as they felt they had no say.

For my mother, it was not being empowered to use the pill thus getting perennially pregnant. For my father, it was a lack of education and limited knowledge of how he could prevent the pregnancies, and generally manage his anger. The lesson here is the truism that we must all seek advice to help us make well-advised choices. We can also learn to share information with our kids so they are empowered to make choices that will keep them in control of their lives. Having children before we have had any experience of life or work rarely bodes well. I am not saying don't do it; just consider the benefits of enjoying your life first. Once you are ready to be responsible for them enjoying their life, you will enjoy contributing to the development of another human being, i.e. you'll enjoy your own life, with them.

This is mind-reading rooms; creating a life that works and re-creating your life so that you become adept at transforming your space, making informed decisions and helping others do the same. Never stop sharing information with others. You'd be surprised at the difference you could make, even if it seems obvious to you. We all have gaps in our knowledge. I have constantly been surprised by people being really helped by things that I think are obvious and have just said in passing. Give people credit for their thinking, but do remember your experience is different from theirs and that tiny bit of info you share could fill their particular knowledge-gap and improve their life.

My Catholic mum wanted to control my wildcard dad. The more she tried, the further he went, finding a job that left her a single parent for the weekdays and some weekends.

When he returned from working away, initially everything was exciting and romantic with mum dressing up like one of the women from Abba in a green maxi-dress, long flaming hair and matching green eyes. My dad was also handsome with curly dark hair and olive skin. My mum and her friends would make the living room look like a party scene with bright lights, loud music and lots of drinks and snacks. It gave them the rare chance of having a social life, even if it was only in their living-room. You see, despite their young ages, and the stress and strain of working and having three young children to be responsible for, they loved each other. But alcohol and general overload meant the morning after wasn't quite the young couple's dream.

They hosted many parties at the house, and we had a great time with cousins stopping over and piling into our beds. Jumping and dancing to the disco beat from the living room downstairs, we had our own party in the bedrooms upstairs. But then the next day the party was very much over with the house in chaos and two sulking, hungover young parents, unwilling to sort it out. And the behaviour exacerbated the hangovers. They would soon start rowing, forgetting about us, thinking about their spiralling headaches, leaving me and my elder sister to wash up the glasses and plates, and pick up bottles and generally the pieces of the night before. We had to help ourselves to breakfast whilst they engaged in a full-scale war.

In this volatile environment, Granny Connolly would step in to make the Sunday roast. This defused the potential for a blow-up and focused us all on delivering the meal, washing vegetables, laying the table and roasting potatoes. Some social interactions require activities to validate individual identity and strengthen group cohesion. Other family members or friends are crucial; thank your supporters. The difference Granny Connolly made to us was huge! Are you a Granny Connolly? Identify people to whom you can make a difference, and people who can make a difference to you.

It was a long-running drama between my mum and dad, with her leaving him, or us leaving them and staying with Granny Connolly, or her throwing him out. But she took him back when I was a kid, especially when he cried on the phone to her... that always worked. The final straw came after baby number four (another girl). I think they both wore each other down in what can only be described as a great example of a terrible marriage! They divorced when I was 14. Mum finally matured enough to recognise that, despite her faults, she did not deserve the beatings he had dished out. Although her life had been a bit easier than the one he had – and she owed him nothing – there was nevertheless a sense of responsibility for him on her part.

I share this story because domestic violence and stressful environments are often swept under the carpet. Domestic violence can come from frustration; a lack of knowledge or feeling that we have to live our lives pretending everything is just great. I hope that this book will provide some assistance to ease the stress and develop communication and support. You can start a Room Reading group in your doctor's surgery, community centre, school… any group can practise mind-reading rooms as part of their therapeutic interventions. Start to develop your oom Plan or help create a Room Plan for others in your Room Reading group.

Key actions: transforming cold spaces by placing objects; adding a splash of colour; letting in light; family activities that develop skills; managing relationships after breakdowns; adding cushions; Room Plans. (Listen to the song *Sorry For Your Loss.*)

7. Mind-reading rooms outside-in

If everywhere you go outside your home is in chaos and dirty, it will impact your behaviour in that community and your home.

To demonstrate the impact of a negative environment outside the home, I want to share a story from Malcolm Gladwell's book, *The Tipping Point*. He reports of a crime wave on the New York subway. Increasingly, otherwise well-behaved people were jumping the turnstiles or simply fare-dodging, and there were regular thefts and physical attacks. Yet, on the train carriages, the number one factor that affected the average person using the underground was identified as... wait for it... graffiti. The solution was to rid carriages of graffiti and then keep them clean. Other activities included public daisy chains (handcuffing) of fare dodgers to each other and establishing simpler systems to arrest and fingerprint the offenders (who the police had not bothered with before because the effort and paperwork weren't worth the trouble for the tiny fare). This new display of zero tolerance along with deep-cleaned carriages and platforms caused the crime wave on the subway to plummet. The environment off and on the trains was transformed. This was, therefore, mind-reading rooms for trains.

Whatever the space, whether it's public or private, ordered or disordered, the degree of cleanliness will impact our behaviour. We must ensure that our public spaces are ordered and complain when they are not. I think that filthy cafes, shops and subways are a reflection of our homes, too. So, if you start to look around properly and you see the dirt and disorder in your workspace or any place, do something about it. Talk to your colleagues and friends about how you want your spaces to look and why.

Food hygiene ratings in cafes and restaurants largely consider the use of kitchen equipment when handling foods. I was amazed to learn that a kitchen can be really dirty but if they are using different knives for preparation of foods (not using the same knives for cooked and uncooked meat, for example) and foods are in sealed containers, this is enough for 'good food hygiene'. I have seen a few commercial kitchens in restaurants that would turn your stomach. In fact, the more order and hygiene we practise at home, the greater the need will be to enjoy this in our public spaces.

House Rules

House Rules must be created by those living alone as well as those living and working in shared spaces. Such rules will keep you on top of simple cleaning and enable you to keep an order that will help you lead a healthier, calmer lifestyle. If you can't be bothered doing it yourself, pay someone else to do it. Don't buy things you don't need and then justify why they need to stay! Please think before you buy that pretty fruit bowl that doesn't have a flat base, which every time you put a piece of fruit in tries to fall off the table. If you want challenges in your life, turn them into physical activities that test your balance not your patience.

Divide up tasks so that each person who lives/works in the space contributes to emptying recycle containers, putting out or bringing in washing, sorting out the shopping, vacuuming communal areas, washing the bathrooms and kitchen areas. Paintings ought to be enjoyed by the whole family if they are displayed in spaces where everyone sees them; so, decide on paintings, furniture and communal objects collectively. Photographs of your loved ones ought to be no older than five years. After this time, transfer them to a photo album. I've had people show me a room and seen several pictures of a toddler. With one lady, she and I actually discussed the toddler at length. Ten minutes later he walked in as a teenager! This completely threw my analysis for a Room Plan. So always check the ages of the family to ensure you have the right information.

It's fine to have one or two images of them as a little one set amongst other more recent photos, or a montage where you see childhood progression over the years. But please don't hang pictures or ornaments above your beds or cots. Given you have lots of wall space to hang items, why choose a place that could pose a hazard? Of course, objects hanging in the home must always be securely fixed! Figurines and pictures ought to be reflective of things we enjoy most.

Kitchens ought to have easy-to-open doors and drawers. Kitchen utensils must be fully utilised; how many items do you have in your cupboards that you rarely (if ever) use? Pans must be limited to five; buy good quality items and use them often for five to ten years. When you're thinking of buying any item for your home, ask yourself if you need it? How long will it last? And, if it lasts five years, will you still use and like it then? Is it comfortable and practical for all those with whom you share your home, and will they like it?

Put the home-keeping rules on a notice or chalk or whiteboard allowing the individual to tick-off completed tasks for all to see. I have heard many times of marriages on the edge of a breakdown because the sister-in-law has come to stay for a while and has 'no idea' how to help keep her brother's home clean while she stays as a guest! This type of misery can be avoided by sitting down at the kitchen table and ensuring everyone's involved in caring for their living space. Excuses such as 'I have never done cleaning before' or 'I don't know how to tidy up' can be dealt with easily; either they do the allocated tasks or they pay someone else to do them. You will find even the most resistant cohabitants will be happy to do a fair share and retain a peaceful clean and vibrant space. Children must always help out with washing, putting used clothes into baskets and, after washing and drying have been done, picking out their own clothes. Have them put away toys and books after use with penalties for leaving stuff around or showing lack of care, such as taking a toy away for a specified time.

Male or female, with or without children, if you find that you're effective in some areas but ineffective in others, ask questions like 'Why?' Don't be a victim of your circumstances, be a detective in them. Mind-reading rooms skills are key to uncovering what's actually going on. Seek the answers in your furniture, drawers and product choices! Keep looking and asking until you have the answers, only then will you know what to do or not do. Has your partner started splashing out on expensive perfumes? Did you find an empty vodka bottle in a stuffed drawer? Does your partner suddenly have regular texts from an unknown friend (irrespective of the gender the friend is supposed to be)? Are your children impossible to manage at home or school? Does your bank balance reflect your business turnover? Do you have moths? Depression? Chaos at home?

Looking at every aspect of your life and arranging your space in a way that reflects what you are aiming for will help you to branch out from a rooted home base. This is best achieved with others who you can share and work with; it's a great way to learn and grow. Join or set up a Roomie or Room Reading group and eventually create a Room Plan.

My children will sort out their clothes, make their beds, and are responsible for the toys and books they have (and they have much less than before our move away from London). They enjoy helping to wash dishes, prepare food, and even set the kitchen table. Vacuuming their bedrooms is good - even if they don't always feel that they enjoy it - they appreciate having created a tidy space to eat, live and play. Angel, aged six, is officially on the home-keeping rota with Darcy, nine, Jet, 10 and Orlando, 13, all proficient. Angel is encouraged to assist in housekeeping, maybe just putting a toy or book away. I turn sock-pairing into a game so that the boys enjoy finding the right – or almost right – pairs! I have them look at labels for identifying trousers and tops belonging to them. Coats are hooked on designated pegs; shoes are on a shoe rack.

These are simple things that help you manage your children to manage themselves, it also teaches them to appreciate what they have... what you have bought for them! Make mealtimes magical with the addition of a vase containing some wildflowers, a little bell to call in your loved ones for the meal and make a gesture in recognition for the food provided by the planet's riches. Mealtimes will become more interesting and the cook may receive thanks. People over the centuries have felt water to possess certain powers. Why not fill a jug and, as the water is flowing into it, think of loving and healing? Each person who drinks from this resonated water should experience a special feeling.

Furniture and key items in mind-reading rooms

Home maintenance in our fast-paced, market-driven world is often overlooked. Once you have your new kitchen, bathroom and living room, maintain it or it becomes another throwaway item. Casserole pots need working lids to operate as designed, and limit them to a 'small', 'medium' and 'large'; baking tins can be housed in the same cupboard as mixing bowls and flour sieves; cereals are best kept in airtight containers; spices keep in labelled jars; cleaning products and cloths under the sink, with child locks if needed.

Quality over Quantity

Sofas are rarely high enough. Consider that you don't want to work hard to get up off it. Beds ought to be solid even if made from hardboards or wood with at least a two-inch gap underneath to allow air to flow around and underneath. I would apply the same rule for cots, sofas and armchairs.

Furniture that dominates a room needs to be replaced unless it's a centrepiece. The number of times I visit a home and I have had to wedge myself between the wall and the sofa to get around the sofa because it fills the room whilst the family makes all kinds of excuses for it staying there. Yet it's preventing them using the space; it is literally blocking them out!

Drawers overstuffed with items no longer worn, or worse, not even wearable or usable, can create blocked energy that prevents a family or an individual's growth. Over-stuffing of drawers or rooms can also create health issues. Cupboards need to be sorted so you know more or less what is inside them and that each item is used regularly. When buying furniture, clothes - any item for your home - consider cost versus payoff. Every object you put into a room must be justified, firstly for its use, then its aesthetics. And, a useful well-made product usually looks good, too.

Organic foods are more expensive than the ordinary chemical-infused foods most consumers buy. So, before I go on about the benefits of organic meat, fruit and vegetables, think about forming a buying group to make organic produce affordable.

In 2013, Newcastle University's study "Higher antioxidant concentrations and less cadmium and pesticide residues in organically-grown crops" in the British Journal of Nutrition was largest ever study of the nutrient content of organic and non-organic foods. The study found organic crops (primarily cereals, fruit and vegetables) and processed foods (e.g. bread, baby food, fruit juice and wine) have more antioxidants compared to their conventionally produced counterparts.

Now, oxidation of our molecules (basically us) can produce free radicals (unfortunately, this is not the sort of free-thinking radical that I want you to become) that may start chain reactions. Antioxidants, on the other hand, will prevent or delay cell damage. A healthy diet and lifestyle can help reduce your chances of getting diabetes, cardiovascular and neurodegenerative diseases and certain cancers. There are many theories about why healthy non-smokers are suddenly told they've got something horrible. Apart from genetics, I think it has a lot to do with the poisons that accumulate inside us. E.g. from non-organic fruit and veg we get many more nitrites and nitrates (leading to stomach cancer) and, perhaps even worse, cadmium. This toxic metal stays in our liver and kidneys and is one of only three metals for which the European Commission has set maximum permitted contamination levels. (The other two are lead and mercury.)

Traces of toxic metals are all around us and pesticide residues and slight contamination from other farms may occur. Still, pesticide residues were four times higher in conventionally – rather than organically – produced crops. Putting all this simply from The Soil Association's website that I can't get out of my head, let's just say that it's great we are top of the food chain so the predators we have to watch out for are unlikely to eat us. The price we pay for our relative security is retaining the residues of the chemicals we feed the animals we eat. And that includes the stress hormones that must be so abundant in the creatures kept in cages where they can't move. (Our own stress is bad enough for us!)

Thanks to documentaries, the coldest human heart now agrees that the 'lower' animals have thoughts and feelings. Then you've seen the secretly-taken videos of some farms or heard the horror stories, even if you didn't want to. Our dietary risk is our victims' payback. I know it can be more expensive, but make an effort for the animals, for yourself, and for the values in your house. Sure, eating is essential and it's often comforting, but it can be healthier and kinder. That must be, if you're eating at home, part of your mind-reading rooms.

8. The burning boy

I knew of a couple who adopted an abandoned boy. His parents died in a car crash. Adopted, he was left by his second parents when their marriage broke down. Adopted again, after seven months, things were going well with his new parents. Too well. So, the boy waited until the couple left to go shopping then burned the house down. Wow! Why?

Labelled by one of the team of experts involved in this case as "a dangerous no-hoper," I wondered if mind-reading rooms could have helped prevent that destructive behaviour. The boy could not cope with a third abandonment. He felt he had to act first. The destruction of the space in which the family had been created and nurtured – and the fear of losing that nurturing yet again – would have been overwhelming.

He acknowledged the couple's love and his place in their home but felt it could never truly be his. Step lightly in your sacred refuge, love and care for your home. In a terrible irony, the boy paid the home his own compliment.

Possible reactions to the boy's behaviour could be anger, frustration, resignation, bewilderment, and concern.

Mind-reading rooms might have helped this boy move beyond the fear of abandonment. Watching him in his home could have given clues as to what was to come. There may well have been a build-up of tension seen in how he used his space, such as uncomfortable clothing, unhealthy food choices, pictures on his wall of desolation, his lyrics (written or listened to), even something as crude as a suitcase that just happens to fit neatly by the door, all say that you are dealing with someone who does not plan to stay forever.

To tie the abandonment of the past to the security of his present, I'd encourage the boy to express himself with his favourite colours in his home. Clothing needs to be relaxed – natural fibres, cotton, wools, canvas, jeans, fitted but not tight cut clothes; this maximises his breathing space and comfort throughout the day. His room ought to be at the heart of the home (I mean, not in an attic or on the way out). This develops his security. It's important that the family cooks, and eats salads, fruits and veg together. I'd suggest growing herbs or veg (in a garden or in window pots). Physically challenging group activities that he can handle will practise taking him outside of his comfort zone and develop physical strength and body presence. Meditation or one-to-one life-coaching in the home generates a safe place for him to share. I'd introduce a family calendar and his own personal diary, with dates for parties, activities involving him and his family, medical appointments and special days such as birthdays of family and friends. In short, I'd blast the present with vibrant energy and colour it with a shared future.

You might not be dealing with such extreme circumstances as these, but if your situation or a friend's has elements of child detachment, introduce some of these ideas; a personal diary, a wall calendar, social gatherings, physical activities, comfortable clothes and maybe a room change to a secure position in the home's heart.

Mind-reading rooms in - and outside of - the home connects and roots us all. This means that the possibility of a life beyond the past or present becomes a probability. Mind-reading rooms focuses on the impact of things like sofas and the colour in the hallway. Whereas,

Family Therapy looks at participants' upsetting comments or actions. This focus can raise awareness of self. But does it complete the complex process of rebalancing? It is unlikely to be enough for long-term benefits, given that our presentation and space must shift in tandem.

I spend time in the home and use the space as the object of transformation. This can deflect blame, indignation, guilt, suffering; in fact, deflect the full range of emotions from the participating members. Such an unconventional way of working has proven effective due to the non-confrontational aspects. I could have called Room Reader 'Object Therapy' but then the transformation shows up in both objects and non-objects. This is because mind-reading rooms is the transformation of a group or individual consciousness through cleaning, re-arranging or changing of furniture, products, pictures, ornaments, people, pets, and space in the home.

I recently met a friend who said she'd spent years struggling with her son who couldn't sleep well at night and had exhausted experts' advice and medicines. She instinctively started to move the furniture in the boy's room. She told me: "I didn't change anything, but the direction of my son's bed and it worked! I was so relieved, my son is sleeping through the night, and everyone in the house is calmer." Mind-reading rooms is preventative and supportive, but it's not a cure-all for medical concerns. Seek medical advice if it's needed. (It's just that I have found mind-reading rooms to be almost always needed.)

We also use the rooms to redistribute the roles taken by the family members; swapping rooms can be fun. Whereas, asking a loved one to leave or have one-to-one therapy (especially if they don't think they need it) might not be so easy. Changing rooms, bits of furniture or colours can really change hearts, as you will see from the stories.

Room Reading groups can also provide these things with people bringing in the pictures or sketches of rooms and sharing their stories and issues. Every time I've attended one, I'm amazed at the speed the audience turns from spectator to expert. You're all naturally connected to the themes and ideas in this book. I just offer working examples and possible solutions as your way to creating Room Plans.

The family get to work in the space and with the space; we look at it together and start to transform it. Because mind-reading rooms is brought to the family, it gets to the core via visual and collective analysis without the family needing to discuss any specific upsets. My clients don't have to meet me. I can learn so much about them just through the rooms they do – or don't – inhabit, the colours they choose, the weight and shape of furniture, how many clothes and shoes they have, what they eat and drink... most of these things can be seen in the home.

What kind of products they like is a key factor in identifying the person's lifestyle; so, I look into the cupboards and fridge. Do I find Pepsi or Coca-Cola? Butter or margarine? Danone or Yakult? Branding, packaging, and colour help me to get to know what the client needs from mind-reading rooms. But why would these choices be so important? Why do companies spend so much on branding (and sometimes even more on rebranding)?

Because branding works. For instance, you see a tin of meat with a sprig of parsley on the front. Does the product inside taste fresher? You see a bottle of savoury sauce with garlic cloves on. Do you taste garlic inside – even if there is none in the product? (Advertising rules vary from country to country.) Taste two margarines with identical ingredients except one is pale white (lard colour), the other has had yellow added so looks like butter. For nearly all of us, the latter will taste better! Imagine Coca-Cola without its deep red can? Do you think it would taste as full with a yellow or white can?

Take the Pepsi Challenge reported in the book *Blink* by Malcolm Gladwell. In the 1980s, the Pepsi Challenge was a sip test designed to enlarge Pepsi's share of what was effectively Coca-Cola's market. Thousands of people across US shopping malls sipped both colas. It was a successful campaign for Pepsi whose market share soared. But the test was flawed. Pepsi is sweeter than Coke and when we take just a sip of something we usually like sweetness. However, over a whole can, this may become cloying. When do you have a whole can of Pepsi or Coke? Often when you're relaxing at home. Forgetting how strong the attachment to the Coke brand and taste was, worried Coke execs had the lab guys tweak a perfect vanilla flavour into something nearer Pepsi's sweet-fruit-burst one.

Worse, the execs changed the name to New Coke. Coca-Cola's efforts failed – costing millions – because Coke fans were angry and upset that their product had been tampered with. Studies have shown that the process of bringing your chosen product into your home will intensify your taste and emotions towards it.

Mind-reading rooms recognises this sensory perception is fundamental to rebalancing homes. Rebalancing is done with deep-cleaning and organising, turning clutter into order by reducing and simplifying our object-choices and helping us to choose organically (rather than by branded manipulation). Share in your Roomie group what you think brand choices mean or say about you, how they impact your life, and the advantages of sharing your thoughts on marketing manipulation. These are ways you can start to be independent of branded products. Look around your kitchen, bedroom or bathroom, there are maybe 30 products that affect your day.

Yet, mind-reading rooms does some manipulating of its own. We manipulate use of space to afford greater freedom of expression in daily life, through containment or expansion, a bigger or smaller bedroom, living room, bathroom, etc. (I am not talking about smashing down walls, just moving objects and people.)

Some people have a whole cupboard of products with irritant signs on them; washing powders, softeners, whiteners, cleaners. Seeing the irritant symbol every time you pour such products onto your clothes might make you feel irritated in those clothes. If its use excessive or goes against a belief that natural products are best, then it certainly will be depressing as it doesn't balance with your values. This emotional imbalance to a product could manifest in skin allergies or breathing problems so simply removing and replacing it could improve health. However, if it's not causing an imbalance (negative emotions or physical conditions), we don't comment because for that family or person it's in balance. Allergies, asthma or unexplained rashes may be dealt with, or improved, by mind-reading rooms. Replace some of your products with ones that will generate a positive response reaction. A commitment to better relationships through choosing brands/products that work for us is the way forward.

I recently read a great book by Matthew Crawford. It also has a great – I mean, long – title: 'The Case For Working With Your Hands Or Why Office Work Is Bad For Us And Fixing Things Feels Good'. Over the last 20 years, craft skills, domestic skills / home economics and woodworking skills have almost disappeared from our education system. We are all white-collar workers now. IT rules! But are we happy? Not according to Matthew, and I certainly agree that only using our brains isn't enough; we must use our minds in tandem with our bodies for optimum use of ourselves.

This next family story highlights the dilemma between the two needs in the workplace, with the husband choosing white-collar work over creativity which gives the family a quicker and higher payoff. The result for this particular family is an environment of deep unhappiness. They feel trapped and helpless. Solace has been sought in buying stuff (which the family can do thanks to the high income), so, they exist in a vicious consumerist cycle. If you find yourself relating to these people, you know what I am going to suggest: set up or join a Room Reading group. You can get help creating a Room Plan, so your dream of giving up your white-collar and stepping into creativity might finally be realised.

The following story also looks at off-loading. This is a subtle yet damaging (and sometimes manipulative) process of getting rid of stuff you don't want by giving it to others, even if they don't need it. Off-loading only helps the off-loader who feels guilty because they have too much stuff. You can allow people to off-load on to you and your family crushing your space and creativity… or you can wise-up.

9. The moth house

Key themes: addressing family relationships that aren't working; choosing clothes that empower rather than restrict your children; why second-hand shoes are a bad idea; limiting clothes, toys, books, and furnishings to release trapped energy; getting rid of moth-related sickness; creating an environment for the parents' home-business.

Our next case involves a whole family living in a good-sized terraced home in south London. The parents, Mick and Patricia, are a loving, devoted couple with traditional roles. He's normally out at work in the City and she's looking after their three little girls. Patricia had been recommended to me for my expertise in moth-removal without chemicals using mind-reading rooms.

I attended the house for a consultation with the couple. It was the weekend. Everyone was home – the three younger children, mummy, daddy and the dog. The children's clothes looked awkward as if the girls were uncomfortable in their skin; the styles, colours and fit were at odds with my first impression of the wearers. The girls were articulate and excited to have a visitor, but there was a level of restraint, a put-on element connected with the clothes. I made a mental note.

The family had an Irish wolfhound. This lovely, giant dog with its long, scraggy hair looked forlorn and out of place in the house. Being so large, he struggled to move freely and soon retreated to his basket. Mick had dark circles under the eyes and pale, slightly sweaty skin. Patricia veered from calmness to confrontational outbursts softened with a swallowed frustration, and she had eczema on her forearms. The house itself appeared packed to the rafters, though I had yet to walk around. I stood in the kitchen doorway between a children's playroom and patio doors leading out into a small garden. Their dad prepared lunch for the girls sitting around the table. They showed me a picture of a family with a dog standing on a beach in the sunset. "This is where we were supposed to be right now," Patricia said, as she swiped uselessly at a moth flying passed her face, "but our plans have all gone awry." Her eyes watered.

Apart from one flimsy set in the master bedroom, the house had no curtains. I could see large moths flying around. They settled on sofas, doors and pictures without a care in the world, they had such a hold on the house. We counted between 20 and 25 full-size females at any one time. These females had produced thousands of larvae in regular cycles under beds, on the dog and in the dog's basket. The house was 'mothful'.

To add to this mix, the couple explained they had been unhappy in the house for the last few years: Despite Mick being a successful banker, both he and his partner were creative and had wanted to set up a business selling craft packages for children to use at home. But, after analysis, they had found out the price of making a quality product was not viable so the whole plan had been shelved.

Now a third child was announced (a surprise pregnancy) ensuring they'd not be going anywhere anytime soon. The large sad-looking dog had been bought in the excitement of the former entrepreneurial plan. Their house was under offer and a dream seaside-home was within view. Yet suddenly the sale of their property fell through, the business plan faltered, and a new baby confirmed the dream was on hold.

The baby girl was very much loved by her parents and siblings, but the house had not been loved. The way they talked about the house and how it looked, showed their resentment. It was packed with clothing under beds, in cupboards and drawers. The family had toys and books enough to open a shop, a library and a nursery.

The house, once a sanctuary, had become a burden that itself kept getting burdened with more and more things from a well-meaning extended family. Cast-off clothes, shoes and toys, extra beds, sofas too large for the room, suitcases, albums, fabrics, ornaments, dining sets, craft items – you name it – they were overwhelmed by it. Hundreds of moths had permeated every single room, and their flutter had made everyone ill. The kids were run-down and did not sleep well, while the whole family had raised dots on their tongues and mouth ulcers. The large dog, bought for outdoor life, was cramped and now he too had become a burden as he needed constant walks. This exhausted Patricia with three very young children.

Having no curtains on the windows also contributed to the family's disturbed sleep. (Why no curtains? I didn't know and nor did they.) The plainly painted interior reflected the lacklustre state of the family's health. So, since mind-reading rooms treats the house like a person, I could honestly say this house was overweight yet undernourished and suffering from exhaustion.

I wandered through the hall. From here I noted the living room door was open, revealing the width of the house. Two tiny streams of water ran the full length of the ceiling. One went down the left wall into the living room; the other trickled down the right wall into the hallway.

Dare I share my thoughts with a successful banker and a sensible middle-class housewife? I took them into the centre of the hall where the living room could also be seen. From there, I pointed to both streams. Taking a deep breath, "The house," I said, "the house is crying."

There was a moment's silence, then a big sigh from both and she said: "You're right, we have treated the house with a total lack of love and care." He added: "Wow, we'd better call a roofer." Although the regular cleaner had been doing a very good job, every room needed a huge declutter and deep-cleaning. And clearly, the roof needed fixing! While I was on a roll with the couple, I said: "You do understand that to get rid of the moths and turn this house into a loving, healthy home, 50% of the total contents have to go?"

The poor dog bought for their proposed beach-life was miserable. I recommended that it would be kind to have him rehomed if no other reasonable way of providing for him could be managed. I couldn't see, even with paying a dog-walker how, given his size, he could be happy without a much larger indoor space.

I was also concerned about Patricia and her sisters. It appeared she could never turn down any item of clothing or shoes they were offered. Her young daughters had enough clothes for an army of zero-to six-year-olds! Too much acceptance, thus building resentment, everyone who walked through this space left feeling emotionally drained. Having 'too many' things in your home, especially if that stuff wasn't what you had chosen (only stuff you'd been given, albeit with kindness) absorbs the energy. Having no curtains further depletes energy as it's constantly escaping through the open windows. The impact is stagnation.

Stagnation has a sickly, feather-light, slow ebb and very little flow – perfect for the materialisation of moths, ill-health and weeping houses. Patricia was on edge; mid-conversation, when moths flew close, she had to try to catch them. This useless habit only added to her and her daughters' distress. And Mick was clearly at his wit's end, so absorbed himself in City work.

I had to move quickly. The family's stress levels were high, and I did not know if my efforts were going to be taken on to the degree required for mind-reading rooms to be effective. Actually, the response from this family was very positive. They did not want to resort to chemical infusions or freezing to rid them of the moths. Once the burden in the house was lifted, the moths would no longer be in control. I constantly hear that other methods to remove moths are ineffective. Such methods deal with only part of the problem and never the cause.

Moths are a major issue now. It's dangerous using poisons, and heating or freezing only rids the client of part of that infestation. As soon as the Rentokil van turns the corner, even with poison, your next infestation is just a flight through the window. The reality is moths and other insects will come into homes and if yours isn't deep-cleaned and ordered, you're inviting them to stay.

Hidden dirt is made of our old skin and toxins. This combination will have moths thriving, laying eggs, feeding on your open shelves, enjoying cotton, cashmere, and they particularly like wool.

Many of us have become resigned to moths, treating them as part of the furniture. They needn't be. Mind-reading rooms can help. Before we conclude with Mick and Patricia, let's take another look at how you can deal with moths...After a deep-clean – described below – and our great results which would have been unattainable by one person, we had cleared the moth-infestation. And, to ensure no further infestations, I put pheromone stickers in the cupboards to catch male moths and stop them breeding.

(There is a bedroom deep-clean full structure ending Chapter 2.)

I asked Patricia that all the children's clothing (items she had been storing under beds and in cupboards) be either sold on eBay or given to charity. Mick had literally hundreds of articles of clothing. I asked him to part with many of his novelty t-shirts, collection of leather jackets, jackets and shirts so reducing his clothing to 8-10 items of trousers or jeans and jackets, 8-10 items of other clothing such as shirts or t-shirts, underwear and socks.

The couple had an excessive amount of kitchen items. I had the family reduce kitchen plates, bowls and cups to a set of 10 each. I suggested three to five pans of varying sizes, and a reduced set of cutlery so knives, forks, large spoons, small spoons went from maybe 25 to exactly 10; kitchen knives from 15 to five; casserole pots from nine to three and so on. I asked them to remove a metal bed from the attic and an awkward looking –actually 'blocked'– sofa in a multi-purpose space.

The girls' room was to become a therapy space for the mother who was practising for her diploma in the living room. This room was a dumping ground for the never-ending 'gifts' brought in so was a wasted potential haven for the family and – because the client massage couch for her holistic practice was surrounded by paraphernalia – whatever good physical work her hands did for her clients, the ambience was disturbed. Thus, we'd move the therapy room into a professionally created space to satisfy clients and family.

The girls were to be moved to the fun attic room so that their play and energy vibrated through the stagnation from the top down. The baby was to stay put. She was identified by me as the rock. She had been born at a difficult time for the family but brought an abundance of joy, energy and light.

I also wanted them to consider having a housekeeper instead of an au-pair and a cleaner. This was because they allowed a series of au-pairs to practically take over the house. The great cleaner they'd had was moving far away so it was an opportunity to transform things.

A housekeeper could also help with the girls. She would not have to live in the family home. Live-out staff are preferable, it's a more professional set-up for all concerned. House-rules tend not to be broken, and the family retains full control of the home. A doula or nanny may be required to live-in for through-the-night support but that is temporary and still needs management.

I recommended that if the couple opted for an au-pair using the room as a trade-off for a low wage, they needed to have the following house-rules: No partners staying over at the family home; the kitchen to be used only at specified times; a bathroom allocated for the au-pair or only used at specified times (clearly, this wouldn't apply to the loo). The idea of restricting people in their space did not appeal to my clients, but the homeowner must retain control of their space, by ensuring staff has boundaries.

Helpful adult siblings living locally or not can be problematic, as can visiting in-laws and parents. In this family, the impact was the heavy burden of feeling one always had to say 'yes' and 'thank you' when it should be a 'no thank you. Our home is our home!'

Individual items and people can have an impact on our health and relationships at home and work. This family was so 'nice' to the siblings, it was stifling them.

I recommended the women (girls and mother) have 8-10 base items of well-cut dresses, skirts or trousers, 8-10 mixed items such as sweaters, t-shirts and cardigans and 8 sets of 100% (preferably organic) cotton underwear, wool or cotton tights and socks.

The girls' grandmother had left a much-loved sewing box in the house. Patricia could not bring herself to sort it out, so I did it for her as part of our decluttering and deep-cleaning. When she told me how much this little box of cotton reels and buttons meant to her, I knew I would find hidden treasure. Sure enough, when I opened the box I did see a strong range of base colours from which I thought the girls would choose. Blues, greens and raspberry were a theme of the cotton reels. The girls had never had the opportunity to choose any colour for themselves. They loved the dresses they had from Auntie but none of these colours, styles or fabrics was chosen for - or by - them.

In memory of the grandmother, I suggested they each choose a colour or two from the box and have a few dresses or skirts made or bought in their chosen one. It is important that children choose their own colours and style as it's part of the process of forming one's identity. You can even buy second-hand clothes in the many charity shops so that your child can pick the colour, style and fabric. The quality and price are secondary to satisfaction. The girls' shoes were another issue; the girls had never had their own shoes!

One quality pair of shoes fitted for one child's feet is better than four pairs of hand-me-downs. The sole of the shoe gets worn down according to how the original owner walks, runs and plays. This can cause damage to the second owner as they walk, run and play in a different way. Following in someone's footsteps is one thing, but standing in their shoes is a definite 'No'! It will affect your child's development physically and mentally.

I recommend a slightly heavy shoe (over a lightweight one) with a bouncy sole. This is especially useful for toddlers and children up to five due to the head having a tendency to lead and weighing proportionately more than the lower legs and feet. The heavier shoe helps to ground them as body/head weight, and balance develops.

The large dog was rehomed via a wonderful adoption process whereby the family met the new parents of the beloved but sad animal. The new family had a larger home and outdoor space along with other dogs for country walks. Both families are settled, and the dog is happier.

My team and I spent four full days with the family, meticulously cleaning every item in every room. Soon, we received email updates from Patricia on the number of moth larvae discovered and removed.

I have also recommended meditation sessions for Mick; a business coaching session for the couple to continue exploring entrepreneurial opportunities; a natural moth-management system is now well established with numbers reduced from thousands of moths to four tiny ones; the roof has been fixed; room changes are happening; the extended family, including siblings, have been around and – for the first time – taken stuff away. This re-balancing of the previous off-loading relationship creates a new level of understanding.

The lady of the house said: "Why did you allow us to control the removal of stuff? Why didn't you just take over, like they do on decluttering and styling shows?"

My reply was based on my mother's yo-yo dieting: "I had to gradually increase your level of commitment to change, and you had to set the pace. If I had taken 50% of all your stuff in one go, you'd have thrown me out of the house! Or, you could have accepted it at first – like a crash diet that works for a few weeks – but then you'd relapse and pile on more weight than you lost."

For any system to work it must become a part of your daily life, otherwise, it's an artificial success. I'm not interested in great theories unless they're proven and accessible in practice.

The work continues. On my last visit, Patricia told me they have more spiders since the house has been deep-cleaned and decluttered. Spiders are a natural part of the ecosystem. Therefore, a few spiders are welcome to devour insects before the insects eat up the house contents.

A new live-out housekeeper was in attendance and Patricia was confident that she had established a transparent professional working relationship with her. I spoke to the new housekeeper and she certainly felt secure and accountable for her duties (all positive signs). The family had experienced the generous act of giving away hundreds of books, toys and clothes. And the girls had made a felt-tip coloured rainbow-butterfly with a smiley face for me.

The girls are out shopping this weekend... for one pair of new shoes each. The parents have had their first meeting with our business coach to forward their ideas. Sometimes plans must change. The family has embraced change, seeing it as a chance to create a different future.

Key actions: Saying 'no thank you' to unwanted items; removing furniture that is too big for a room; reducing clutter to release trapped energy; re-homing unhappy pets; having business coaching; room changes; adding colour; deep-cleaning schedule for any room.

10. Photo-analysis for shorter case-histories

I began to realise I could analyse homes just from photographs or even descriptions. Tracey Carter invited me to her all-female small business enterprise group. Tracey told attendees to bring in mobile or laptop photos of rooms or describe their space and issues. Here's what happened:

Time-Warps and Mind-reading rooms

A woman, aged 42, had a room that looked like an 18-year-old's. She is a teacher but people treated her like a teenager. She could not quite work out why despite her qualifications and position, practically everyone, including her family and young friends, saw her as a woman lacking experience and needing guidance and protection. This had been going on for years!

She brought along some photos of her bedroom and I noted from them and her clothes that she was stuck in her past. I suggested she create a scrapbook and write down her memories from the age of 18 as a way of connecting her past with her present. I'm not an analyst so I cannot tell you why she got stuck, but we see the impact of her past on her so my mind-reading rooms analysis is based on this evidence. This woman dressed like a teenager, her room looked like that of a teenager. She couldn't see why the world treated her like one. But all in our Room Reading group saw clearly.

I advised that she ought to consider finding other flatmates as her current flatmates were 18 to 20! I felt that this was not helping her to be seen as a mature adult. I suggested she start collecting age-appropriate items that she liked to connect her with her real age and professional ability. These changes have resulted in her forming more mature friendships, moving house, and finding a man of a similar age and profession.

Creating spaces that invite relationships and reflect you

A woman wanted a relationship but told me that each time she brought a man home he quickly made an excuse and left. We all looked at her room in the photo on her mobile. We noted that she had no pictures, no cushions, no warmth yet the woman herself was dressed vibrantly. I explained that this was causing a disconnection between how she appeared and her home. When she would leave the living room to make tea, each man found this room discomforting and started to doubt the initial judgement he'd made of the lady. Everyone understood how this was happening. She simply hid her self-expression at home. This did not match her outside appearance. I advised her to choose some fabrics and colours she liked and start to decorate her living room. She has set up a Roomie group with two other people and they are working on this and other issues.

Bachelor-pad problems

A young lady and her partner had their own flats and wanted to move into a new home together. However, they argued constantly about his and her singleton-furniture and the memories of past loves being brought into the new space. I advised that you can clean and transform items like a sofa or a table with cushions, table mats, flowers and so on. Beds should be chosen by both current partners. (For a full discussion of this, see Chapter 13.)

Any historic bedding (especially the mattress) ought to be discarded in favour of a new one, and one or two new bedding sets. Pictures of previous partners can be placed in albums. The space ought to be created by both partners and seen as a work in progress.

Making room for a new partner to manifest

A woman wanted to find a new partner but pictures (of two rooms) showed her home was packed to the rafters. I explained that she needed to reduce the items in her space by 50% and focus on the things her anticipated partner might like. She could start to create a space that invited her ideal man into her world. This is done by starting to collect in a scrapbook the things he likes, the food he eats, what kind of job he does. Does he like to watch old movies? (Do watch some old movies!) Does he like home cooking? Have a Room Reading group dinner party and invite people to bring a friend. Start creating your space and mind such that it materialises in your matter (the home). Have fun, play with this creative process.

Extensions and 'special days'

A lady wanted to build an extension to her large three-bedroom house. She said her space was not big enough for her and her family. I hear this a lot! Yet she went on to describe her family and large kitchen, diner and living rooms. Please think twice before creating more space with extensions. Reduce what you have in your existing space first! Kitchens do not need to be full of cupboards and giant fridges. Pare down the space and reduce clutter, clothes, shoes, before taking out loans that will increase your mortgage and stress levels. Check if building your new extension or renovating your bathroom is actually just an excuse for not addressing other issues in the home. Use Room Reading groups to assess and make the best of what you have before splashing out or breaking down.

Here I'll explain why Roomies are less likely to engage with 'special days.' I have often encountered people who lose loved ones or experienced a dramatic event on a 'special day.' My advice is, yes, celebrate, but keep it within the range of normality rather than be excessive. Then any day is kept in perspective to the rest of the year. It takes pressure off us to 'buy-in' to marketing hype and keeps celebrations organic. Hyped existence increases depression and suicide rates as we aim to reach ever-greater heights of happiness.

Consider the impact on the environment, too. Christmas trees – still alive and strong – tossed out onto the pavement are left to wither and die after the celebrations. Food wasted and/or over-consumed leaves us depressed and bloated. A German lady told me they have nothing like the number of parties we have here in the UK. She found it all unnerving and shared how her husband had lost his mother and she'd had to deal with a management issue at work. The couple, living in the UK, had needed the 'holiday period' to simply relax and recharge batteries but had been challenged by 'festive frenzy'.

An American friend told me of a couple who had spent years childless and adored the precious daughter they eventually had. It was 'Thanksgiving Day' and the child was playing just outside the family home. A drunk driver – himself celebrating Thanksgiving Day – mounted the kerb. The pain of the death of their daughter on that day is amplified every year by the sound of everyone else's celebrations.

Make your celebrations mindful so others don't feel isolated. And courteously invite people within your vicinity to outdoor parties, especially if they live next door (that way, even if they don't want to come, at least you've prepared them for the date.) Festive celebrations lend themselves to buffet-style dining where you can extend your generosity to the wider community and get to know the locals. Keep alcohol minimal, replacing it with non-alcoholic cocktails or fresh juices. See a party as a chance to feed people with quality homemade foods that will inspire them. The Standard American Diet (SAD) might be better used as a checklist for what not to eat given that following this diet has made a large section of the West ill.

Children's parties should defiantly break with the sugar-craze and party-bags. Go on, get your friends and neighbours talking about your vegetable burgers and salad, and how you explained to the fast-food-kids that your family 'just don't do party bags.' Make a donation to a favourite kids' charity and share that with your friends and parents. They will soon be following your example and sharing games and memories as opposed to 'cheap tat' treats and more sugar-saturated sweets. Make cakes out of natural products like fruits, nuts, seeds and – being mindful of nut-allergies – have one nut-free cake. Keep decorations simple, engagement consistent and emotional crashes low! Observing the Standard American Diet parties for adults and children, you will notice that those fuelled on quick highs (alcohol, sugar, barbequed meats) often result in tension and anxiety potentially even resulting in the partygoers fighting or crying. I have been to some parties where upset sugar-'n'-fast-food-kids are being coaxed into unnatural 'false cheese' smiles. It's always awkward to watch those desperate-to-please-parents during their kids' photo-call. At least if we cut down the junk, you will get a picture that is truly organic as opposed to the highs and lows of the quick consumer fixes that truly leave us SAD.

At a Room Reading group, a Muslim lady shared how her brother aged 33 had a headache. It was three days before the start of Eid. He went to hospital and was diagnosed with an inoperable brain tumour. On the first of Eid he died. Again, whatever your beliefs, your own celebrations should be sensitive of neighbours. Incidentally, what would we do if a natural disaster or terrorist incident like 9/11 occurred on a 'special day'. Would the bells ring as loud?

Sometimes tragedies simply happen, and we struggle to make any sense of them. Only a few days before I thought I had finished this book, a man shared with me how he had lost his children and parents in a house fire. He was studying away from home and had a phone call telling of the tragedy. Although she survived, his wife was burned, but the marriage ended not long after as the same question returned over and over: 'Why'? We don't have all the answers. We can only sympathise with his pain at his loss of most of his family and then his marriage. My greatest wish is that other couples will find comfort in a Room Reading group to ease the pain and suffering of loss. He told me the inquiry thought it likely one of the children had lit a match in a bedroom. We cannot be everywhere and know everything. However, especially in the West we have become a 'nanny state.' Children are treated like pampered pooches. They have little sense of danger. We need to take back control of our children. It is important that our children and parents have the right to decide when a child can walk to school alone; when a child can light a match or build a fire; can be left in a room without constant parental engagement.

Right now, our children lack confidence in their environments; they explore hidden away in case they are stopped. And this, in itself, has developed from dangerous, dumbing-down politics resulting in passive parenting. As the next generation, children must be empowered to take risks in order to learn. Parents should not be criminalised by the state for experimenting with boundaries and safety so that their children are actively aware and can assess danger. Please discuss these and other parenting issues in your Room Reading group so that collective agreement can be reached, and social support gathered to help us to better manage our children in different environments.

In Mauritius, children take boats across rivers and cross roads safely from the age of five. So why must I accompany my nine-year-old from one building to another in an enclosed area with no traffic and no roads, less than 100 metres away, with cameras all around? I am told by the school: "It's all about the insurance policy!" I assume they are worried about someone suing them? But if I as the parent am taking the perceived risk, where is the harm? The impact on my son is that he feels disempowered. He is frustrated that he is not trusted with his own safety to walk 100 metres. Then when they started secondary school at 11-12, I was worried sick that my eldest, Orlando, had not practised managing his safety on the roads. So, what seems like 'care' is actually damaging. In the longer term, 'nanny states' simply create passive societies where people expect someone else to tell them how to think and behave. Orlando felt overly cautious with his sudden freedom after state safety-indoctrination. And he had no proper experience on his own of how to use a bus or get from A to B without Mummy! You might think caution is a good thing. Well, it is, but the truth is also that wanting to survive is a built-in desire that naturally encourages caution. Sadly, Orlando's over-cautiousness now came from fear or uncertainty in his own natural abilities.

Curtailing our survival instincts ensure two types of people: conformists without creativity, or extremists without empathy. Police cautions are often used to define our parental rights to decide on what is safe for our children. But it is not the duty of the police or the state or even educators, it is the parent's duty to decide on such matters. We must recover our right to parent and to make mistakes. Education, policy and policing must be based on the facts that most parents only want the best for their children.

In your Room Reading group create a Parent & Child Charter and decide on what you think is working in your school, community or wider area and what structures would improve the environment such that children are empowered to take reasonable risks. How can we improve road safety? How can children be allowed to manage risks in a safe way like understanding ways to build a fire? Light a match? What other changes would your Room Reading group make?

11. Torn (mind and body)

Key themes: Pregnancy; pre/post-natal depression; caesarean; water births; expectations; magazine influences; managing changes.

We might have started with the perfect space, but it can become out of balance because of a stressful life event. This story explores how post-natal depression impacted furniture choices and how this, in turn, exacerbated the depression until the owner started to recognise where she had gone wrong.

This young couple lived in a large maisonette with a balcony and roof terrace on the edge of Hampstead Heath in London. The couple had, until now, a wonderful marriage. He was very considerate and loving. They worked with an architect to design a roof-garden, new loft-windows and a new bedroom. The 30-year-old lady of the house had recently had a beautiful boy.

She had bought several pregnancy magazines and became obsessed with ensuring she only put on a tiny amount of weight. Just like the stars, she wanted to ping back into her great pre-pregnancy shape. She spent a fortune on decorations for the new baby and bought into the many gadgets, baby toys and designer baby clothes. But she struggled to stop or even reduce the amount of food she was eating and, in her mirror, felt she looked enormous! This 'failure' grew with sleepless nights. And she hated the stretch-marks that seemed to be covering every inch of her once-smooth soft skin.

She and her husband had planned a natural birth in a water-pool but this did not happen. In fact, her stress levels resulted in complications leading to an emergency caesarean. Also, since she had spoken of the perfect natural birth, and her husband and his mother were now watching, she felt she was letting them down. So, when her son was lifted out of the 'bag' – her abdomen open wide for all to see – she could not feel him nor did she have the confidence to ask for him. He was checked and handed over to her mother-in-law as she tearfully looked on whilst her belly was stapled back together.

She returned to full physical health apart from the heavy c-section scar and stretch-marks; she lost some of the pregnancy weight; but was not relaxed. It was such a shocking experience that the post-natal depression was exacerbated. This was reflected by her need to replace two items of furniture: the comfy sofa bed once lounged on was replaced by a heavy, uncomfortable, narrow, black suede, three-piece suite with broken springs; a cosy bed once filled with love was replaced by a scary-looking, giant, gothic, metal bed that – when she lay in it – made her feel part of a gargoyle and gave her nightmares. She hardly woke each morning feeling like the perfect mother!

Often when we are depressed, we don't know it. She didn't. But her new choices in furniture, alien to her, reflected her state of mind. In fact, they added to her depression. That's why mind-reading rooms is so effective at balancing imbalance. I am not saying these items of furniture or the colours would always indicate depression. Mind-reading rooms looks at the whole before making suggestions. If the overall appearance of a room is energised and balanced, neither overstuffed with items nor bare, you're on the right track. So, before you rush to replace your furniture, always ask yourself: 'Is this colour or style one that I will enjoy and feel happy with?' If 'Yes', then ask: 'Why is that?'. Write it down and share with others in your home or

Room Reading group and get feedback. Only then will you truly know if your emotional response is positive. Furniture is an investment so take time before choosing. Unwise decisions and resistance to ask others what they think about your proposed choices can have huge implications.

For the young couple, the gothic bed was powerful. It surely would encourage some much-needed passion, but its overbearing appearance grew and grew. The bed became a passion-killer. When she took her son from his cot to feed him in the metal monstrosity, she felt uneasy. She regretted that they had chosen this bed (the one they'd had was perfect). The couple was now literally enveloped in furniture imbued with a newly projected unhappiness.

Inanimate objects have a life. They have a past. They live in our present and help shape our future. When choosing furniture for the home, think carefully about what it will or won't provide. I strongly suggest furniture and decorations are chosen at stable times. We know mind-reading rooms isn't about styling or interior design, but that doesn't mean we are not interested in furniture choices. The scary bed was wreaking havoc on this marriage and the black, un-sprung, leaden sofa reflected her deep depression. The sofa certainly never said to her husband: *Come here. Sit, lean back on my arm while taking your wife in your own warm arms. And here's some chocolate.*

If something is off in the home, it will be reflected in the objects and people inhabiting that space. In the same way, when things are in balance, a room and its inhabitants shine with energy. Guests will love to visit your home more often and many happy times will be shared.

Something see-able is probably movable; and something movable is definitely manageable.

She attended a Room Reading group at her local health clinic and I showed her how her mind was reflected in her home. She started to see the impact of the furniture – the hard, overbearing metal bed, the black heavy stiff broken sofa – she now had a chance at getting on the right track. She continued to attend the Room Reading group with other women who had experienced depression. They transformed their homes; the mutual support allowed them to express themselves in a safe space. I am so passionate about setting up Room Reading groups. Getting together to learn and share is a great way of practising mind-reading rooms.

Mind-reading rooms is mainly practical and all who enter the home in tune with the plans – from flower arranger to carpenter – are part of a Room Reading group. Deep-cleansing cannot be compared with any other type of cleaning. We treat the house as if it is a person. We bathe it with hundreds of lint-free (dust-free rags) and non-toxic mixtures that energise the space. The deep-cleansing has a dual purpose: it allows both observation and meticulous management of the space. Mind-reading rooms isn't just about the introduction or development of structures and systems in the home – though this underpins our therapeutic interventions – nor is mind-reading rooms a styling or design service; we have no interest in putting a professional gloss on shaky foundations.

Key actions: Room Reading groups; recognising signs in the home; timing of furniture changes; assessing your space; mind-reading furniture. (Listen to the song *Clinically Spontaneous.)*

12. The gilded cage

Key themes: cross cultures; westernisation; unhappy marriages; how we unconsciously mimic paintings and ornaments in the home; disturbed rhythms created by inanimate objects and animals; managing endings and new partners.

Sometimes we find our past and future colliding, especially when we have experienced major traumas that challenge all we thought we should be. Here is a story of a couple who sought refuge in the UK. He sought a traditional marriage and she sought creative freedom. How was their unhappiness showing up in the space? And how could the space transform their lives so they could 'grow their separate ways'?

The flat was on the 10th floor of a 20-storey block. The lift was unpleasant; a strong disinfectant failed to cover last night's urine. I was glad to enter the cleaner communal hallway that led to my client's front door. The master bedroom was opulent with fancy frills on the bed and curtains. The second bedroom had been transformed into her office and was full of legal books and a computer desk and screen. The bathroom was separate from the loo, old in design but clean and pleasant enough. The kitchen was decent and functional. The living room was large and had a balcony. A gilded cage with six pretty, tiny birds erupted into sound as the door to the room opened. Behind these finches was a life-size carpet portrait of a beautiful yet sad woman carrying a large water urn on her right shoulder. She had bare feet and long dark hair and was a mixture of seduction and servitude.

I thought how lovely the caged finches were but, after a short time, I became irritated by their unending chatter and movement. I reflected on how this constant energy affected my thinking. It made me dizzy, my thoughts became fragmented. It was the festive season and the lights on a Christmas tree were set to flicker to a very fast rhythm. These flashing lights, added to the chirping and flutter of the finches, intensified my inability to think straight. The picture of the sad-looking lady carrying a large water pot on her shoulder hung on the wall. But this was no ordinary 'picture on a wall.' It was a life-size tapestry woven into a carpet that was as big and heavy as the water pot on the forlorn, barefoot, raggedly-dressed woman's shoulder.

A sense of heaviness washed over me as I looked at the picture of the weighted woman. My client, Lanja, stood with me in her lounge. The Christmas lights flickered on her face. They must've been flickering on mine, too. Her expression reflected the forlorn woman's. My client's right shoulder dropped distinctly. Had she had a recent accident? Any slight deformity noted through the years? No. It wasn't a coincidence that this was the same shoulder as the lost woman on the wall. She said her chronic shoulder pain could neither be explained nor cured. It left her irritable and lacking sleep. If I didn't act fast, she may be stuck on prescribed medication, increasing her belief that she was powerless.

"How's your thinking?" I asked.

"Thoughts are all over the place." she said, "I cannot settle for even a moment. I cannot breathe. I have real pain in my shoulder; the stress is making me not enjoy my life."

Her eight-year marriage to a taxi driver was stifling her. She was a creative woman who had forced herself to study law in order to provide for her nine-year-old son. She was indeed burdening herself. I asked her to look at the picture. Do you recognise anyone?"

She smiled for the first time: "It's been up for a year. But, yes, I feel like the woman. I really do."

"How about taking it down?"

Lanja looked a little uncertain.

"Take it down," I said gently, "and please find a new home for the caged birds. They are stopping you thinking straight. Can you still the flashing Christmas lights?"

She said nothing but looked open to it.

"Let me know how you get on," I concluded.

Lanja knew she needed help but didn't know it was deliverable through mind-reading rooms. She'd called me, and I told her three things: rehome the birds, remove the picture, reduce the lights.

Having done all I asked, Lanja called later that same week. She was already feeling a weight had been lifted off her shoulders, and able to start to create a life with less stress.

Mind-reading rooms with a willing client can be quickly effective. I continued to work with Lanja; this involved a deep-clean and declutter of the home and an honest review of her relationship with her husband during the process. We interact with clients whilst working, which takes the edge off difficult conversations. He was a great guy but unsuited to Lanja. She'd married him at 16 because she was pregnant. Both were refugees from Kurdistan to the UK. They knew little of the new culture but, whilst retaining her own cultural identity, my client was able to adapt much more than he could.

Retaining his views on women and their role in the home, he worked, then expected dinner when he came home each day, and that she kept the house in good order. But the relationship lacked stimulation for her; she was well-read, he less so. I worked with them through an amicable split. He has since re-married a traditional lady who enjoys his requirements and wants nothing more than a breadwinner. And Lanja has re-married a classical musician from her country of origin, Kurdistan. They live in London growing garden vegetables and they lead a creative life. Her son moves between his parents. This has been a time of growth and taught him to adapt to the ups and downs of life positively due to both parents and the new partners being committed to his well-being.

A good match for a long-term relationship is one where both parties have emotional, intellectual and social relatedness. A child in an unbalanced marriage suffers by trying to please both parents, then struggles to identify him/herself.

My client is now enjoying folk singing and no longer taking medication. In fact, Lanja is a star in Kurdistan! She's had a cultural journey through war in Kurdistan and peace here in the UK, but then she faced her internal battle when she wanted more than she had. We have a duty to ourselves to listen to our hearts and follow our dreams. Lanja has finally listened to hers and is now queen of her life and wears her little crown.

Key actions: Remove the weighted-woman tapestry; rehome birds; reduce flashing Christmas lights; accept relationships; manage change. (Listen to the song *Own Little Crown.)*

13. Making new spaces

Key themes: new beginnings, adventures, embracing change.

I bought and moved into a unique house at Poet's Corner, 96 Milton Street. For 50 years, it had remained untouched with only one previous owner, a lady called Violet. She had died, leaving me the opportunity to slowly peel away the layers creating my future home. With mind-reading rooms, we respect the history of a house. We don't rush in and tear it to pieces. The house must be acknowledged and cleansed of its past to fully create its future. You may choose to leave some colours on the walls. In this case, you'd add your own mark, so it becomes your creation. Anything that gives off a bad vibe – makes you feel uneasy – should be removed as soon as possible.

Each room had original, working fireplaces; original, heavy, wooden doors; and beautiful, carved surrounds and skirting. The house was full of loving energy. I felt that a part of Violet was with me. I don't believe in ghosts, but that the energy and creativity of those passed can remain if we want it to.

We know we won't live forever and most of us wouldn't want to. Still, death is so obscured - actually, underrated - these days. I am always reminded when someone dies of how fragile we are; leaves in the breeze. I hope that each one of you will reflect on the beauty of death and how those who've passed on live on through us. And death allows those around us to realise we can move forward and make new friendships, new loves, new children. Even when the person died was disliked or hated, they still – through their mistakes – teach us something in death: how not to live.

My Nanny Sinnott made cookies to die for. She'd never give up her secret recipe. But, once she knew she was dying, she wanted to leave one of the joys of life behind, firstly, for those she loved, then everyone. So, the cookie recipe is clearly engraved on her tombstone. Still, I'm quietly confident that when someone writes the recipe down, takes it home and makes those cookies, my Nanny Sinnott is berating their efforts!

Because in our daily life others rarely get the distinction of our life, in death, our power can be fully experienced. In our death, a magical moment of clarity around us appears in a way it would not have done in life, for life keeps us busy with the minutiae of everyday events. And that is exactly how things should be.

I hope that when I die those around me will keep smiling, stay hearty and say, 'Let's get on with life. No stopping to cry for Hannah; she wouldn't have wanted that. I expect to be living through the inspiration you have taken from this book! Knowing everything you did in life lives on encapsulated in an object, colour or memory is a comforting thought when dealing with the inevitable.

In your Room Reading group take time to talk and share about death. Share the life and inspiration of those you have been fortunate to know. Collect or write poetry, photos and other snippets for your Room Journal or Scrapbook.

At 96 Milton Street, the garden was huge and overgrown. I never fully got around to working on it although I did enjoy sunbathing there and felt secure in the high grass.

Aged 24, I met a handsome sailor and a roofer. In the seven-year relationship, we sometimes lived in his house, other times in mine. His house was on a corner and gave the feeling that we were on a ship! It suited his personality. The energy of the house was very much towards the helm, with him and I steering there; he the captain, me his mate. We had pale, comfy, pink sofas encouraging open conversation. This, coupled with our free-standing claw-foot bath, meant romantic candlelit encounters. Wooden floors and rugs we collected from the Greek Islands and Turkey adorned our treasured homes. My house was for the winter seasons with heavy floral wallpapers stripped floors and doors and a new white kitchen. We painted the bedroom together in a deep plum-red, resulting in a safe and sexy place. We had working fires in both our homes and enjoyed cooking together – and then the meal itself – in front of the fires we built.

I did not appreciate at the time how extraordinarily lucky we were. We both had our own houses and money enough to create them how we wanted. I worry now if my children will ever get close to having an affordable home. But I want to address the less perfect situations when a couple who have had their own space have to decide whether to move into a shared space, or not.

A couple attended a Room Reading group with pictures of each home. 'Mary and Janice' had been in a relationship for three years and wanted to marry and have children. But neither woman could agree on what was to go into the new home.

We looked at the pictures and I noted Mary was particularly attached to her Louis VIX bed. But Janice was furious even at the thought of it coming into their new home. Janice had not had the opportunity before to explore why she felt so strongly about not having Mary's old bed. Mary had reservations about several of Janice's belongings, too! Oh dear.

The problem was the same for both women. They did not want to bring the memories of their significant other's past relationships into the present. I've seen this acrimony many times over the transition from single living to partnerships.

Many couples split as the tension around such objects mounts over time in the new space. So, let's suggest some solutions. Firstly, I'm with Mary on the bed issue. It's a bad idea to bring a well-used bed into the nest of a new relationship. I am not suggesting you change your bed for every relationship, but for 'the one' you certainly should. A possible alternative is to deep-clean the whole bed and change the mattress.

The mattress carries a physical memory of activities and cannot be 'cleaned'. In particular, the physical activity is sexual and it's this combination that can sometimes be fatal to bring into a new shared space.

Cleaning has a stronger significance than just 'cleaning.' When it's done with mindfulness and a consciousness where you are literally wiping away the past to create the new. Always buy new bedding because, even though you can wash it, memories are connected with colour, fabric and age. I recommend ideally choosing a bed together when you're moving into a shared home. Buying bedding together is romantic and getting rid of all the old stuff can be a shared experience. Of course, it can be hard to part with treasures from past loves. This is where communication and compromise is key. Now you understand the significance of objects, you can have more empathy and empowerment to find a way that fully acknowledges each person's feelings.

The other tricky situation is when a couple inherits furniture from well-meaning relatives. Janice had been given a "lovely sofa" from her mother and there was "no way" she could part with it. The sofa was made from expensive materials and had excellent design qualities according to mind-reading rooms. It was functional, practical, certainly worthy of continued use. It would also save them money if they could re-create it. So, given we are not experts in upholstery, what could we do to make the sofa work for Mary who was opposed to it? I suggested we start by simply adding some cushions in her favourite colour, or a throw so the engineering of the sofa could be enjoyed without the fabric design. Over time, maybe the sofa is replaced but don't chuck it out if it's usable and can be re-created simply. Don't make it – or the owner – a hostile target.

The other object of discontent was a writing pen from Janice's former lover. Mary went green every time she saw Janice with the pen especially when she used to suck the tip! These kinds of objects seem harmless but cause acrimony as they are held so dear by the owners. My suggestion is, if you have such an object, you don't have to tell your partner its significance to you. Or keep it well out of the way. Or give it as a special gift… just not to your partner! Of course, you could give it to your partner and say nothing of its significance. Who'd know? You would. And this knowledge would always bother you for two reasons: you might have a (little) conscience that you'd not acted fairly, and you might have a (little) fear that, one day, someone or something would know the real origin or owner of the gift… I recall attending a wedding party where the ex-wife complimented the new bride on her engagement ring. "How lovely," she exclaimed looking at the ring, "that used to be mine."

Second-hand objects should always be 'cleaned'. This ensures that the past associated with the object has been removed. Any objects, whether second-hand or new, that make you feel uncomfortable or give you a bad state of mind, need to be replaced, cleaned or re-created.

Some ideas within your Room Reading group: write down what objects you could not cope with being in your new space, and any objects that could be 'cleaned' or 're-created'. Start to find alternatives to these objects together.

Key actions: respecting your space; creating romance; managing objects in new relationships; cleaning and re-creating objects (second-hand or new).

14. Spotless Organic Ltd

I started a little cleaning company that would use chemical-free products and evolve into a moth-&-home-management service with ethical, practical services. My small team delivered therapeutic cleaning services. We would make dirty houses spotless organically. Spotless Organic was born.

The life of a cleaning company is a precarious one. Cleaners tend to be uneducated, untrained and their companies unorganised. The standards of training in the UK are limited to basic courses that rarely address team skills. These team skills are an essential complex system that requires the input of a team leader, and a technique must be in place to get the best results. Sadly, cleaning is often the bottom of any list of priorities until a cleaning company is invited to take on a job. Post-tenancy cleaning is an example of how a cleaning company is scapegoated by the tenants, landlords and estate agents with the helpful assistance of the inventory clerk's report. None of these people is specially trained to assess cleaning standards.

The market is dictated by price, fear and ignorance. Inventory clerks can destroy a cleaning company with unfair assessments from photographs of a property. Inventories can therefore be nonsense as they are based on how a property looked at the start of a previous tenancy. (They will have taken the report from another inventory company and expect the property to look the same as it did at that time, usually a year earlier.) When it comes to assessing the cleaning, they take little account of how the property has been treated in the interim. The other problem with filth is that it doesn't show up well, so something can look OK on a picture but actually be quite dirty.

Assessments focus on the items left in the property when the clerk first visits. Only on the second and final visit do they take note of the cleaning. This means the cleaning company has already cleaned it! The cleaning ought to be properly assessed by a cleaning expert when the clerk is checking items on their inventory, during that first visit. This way, the cleaning company can work to assess the level of filth, drawing the inventory clerk's attention and thus managing expectations before the actual clean takes place. Price will reflect the level of work required and lead to realistic expectations – mutually agreed with the clerk – for all those involved. Levels of cleanliness could be assessed by looking inside radiator panels, looking at the fridge and washing machine rubbers, inside the machine's soap-drawer, and running a finger over kitchen unit tops. These areas reveal the true standard of work needed as opposed to a cursory look around. Toxic chemicals ought to be restricted. Cleaners use lots every day.

Estate agents – also largely untrained – don't care about cleaning. Once they have new tenants moving in, their commission is certain. And landlords are often out of touch with the state of a property, even if they live locally. Tenants have few cleaning skills and little incentive to maintain a property, especially if it was dirty when they moved in. It's only when they leave that all parties start to 'care'. Deposits are suddenly at stake for the tenant, the landlord worries about replacing current tenants and getting the best rent, the estate agent wants new tenants quickly and, although they are usually instructed by the estate agent, inventory clerks want to appear independent. It's a recipe for disaster and the cleaning company bears the brunt.

However, the long-term cost is on the landlord whose property will surely suffer mould, rot, moths and mice, windows will need replacing sooner, decorations will fall apart, appliances become so saturated in dirt that rubbers and compartments cannot be used, furniture and curtains will need renewing often, and – worse than all that expense – the feeling no-one really cares about anything. The cleaning company will valiantly battle to recover the property and will fail or do enough to get it passed by the clerk. But then, after years, the property is so bad, its condition can no longer be stepped over. It's worrying for me to verify that over 70% of properties in London are dirty.

The impact of living in a dirty home should not be underestimated. Just to be clear, the properties I talk about are not, generally speaking, from low housing stocks or social housing. The properties we clean are above average in terms of value and location. We have become blind to filth, helpless to what is required to keep a household healthy. Single domestic cleaners cannot keep a home deep-cleaned, nor can a single working person.

Meanwhile just consider that if a home has been deep-cleaned and ordered with simple well-made furniture, that incidence of depression, suicide or violence are reduced. The importance of deep-cleaning every three to six months ought to be part of every tenancy agreement. And if it was carried out by a cleaning company paid as an expert, this would result in higher standards of mental health and housing stock throughout the UK, USA and Europe.

Some landlords have started to factor in the cost of filth with expensive items being replaced yearly! But, sadly, the property itself will still be filthy even if it has a new fridge and landlords will still penny-pinch on the cleaning. These choices lead to generally poor standards, a lack of confidence in cleaning companies, and the fact it's price-driven makes a new fridge (costing a few hundred pounds) seem like a safer investment than a proper deep-clean (costing a few thousand).

Spotless Organic Ltd spent its early years in this miserable market. All were subject to us changing a filthy, dilapidated flat or house and its gross contents back to new for a few hundred pounds, in the hope that the estate agent would give us more 'great' work.

We were touting for business under the direction of my business partner who set the appallingly low prices and counted the money whilst I worked eleven hours a day. But he had knowledge and experience in commercial cleaning, so I assumed he must be right. JAC Strattons is a respectable Japanese Estate Agent with good quality service (my partner assured me). Now back in shape after my fourth son's birth, I attended Strattons' offices wearing a well-cut suit. My cherry-red briefcase was full of our great, organic, cleaning products. I was determined I'd use all my skills to secure a much-needed deal.

Sachiko, a petite lady in her 30s, liked our products and committed teamwork. Her manager was a handsome young man. I was keen to cover the seven branches they had throughout London and, just like any other cleaning business, willing to prove we could do the best job. I gulped the tea Sachiko had poured. I felt having four young children (still having to wear a medical support after my c-section for the last one), nine staff and working 11 hours, six days a week, with family shopping and chores on the seventh, had all taken its toll.

Sachiko soon presented us with the perfect opportunity to do the impossible. A cleaning test is designed to ensure you're the right kind of cleaning company, so your staff turn up at the agreed time, in uniform, and perform miracles. You can already understand why so many cleaning companies only do domestic work – easy money with little or no comebacks. I was taking full responsibility for my service-delivery with trained staff and accountability, but still we struggled with limited resources. Few companies have training resources unless they have investment. Even then, limited knowledge results in failures. These failures are covered by monitoring techniques that look good on paper in the commercial market but mean little in reality and, of course, managers take other managers out for drinks to cover the cracks.

In both the domestic and commercial market another major problem is the frequency of cleaner turnover, this is often three-weekly. Low pay and unfair conditions have the cleaners always trying – mostly failing – to find a better job.

All our staff had been with us from the start and we had been trading for two years so we were a force to be reckoned with. However, passing this cleaning test would ensure we would lose to another cleaning company one day soon. This is the over-crowded, unmaintained, untrained and self-defeating industry in the UK.

The call came from Sachiko and I was ready with my team headed by my then-husband, John. Sachiko explained this was a property she'd just taken on.

Maybe the property or landlord was a new contract, but it is common practice by estate agents to ensure the stakes could not be higher and that I was responsible for the outcome of the cleaning. If we failed that would have been the end of the relationship with JAC

Strattons. I have worked in hundreds of properties over the years and cannot over-emphasise how much damage can be caused by lack of deep-cleaning in an over-occupied property. I was about to see a property that would have been better to tear down and rebuild, such was the level of dilapidation, all caused by a lack of care. Properties are left by lazy, arrogant individuals and groups such as students or families who are so caught up in their own rubbish, they don't notice the filth. Then they walk away and do it all again in the next property leaving a cleaning company to scrape back the years or fold trying.

It's demonstrably the case that our mental and physical health is affected by our surroundings. Relationships at home and work are impacted by the level of dirt and disorder we live in. Clean, ordered homes help create clean, ordered minds, families and workers. Disorder and dirt create chaos at home and beyond.

If this property had been assessed first by me, I would have written a report and justified it taking weeks as opposed to days to deep-clean.

John was the team leader. Kin, (second in command), wore the veil and was an Ethiopian refugee. We gave Kin her first job and transformed her life during our three years together. I had Tanya, a brilliant girl from Cyprus who had been unfairly treated by several cleaning companies that were themselves being abused by several estate agents. And Alex, a new trainee who became an experienced and knowledgeable team member, Nick a lovely London geezer, and Fowzia another refugee in a veil. They were all excellent team players, hard-working, polite and skilled in housekeeping.

We would normally have only three members of the team on one job but, given the opportunity, I was taking no chances. David, my experienced business partner and former shareholder, was equally keen for us to ‘get it right’. David claimed he had great experience of cleaning teams, but his year with the company cost me much more than his well-meaning involvement. David was another thorn in my side as he dragged me away from the direction of mind-reading rooms and into the world of cheap commercial cleaning, endless complaints, and potential liability. One can imagine the facilities managers penny-pinching yet cherry-picking as the market is saturated with cleaning lambs ready to commit themselves to the commercial slaughter. It’s the individual cleaners who get abused and disempowered with early starts, overloaded expectations, unacceptable personal and professional demands, poor pay, and low or no job satisfaction. Then there are the toxic chemicals which they’re expected to use. The impact is not only on the cleaner; the office workers who spend half their lives in these commercial spaces, often suffer too, with poor cleaning and toxic environments exacerbated by luxurious air conditioning that will ensure bacteria and dirt are well-circulated for everyone to inhale. If only these big companies would invest in some deep-cleaning, they would find their workforce thanking them with fewer days off and higher productivity. Not only that, a company that behaves well and employs an ethical practice could instil this ethic in its workforce.

My team at least had a technique and non-toxic products, but it wasn’t enough! Even with David, who wanted to undercut any other company to get deals – thus ensuring our survival long enough to prove our skills – we still never stood a chance of getting noticed. Although good quality cleaning is about technique, for everyone else it’s about price, and there is always some other cleaning company willing to do the impossible for an equally impossible price.

Trouble is, the market cannot stand the long-term abuse of workers and buildings. Spotless Organic was called into the international Arabic hotel chain, Jumeirah, selling apartment-style living for £11,000 a week and budgeting just £6 – yes, six – a day for cleaning the same. Rooms are turned upside down by decadent guests on drunken or drug-fuelled rampages. These rooms have to be redecorated monthly costing five to ten times more than we would charge for deep-cleaning. Jumeirah is choosing to decorate because they cannot clean to a high enough standard. The redecoration costs will mean the room is constantly toxified with paints and non-eco-building materials. Jumeirah has a written agreement with all staff to comply, as best they physically can, with anything a guest demands. The French head housekeeper in 2013, Daniele Buaron, told me she feared for her cleaners' mental and physical health. The young women, Daniele explained to me, were often found in tears sitting in these apartments, overwhelmed by the amount of debauchery left for them to clean up.

I assured her my staff would not crumble, so Daniele and I created a price list to reduce the decoration costs with quality cleaning and mentally stable staff. But the hotel bosses feared exposure if they reached out to Spotless Organic. I even offered to take on all their 100 cleaning staff and retrain them. This would have protected them from compromises because Spotless Organic would be outside contractors thus not obliged to sign-up to Jumeirah's subtle exploitation.

Imagine you're an 18-year-old from, say, Eastern Europe where low pay is common... you come to London to find work with a full job description, clauses, penalties and perks plus a line or two verbally highlighted by your interviewer on the importance of adhering to this specific agreement (ensuring guests' happiness is one reason why the Jumeirah brand is so successful). Eager to please and wanting to become part of such a high-end service, you happily agree to comply at all times. It's unlikely you'd think you're agreeing to compromise yourself.

But then some months into your new job when you have enough money to pay rent and buy food, a customer requests that you relax after a hard morning's work: "Please, come, sit on the bed and try a little champagne with me." Then you recall the agreement. You break the rules to make the rules; you take your first sip... Once you have been paid a cash tip for your services, it's easy to do it again. Of course, this demoralises the staff and damages them long-term.

I am suggesting that staff are compromising themselves by doing more than the actual job description. For example, cleaners are not supposed to drink alcohol when cleaning a room but they are doing it! Compromising ourselves creates stress and the potential to further compromises.

Jumeirah has opened their own academy for training in hospitality but they worried about letting me in, so the nasty farce continued and my proposal was swept under each room's £30,000 rug.

JAC Strattons is probably one of the better agents so I decided to use them as a marker for the rest of the industry.

The team had arrived at the test property. A large house with three double bedrooms would normally take a day with three staff, even if it were in a bad condition. Day one at this property had not even scratched the surface. The team started in the downstairs loo – literally the smallest room – and, when I phoned them from the office at the end of the day, they had just about finished it. I was perplexed at the lack of progress. I decided to attend the property the next day. I have been housekeeping since the age of four. Up to that point in my life, I had never seen a property contaminated with ingrained filth so bad it led to the total dilapidation of the property. I used to watch Hammer House of Horrors when I was a kid, but I didn't believe the vile sets created could ever truly represent real-life homes.

Each one of my team had suffered discrimination, violence, addictions and low pay. Fowzia and Kin had grown in confidence and were relieved to be contributing to this country after escaping bad marriages and living on state handouts; working with me was a chance of freedom. Nick used to be a painter and decorator who drove his teammates; nothing was too much trouble for him. Alex our newest member had wealthy parents and top private schooling but ADHD had kept his achievements low, so he had a chance to shine with us. Tanya wanted to work without fear, having experienced verbal threats and actual attacks from two previous cleaning companies; she became a team leader. You already know something of John, my husband, a committed Team Leader.

I did my best to provide leadership and training both internally and externally, but it wasn't enough. We had no support in any form from the government and even the dreaded congestion charge and limited parking across London left us – like many small business owners – in a constantly compromised position because some specialist jobs can only be delivered well during daylight hours. So much for supporting new business! No wonder most people don't want to even try. I am hoping this book will help raise the profile of cleaners and service companies with a small or, as in my case, no budget.

I started Spotless Organic by knocking on doors every afternoon, into the early evening, until someone gave me a contract. In the first two years of the company, I had no set-up capital. An interest-free loan would have enabled me to employ help to do the admin, bookkeeping, payment-chasing and marketing and sales. I saved every penny that came in to buy much-needed cleaning equipment, the rest paid staff. The business only became profitable enough to pay me after its fourth year of trading. We had no infrastructure. I couldn't get a loan from the government, or my bank who also claimed to support small businesses. Many of us will have unsuitable personal credit ratings. This can be due to not having higher purchase or credit agreements. Banks are largely designed to profit only the rich shareholders, and ensure the poor man with the fewest resources stays that way. I had a 20-year history with my bank and stayed within my overdraft. I was expected to run my small business as though I had the staff of my two UK giant contractors, Countrywide and Barnard Marcus. In short, I had to wear too many hats when only a couple of them fitted.

When I opened my first Spotless Organic shop in 2013, I was further burdened with all the demands of business rates, VAT, insurance, employment law. Within a year, I had closed down the shop and retreated to my home base. It isn't that I didn't want to comply with the multitude of regulations or pay my taxes, there were just too many. I hope that the cleaning industry is shaken up. It will take some big budgets to transform the industry and raise the appalling standards of cleanliness seen in buildings across London.

I arrived at the cleaning test-house in south London. From the outside, it looked OK. I pushed the front door open and entered the Hammer House of Horror hallway. My staff was all around me holding barely visible items with the amount of cleaning far outweighing each item's worth. Toilet brush holders, bins and a light-fitting were revealing themselves like diamonds in the dirt. As I looked up the stairs, the sight that met my eyes had me thinking perhaps Frankenstein's monster lived here. The walls – what I could see of them – were as rounded and high as the staircase that sat within them. Layers of cobwebs, five inches deep, covered the ceiling along and down the curving walls. Obviously, the cobwebs hid the wallpaper or paint completely. On top of this was a thick covering of dust that must have gathered over at least three years. The sheer magnitude of the cobwebs was astonishing. Literally, years upon years of built-up webs undisturbed by the inhabitants who, we were told, had only just moved out, although some spiders remained in residence.

I armed myself with a lamb's wool long stick and tapped the cobwebbed wall. The stick bounced off the webs, leaving the cobwebs perfectly intact. Well, at least that tapping didn't create any dust – it was all safely cocooned in the cobweb! For all the team knew, small rodents were captured in there. I wandered into the bedroom and tapped my pen on the side of a ceiling lamp. The lamp was once full of tiny holes. These were now black spots of microscopic dust that had filled up the holes over years for a snug home. My pen (now a scientific tool) tapped the side of the lamp and released a plume of the black dust spots. This clouded around the lamp like a mini-bomb encasing my head, and engaging me in a coughing fit.

The entrenched dirt formed a 'protective layer' between the paint and the wood or the walls. Painting would've been impossible. Imagine trying to sandpaper grease? Well, that would take more than twice the time and effort compared to a clean dry surface. If you've painted, only to find it peeling off in weeks, it will be because the surfaces have not been cleaned before sanding.

I phoned Sachiko: 'Hi Sachiko, have you seen this property?' Sachiko had, so knew how dilapidated it was. I should have walked out there and then with my team, but my ego, my hunger, my promise to deliver the undeliverable would not let me or my team do that. "It will take more time than we thought," I said.

"Oh, yes, sorry about that," she replied. "How long?"

"It's difficult to say but at least three or four days." The irony is this would be the first of a catalogue of dilapidated properties we'd see. Mould, moths and mayhem ensure the property will cost thousands to rectify. But in a false economy, who cares? Property owners and cleaners are led by ineffective cleaning companies, driven by price over skill. It will take a brave new breed of traditional deep-cleaning companies to set-up and make a stand for quality service. And intelligent landlords ideally who have read this book will have to understand the need for long-term investment. How about a new English Green Cleaning Guild? Someone should invest in an organisation that sets and maintains real cleaning standards.

Most jobs involve a cleaning process. A dentist scrubs and cleans teeth removing debris; a heart surgeon unblocks pipes and valves; a hairdresser cleans and cuts hair; a chef cleans tools and food then cooks; and a cosmetic surgeon removes fat then scrapes away the years.

The kitchen of the Hammer House was filled with human grease and cooking oils mixed with human debris such as skin and hair. Through our skin, we release toxins from the body. And we shed our skin all the time. Skin-flakes are a major contributor of dust and dirt in homes. In the face of such filth, armed with our technique, my staff soldiered on. The technique is described in detail earlier but to recap: stick close together, work from the top down, and use clean cloths every time the cloth is dirty. We would win this house back and get the contract. It took six full days of very hard work to scrape, scrub, and re-clean every inch of that house. But it only put a noose around our necks; apparently, nothing would be too much to handle now.

JAC Stratton gave us lots of work over a two-year period and Sachiko and I enjoyed a good relationship. But eventually we would be given a property with such a magnitude of filth and, caught unawares – used to dealing with mostly reasonable properties – we would fail. If a property could have relatives, the house we were asked to revive would have been the bigger, uglier brother of the one recovered by us two years earlier.

An emergency clean had been ordered to start in the middle of the same day. We would not normally do this because of limited natural light and preparation time but the manager was insistent, and Sachiko was unusually not around so I had to take his instructions. The new tenant, an irate Spanish woman, was already moving in. My team attended late afternoon. Several lights were faulty, and the team stayed till midnight!

But the next day the phone was ringing. Sachiko wasn't happy, her Spanish client even less so. I was asked to attend the property. The Spanish lady had chosen this property to justify her anger with my staff. (She was always to be angry). She manhandled John, grabbing him by the collar and shoving him into a filthy living room to re-clean the carpets for the third time (the dirt just kept coming up). She denigrated the other staff and generally made us wholly responsible for her anger. I managed to contain myself and, ignoring the rude tenant, explained to the attending landlady and Sachiko that the staff was fighting a battle to get this filthy place turned around. It would take days, even weeks of cleaning and re-cleaning to get the built-on dirt and thick sticky dust off every item. Still, the Spaniard was baying for our blood. And she got it!

The Strattons' manager who had persuaded us to do the clean in the middle of the day was dismissed and, shortly after – despite my long report explaining why we'd failed – so were we. David (my business advisor) and I were on bad terms by now. He liked to come in and give orders as to what we were doing wrong. I was miserable, still working without pay, 14-hour days – from 7.30am until after 11.00pm – and staff had lost their morale. I wanted David out before he killed our chances of moving forward with his cheap 'n' cheerful prices. And his minimal contribution to the company was now unacceptable.

I had given him a 50% share of nothing when the company was first setting up, but it had cost him no more than a few hours of his time a week. Since then, with his help, we had a lot more money and I was getting closer to being paid, but my self-worth was low. I had now to buy back the share I had given him for free. I found an investor and sold a 25% share for £15,000. To get his former-50% back, I had to pay the whole £15,000 to David. Now I had a 75% share of the company. His profits were high! Another hard year would pass before I came into my own and even longer before others would understand mind-reading rooms.

With 14-hour days on telephones and a computer, I turned into a workaholic escaping from the cracks in the marriage for a few more years, losing myself in managing staff, estate agents, and kids, and letting John's homemade curries and Indian bread repress my uncertainty. Why, when I was working so hard and making so much money, did I see none of it? I had had no time to spend any. I caught myself a few times in the mirror, now overweight, over 40, and overworked with four kids and a cleaning company, doing my best. mind-reading rooms and I were lost. A Room Read of my own home confirmed my worst fears. The money was being spent in large amounts on uncontrollable gambling by my husband. Yes, the evidence had always been in my space. It was the real root of years of untold heartache to me and my children. And now it was well beyond the point of Room Reader. No glitzy cushion could turn the losses and red herrings around.

But, thanks to my mind-reading rooms, I was now not in denial of the facts before me (even if he continued to pretend all was well, giving us no chance to sit down and arrange our finances). The banks had already instructed the sale of everything. I found thousands of betting slips hidden in drawers and gym bags; scratch-cards scattered behind and on top of wardrobes; and stomach-churning eviction letters folded neatly in suit pockets. I quickly sold my cherished family home to pay off what was owed. I decided we'd all go to John's home in Mauritius.

With a heavy heart, a month later, I returned without him. I closed the business knowing that managing four children alone would be more than enough for me. So, everything I had worked for those last eight years had evaporated. On reflection, I want to assure you that had I not had the infrastructure issues, the gambler and the appalling markets to wrangle with, this business could have been much more profitable. So, I hope that you or a friend will use this book as guidance for what works – and what doesn't – in a deep-cleaning business. Many of the jobs we did after David's and John's exit and out of the estate agency market were highly profitable, so I had really started to make inroads into the domestic market offering my specialist services. The demand for these services is high. Through mind-reading rooms, Spotless Organic will be revived and thrive in a thousand new organic deep-cleaning ventures.

15. Keeping up with the Joneses

As a child, I enjoyed escaping into my world of rooms, creating and re-creating better, safer spaces with my toys. I became good at this. I understood, for example, a window needed curtains that opened each day and closed at night. This ritual brings in energy at morning light and closes off negativity (darkness), resting the room. To see this, keep the curtains in a few rooms closed all day. The space has a different energy to it without the benefit of natural light. It feels dead. If that is the impact on the room, what's the impact on you?

Granny Connolly and my sisters worked weekends to smooth and soften the energy throughout the home. This ongoing activity included monthly deep-cleaning as a big part of that cleansing, nurturing process. It wasn't all work though. I remember our street party at Queen Elizabeth's Silver Jubilee. It stretched the whole mile-length of Cunningham Road. The tables were covered in white paper with a red stripe down the centre. The paper plates were covered with white triangles of cheese and ham, and mini-sausages on sticks. Then fairy cakes topped with lemon icing sprinkles were washed down with orange squash. All the kids were given a Silver Jubilee coin to keep as memorabilia. Some of us tried to spend the giant coin. I knew Queen Elizabeth – the lady who lived in Buckingham Palace – had paid for me and my friends to have a big party. I was so looking forward to meeting her, and I even wore a girly dress I hoped she'd like. I waited the whole day. Only when I was sure she wasn't showing up did I go straight home and change back into dungarees.

Community partying has a positive element to developing support networks. We don't need royal patronage to enjoy this. Schools are a great place to generate social events. Have a street party; whether it highlights a charity or a day. Go on, knock on your neighbour's door.

On normal days, we thoroughly enjoyed life with fizzy pop deliveries and ice cream vans. In fact, virtually all services came to our door 30 years ago. Window cleaners, insurance collectors, Avon ladies, Tupperware or Bettaware sales-ladies, bible-bashers, encyclopaedia or window salesmen, vegetable vans, milk floats – you name it, people and goods arrived without hesitation at our open doors and in our homes.

However, even then, the beginnings of selective entry to the home had begun. My mother was terrified of gypsies who came with sprigs of lavender offering to tell her fortune. Nor was she keen on having dad's mother and stepfather around. I think she thought she was better than them (my father's parents). The keeping up with the Joneses syndrome returns. Just because another person has a different way of living from you, don't mean it ain't right.

Gypsy families are often seen as unwanted outsiders because of their desire to travel. Many people will also cite the rise in crime or mess left by travelling communities as a vindication of society's collective opinion. Consider that we just don't like change, and travelling people do. Often, these people are not being provided with designated plots. I think the solution lies in ensuring designated areas are mapped-out and properly maintained by the local council. I do not believe gypsies are more inclined to criminality than the rest of us. When I was a child we had regular travellers to Widnes and had a lot of fun. They are more adventurous than the rest of us and can imaginatively play without the need for the latest toy or gadget. I found them to be close-knit and supportive of their offspring. They were a hard-working group of people collecting our metal rubbish and tarring our paths. They seemed to look on the bright side of life and had ponies and interesting accents. They may be lacking some education – and business may have changed – but the right for them to live the way they have chosen to has not.

Nanny and Grandad Sinnott had a need for pets, stuff and people. It worked for them, they always seemed happy when I was around. The funny thing is that dad's family name, Sinnott, is connected to Irish tinkers so Mum was probably sleeping with her fears, even though they were imagined. Nanny Sinnott and her family lived in Runcorn across the bridge from my hometown. Nanny and Grandad Sinnott were extraordinarily warm and inquisitive.

Nanny was the very opposite of Granny Connolly. Nanny was a collector of everything: people, stray dogs, furniture, pictures and ornaments. Nanny Sinnott had a large appetite for social gatherings and thickly buttered white bread. Although she was as good at cooking as Granny Connolly, she often ate between and after meals. She was so large she needed helping through doors. Her house was packed with memorabilia, car-parts, second and third fridges, clothes, dogs and people. Visiting Granny Sinnott's house was like going into a warm and friendly food-serving, doggie-friendly junk-shop. My grandfather was a mechanic and a heavy drinker, although I have been told by many people in their late fifties and sixties drinking in the pub and home was routine for men and women.

So, when he and my nan decided to become Mormons and lead a Mormon Church congregation, he stopped all that because Mormons don't drink (never mind alcohol, they won't even touch caffeine). I remember going to hear him speak in the Mormon Church and Nan was always cooking interesting foods for the never-ending stream of American missionaries. I always had a lot of fun at her house. Most evenings she had about ten people with her own grandchildren and the latest arrivals from Salt Lake City. Unfortunately, Nan could not stop eating and was obese in her forties. She died at a young age due to health complications.

Grandad Sinnott was my father's stepfather and I am told he often beat my father. With my Nan to guide him, Grandad did change a lot over the years. He took on her four children because she was another war widow. He stopped drinking and was always kind to us. My dad, along with his siblings, kept the name Jackson from their biological father. Perhaps it was my father's way of ensuring grandad Sinnott never forgot the hurt caused.

This part of my family was comfortable with chaos, which shows that mind-reading rooms is not about moral high ground. So here I invoke the cliché *if it's not broke, don't fix it.* I am also keen to show you a little more of my father's influence and how my mother's snobbery meant that the positive and potentially supportive elements of his family were lost over the years.

We often find ourselves in conflict with unusual mixes in the family. It is easy to give up or hide out but try to harness the positive elements especially if you have children involved. Discuss the issues in your Room Reading group and always try to find a way that ensures the best interest of all the parties. I think my mother could have helped her relationship with my father if she had been less critical of his parents. At least his children would have enjoyed many more fun and interesting times at nanny Sinnott's house. Never compare your family to other people's; your family is what it is. Look at the difficulties the 'royal family' have faced over the last thirty years! So, lower your expectations and enjoy what you have. Remember, the perfect Jones families and lifestyles only exist in artificially created environments lasting for seconds in a magazine photo, minutes in a pop-video, an hour in a drama or a film rather than the reality of a lifetime.

I don't remember seeing an official street-cleaner on the side roads. Steps and pavements were cleaned by each person doing their bit outside their front door. Why's this gone?

Big companies are not automatically safer than local ones, they just have bigger marketing budgets. Big supermarkets are designed to make us spend as much as possible. The clue is in the name 'Super'. As we have become wiser to market manipulation, they are disguising themselves as 'markets' and 'local stores' but it's not just the size of the stores, it's the way they are set out. The aim is to have you buying things you don't need. Buying foods that are *two for the price of one* condition you to buy and then eat or waste more food. Of course, food stores are designed to have us thinking about food more so that we eat more than we need to. It is the same with clothing stores. Walking down Oxford Street in London is heavenly for some; for others, it's like a beautifully bad dream; a world of perfect models designed to make us feel inadequate, so we buy another new dress, trousers or top. Have you noticed how much harder it is to buy the basic items we actually need? Like quality underwear and socks or shoes for children? The focus of most High Streets isn't service provision, it's simply ensuring there are enough perfect images to convince you you're lacking something.

If you buy the item the model is wearing, yes, for a moment you feel better, but the cost of the item often outweighs the benefit. We are responding to our environment. We can have more by powerfully choosing things we really need over what we're told we want.

Please buy local and engage locally; it is key to developing sustainable communities, work opportunities and work ethics. Our lives are more connected when we generate useful services that help us all locally. You can make a difference by taking on a local service provider over the big names. If you can, get together with people and learn or share skills to produce local jobs and growing sites for vegetables and fruits; learn to manage chickens for free-range meat and eggs. Start petitioning government to create more local jobs and to tighten regulation on pesticides and encourage greater production of home grown organic foods; connect with your nearest local farms and arrange to bulk buy foods with neighbours to save money; join a transition town group or similar organisation to learn how to grow your own foods; and set up a Room Reading group.

The mind-reading rooms model generates and empowers ways of being. This model can be used outside the home in the local community. I'd like to see government setting up funding initiatives, entrepreneurial workshops run by business leaders to inspire a generation of freethinkers. It doesn't have to be big, just practical to provide something for the community. For example, home-visiting services like bike repairs, window and other types of cleaners, gardeners, childminders, carers, plumbers, clothes-makers, or sellers, carpenters, cooks, artists, computer technicians – the list is endless. The focus provides what's missing holistically and at ground-level. I'm not suggesting these things don't exist now; we should simply shine a light on this as the key to relieving local communities of the burden of unemployment and of having to rely on corporations and institutions.

Go to a so-called less developed country and you'll feel the buzz of work – all age groups earning a living and usually having fun! They have the extremes too, such as slave-labour, but this is largely created and dominated by either corporations or governments. Big corporations and marketing have damaged our capacity to engage in conversation and local needs.

Islington Council in North London used to sub-contract estate work to a big company, but the big company had no connection with the local tenants they serviced. Some out-of-work tenants felt upset and frustrated they had lost their jobs to the big company and had to let them into their homes to carry out maintenance works. Islington reviewed this position and - at least when I was there - returned to in-house services. It's great to see local people being employed, having pride in doing a good job where they work and live. Mind-reading rooms encourages people to support such local policies and practices. You can encourage your local representatives to make such community-conscious decisions.

We need each other's input and the more hands-on we are, the better. It's human nature; we evolve in teams; we thrive in co-operative spaces. Monopolies based on a dominant group results in extremes. These oligarchic concepts – be they religious, royal, political or celebrity hyped – don't work because they have little connection with ordinary life and don't meet people's daily needs. Ordinary life ought to lead *us,* not power-hungry leaders or groups.

Collective responsibility within communities works and right now we have an opportunity to really engage with this. Room Plans can transform more than the homes we live in. In the past in schools, girls had to focus on home-economics, sewing and typing. Boys did woodwork. I was bored. Rejecting the frills of homemade dresses and engaging instead in rough 'n tumble, I was what many would describe as a tomboy. "Why couldn't I do woodwork?"

I loved my local community centre, a nondescript building surrounded by hills. It served local kids with impromptu discos and social activities. Running along the top of the hill, which was very high for a child, I experienced a sense of empowerment and exhilaration. I pushed myself – breathing, balance and bravery – as far as I could, even slipping once or twice and falling down the hill. Mind-reading rooms advocates running out of your comfort zone, too.

I suppose I was self-conscious that other kids might have more than me. The keeping up with the Joneses syndrome has escalated. Today I feel my kids are in an unspoken class war! Who have better holidays, designer shoes, house – even haircut? In short, kids are asking, 'Am I good enough to exist near you?' Money is over-valued. I want my sons to value people because they've compassion and understanding.

Mind-reading rooms creates compassion in the home; the Room Plan provide structures applicable by anyone. The benefits are strength and love formulated in the home then taken beyond, impacting and improving communities.

See this book as an opportunity to better relate to your family. Our underestimation of the complexity of human relationships is part of our process of disconnection; this disconnection has made us more extreme in our views and less empathetic to each other. Let us embrace and consider difference an essential part of the tapestry of life in our global village. Always look to finding resolutions in our personal space. That will transform life beyond our homes and communities. Media and politicians often have hidden agendas in promoting or demoting different groups. It is easier with the internet to judge what is actually happening. Don't believe everything you hear even from official sources. We must learn to read between the lines, to ask questions. This will help us differentiate propaganda from reality at home and beyond.

Room Reading groups can build up a list of experts so that local people are employed on references given by other locals. Websites are fine, but you never know who's written their testimonials, or why. With Roomies, you're genuinely responsible to each other. Room Reading groups are created for you, by you. They should have no – or minimal – joining fees. Community centres or health clinics will ensure they are regularly advertised. The bigger our group, the greater the support. Nothing is more important to us than our very life and the birth of new family members, yet the world we now live in has left us open to isolation, limited services locally, and jeopardising the comfort of our final moments. Mind-reading rooms offers communities a self-help structure for us to lead more expressive and authentic lives. It's not a one-size-fits-all methodology. It's about connecting with others in a practical way.

16. The little mouse business

Key themes: business choice; inspiration; searching for the heart of the business; why people love independent business owners.

Do you have your own business? If you have a business that doesn't touch, move and inspire you, you're in the wrong one. I cannot imagine sitting in a shop five or six days a week surrounded by things I have little or no connection with. People are drawn into shops because they are inspired by your love of the things you're selling. The big stores are experts at this, but they also use techniques to make shoppers feel inadequate, like super-sized images of stunning people wearing their clothes. Individual shops can put themselves at an advantage over the giants. They can be created from inspiration and the personal touch without those nasty elements that the giants use to have us desperate to buy happiness. Such inspired businesses will genuinely make a difference to you because they are created with love for the products.

To create a powerful business, do what really you most love to do! Bake cakes. Make jams. Cheeses. It could be fixing bikes or clocks or making beautiful pottery. Whether you've a cleaning, a legal or dental business, you should have the energy and inspiration to make a difference to all those who buy from you beyond (sometimes well beyond) the transaction. What really makes you happy? If you have an unhappy shop you will sell misery. You will only make enough money to survive. It will be reflected in your home as well as your business and, of course, your life.

I think, if I had had a business Roomie, I would have found the necessary support to identify that someone (sadly, my husband) was stealing from the company accounts. Even more importantly, I would have created a support network to deal with the accounts more effectively and emotionally help me through the turmoil of having to rid myself of my husband. Of course, I hope that you might even keep your partner! It is all about balance. We have to be realistic about what is manageable and achievable in the circumstances. What's clear is that setting up a Roomie group of like-minded people will help you deal with the issues you face much more powerfully than ruminating over and/or repressing your unexpressed desires.

Work through Room Reader with your Roomies to add value to your community. It's wonderful to run a marathon for charity, but it requires a lot of training and energy and may take you away from your own needs. The Roomie group is inclusive, developmental and will start face-to-face interactions that translate into better lives and business. Many third-world countries are filled with entrepreneurs. Surely, if they can make an inspired living, we in the West can do this too. So, now is the time to plan your new business or re-create your existing one. The number of highly intelligent people with a lovely personality and energy working as cashiers for minimum pay has to drop. The number of new small business owners in the UK and beyond has to grow. Remember, I started my business without a penny. A third world business owner finds the required materials and starts by selling to his neighbour.

Why don't you start like that, see how you get on?

A little mouse makes his home with scraps and has a wonderful life save an occasional encounter with a cat. Rather like the capitalist system, the cat may seem innocent, but has sharp claws and teeth. Some businesses thrive on subversive tactics and do not add value to you in terms of personal growth, health and well-being. Cats can be domesticated to great effect and so can a business. Make things that can genuinely add value to your life and your customers. Keep it connected to a genuine need for making a difference and watch it grow. Little mouse, little mouse, you can make your business or your house in so many places. You survive and thrive with your hugely creative and inquisitive mind.

A shop owner who I met began on the right track, but over many years got side-tracked by pleasing others before pleasing herself. How can any of us help anyone else if we are aiming to provide for the unknown customer who may or may not walk into your business?

You must please yourself first. Keep doing what you love, and your business will keep you and others happiest. Every six months, review what you're creating. Keep refining and defining your gift shared with your customers. Whatever your town, whatever your home or business, you can learn to mind-read your rooms. Use a Roomie group to develop your ideas. Remember that a Roomie group is simply about sharing and getting help to improve your life and those around you. Mind-reading rooms is active, so don't just sit down and moan! Network with love, create events for fun. Share with others and see how your life will flourish.

I wandered into a large shop in Exeter. It was a mishmash of incomplete ideas; second-hand, then new clothes with candles, a vintage duvet cover in the window, silver necklaces and earrings placed on top of antiquarian books.

The lady was simply and prettily dressed. We chatted about her lack of energy. Her life seemed to be in transition. She explained that the shop had originally been full of homestyle items but over the years found herself trying to please her customers, even to the detriment of her inspiration.

The shop was spacious yet was too busy with all the different elements going on. It was difficult to focus on any one thing. I went over to a large tabled area in the shop's centre where I picked up an oversized matchbox trinket. Inside was a sweetly dressed mouse with his little pillow and blanket. It was the most adorable thing in the whole shop, and I felt that it represented the true direction of its owner. We talked a little more and she told me she loves to listen to the Archers at bedtime. She also liked to read books.

I promised her I would return within a few days and advise her what she could do. Meantime, I recommended Sadghuru's free online meditations and vitamins like magnesium, D3, B12, B6 and sea kelp. These things helped soothe anxiety and calm the energy of the mind.

Of course, I could have told her there and then what to do but I wanted to wait a few days to ensure she listened intently. I went back the day after her birthday and explained that the mouse was the key to transforming her business, that the dresses she chose to please others were far less inspiring to her. And I said she had to take a risk. "People buy into your inspiration and that is only apparent in your choice of vintage duvets in the window, your lovely scented candles and soaps and your love of books, radios and bedtime!"

I suggested she start to invest in beautiful bedding and put a bed in the centre of the shop. She would dress up the bed every few days with sumptuous pillows edged with lace. She could sell towel sets and bathrobes maybe even nightwear, all with a vintage mousey cosiness. I imagined Roberts radios and nostalgic things like bedtime books and bath-time soaks to get people in the mood for reading or listening or love.

The lady agreed to my plans and was a little surprised that I could have been so accurate in my estimations of her space and objects. But the message was clear. So, as I left, I said: "A little mouse told me".

Key actions: developing the heart of the business; dumping elements not coming from you; the need for teamwork or a monthly Roomie group.

17. International mind-reading rooms (of a shanty house)

Key themes: creating our first Room Reading group; recycling; ordering a home; comforting additions.

Mauritius is an exotic country, an island nation in the Indian Ocean about 2,000 kilometres off the south-east coast of the African continent, so beautiful and simple in many ways. I love that the government has put signs with messages on side roads and in parks such as 'Be nice to each other', 'Show you care', 'Smile, make people happy'. Imagine if all the advertising we are bombarded with were replaced by simple messages that have a single motive: to generate peace. I recall being a bit annoyed about something one day, but then a sign caught my eye: 'Be nice' and I thought: 'Yes, this is silly.' I was able to drop my annoyance right then.

My ex-mother-in-law, Danwantee, was an extraordinary little Hindi farming lady. She has lived without money for all her life, raised six children herself and entrusted two more to adoption in France. Danwantee has re-connected with one of them and lives with the hope of one day knowing her other daughter and adoptive parents. I love Danwantee's stamina, her willingness and ability to generate something from nothing, and the fact this lady smiles from an open heart. Her husband had several wives on the Island. He did provide his children with food and craft skills, but he died in an accident leaving all his wives alone with 11 children between them. Danwantee became mother and father to her children. She milked goats on her land and walked miles to grasslands from early morning through hot afternoons to feed them. In the evenings, she had to chop down branches of trees to make fires for cooking rice or baking bread. Then at weekends, she bartered for fruits and vegetables with the goats' milk. The children would be with her throughout her endeavours.

She washed other people's clothes on rocks, always keeping her dignity despite her difficult life. Her shanty house was established on a small piece of land built with cheap materials by her husband and sons, later recognised and supported by the Mauritian government who modernised some parts and allowed the cheap purchase by the occupants. Danwantee had not been able to purchase the land but maybe one day she, her children or grandchildren would.

I was excited about providing her with a Room Plan. The house was very basic; the walls were made from hardboard. It had an outside loo and shower, some land used to recycle plastic bottles, chickens for eggs and meat, a dog to keep predators (other dogs) out, and a tin roof.

The house was worn but sweet. I gathered a team of locals and during deep-cleaning bedrooms and living rooms of my mother-in-law's spacious but sparse house, they started to experience Mind-reading rooms in action. We removed some junk (under protest) to an outside area; I replaced a sofa made of what looked like twigs with a luxurious black velvet one that had gold leaves; the paperwork was messily stacked into corners of wardrobes, so we bought her a hand-varnished TV table with drawers for it all; clothes were sorted into usable and 'past it'. We bought her a fridge, and a new whistling kettle so if she ever started to forget, she'd hear the water was ready. I wanted, and still want, for her to spend the rest of her life with some luxury around because I can provide it. Giving her grandchildren was a gift from me.

House-junk apart, we cleared the outside gardens of rubbish and planted flowers, herbs, and lettuce. She has Aloe Vera plants around the house so, despite the poverty she has lived in, a sense of healing prevailed. My boys love the chickens and collecting fresh eggs daily to eat with Grandma.

All the local people live in hexagon-shaped clusters like the inside of a beehive. I can find out where my children are by asking six different neighbours all at the same time! Collective responsibility prevails here, with an emphasis on support as opposed to blame. Businesses are run at home from bread-making to selling fruit 'n' veg, or fresh fish. You can survive here with very little money. Danwantee did everything to teach her children; from appreciating the fun of swimming to the dangers of the Indian Ocean, from catching fish to building a fire, from cleaning clothes on the rocks to keeping her family safe.

My cafe kids – used to eating out and having all the latest gadgets – have stopped asking me to buy material possessions and instant (fast food) gratifications; they have learned how to grow veg, how to be safe in the sea, where eggs and chickens come from (even asking which came first) and that simple living can be fun. I had stopped worrying about where the children are and who they are with. I'm not suggesting we all move to Mauritius, but we can learn from so-called third world countries that commercialisation is making first-world nations greedy, over-stimulated and disconnected.

Disconnected to ourselves, we start to seek more intense pleasure; we even want more pain. This is seen in the boom of body-piercing (other than the ear) by one in 10 young women. We've also seen an escalation in tattoos that cover more than a third of the body amongst both sexes. We escape from mental suffering by denying our present. Transfixed by unreal futures depicted in pop videos and commercials, depression amongst young people is rife as they aspire to unreality. Another extreme is the use of religion to wage wars and restrict vulnerable groups (often women, children, and other marginalised groups). Such opposing positions must be balanced with the nuts and bolts of daily life because it's nuts and bolts that make life interesting and rewarding, not the fizz of coke or a particular ideology.

We painted the house in pale blue and lilac. We bought a sign with Danwantee Tohuls' name and address on it surrounded by little flowers. We built her a front gate from the junk we found. I bought her a lounger and threw out the old cushions she used to put outside on the ground. I provided my mother-in-law with the dignity and honour she had not had, or asked for, but deserved. It cost very little to transform this woman's life in a simple but profound way. Gathering energy from those around her and empowering them to deliver the service to this paragon of motherhood was beautiful. Some mothers face poverty, addiction or wars with their children, but I know, whatever it is they are dealing with, they will make sacrifices. Everyone calls Danwantee their mother because even now, though her age prevents her from teaching other children how to swim, cook and clean, she will keep them safe.

Danwantee Tohul passed away in March 2017 so she never got to hear her story in the book or enjoy the song dedicated to her and mothers everywhere. Please share this story and song as a way of expressing gratitude to all mothers every day. And always treat mothers with respect and gratitude because they are giving birth and creating the future for of our children to live in peace now. Help mothers around you to become better versions of themselves by supporting, sharing and nurturing them whenever you can. Never judge your mother, no matter how bad a job you think she did, she must have done her best. Help all mothers to be peaceful and heard throughout the world but especially at home.

Key actions: Setting up a Room Reading group, mind-reading rooms in- & outside. (Listen to the song *Motherhood*.)

18. The magpie

Key themes: obsessive behaviour, lack of self-expression, addictions, lies, mortgages, relationships.

Gambling is popular all over the world and sadly it has been normalised by things like the 'health lottery' and 'national lottery' in the UK. We never question the morality of buying raffle tickets or consider the long-term implications of quick-fix solutions to getting what we want. More importantly, schools hold events centred around tombola, raffle tickets, and sports cards where no skill is needed to enter. It's gambling. Why do we parents and teachers not see that children are being conditioned to think that gambling is OK, or worse, good?

How could it not be a good thing with such wonderful charities as 'The Health Lottery'? But for the few people or organisations it helps, there is a massive hidden cost to those who have become addicted to winning and losing everything. Out-of-control gambling destroys lives. And if you think you're immune and in control, think again. It is a very fine line between control and addiction. Any activity requiring little involvement for a big payoff is likely to be bad for us mentally and physically. If you or a partner has a gambling problem, do not ignore it. Do not underestimate its power to destroy all you have created on the fall of the dice, the running of the race, the buying of the scratch-card, and the next, and just one more.

Seek professional help and join a Room Reading group to find the excitement of creating your home so you really control your finances.

A man lived with his wife and three daughters in a comfortable cottage. The front garden was large compared to the cottage (the only one of its kind on a crowded street of relatively giant houses). It had two large trees in the front. Set back from the road it looked cosy and inviting. When I knocked on the door, a nervous-sounding "lady of the house" thus announced herself and ushered me in.

We went through a door to the right of the hallway and entered the living room. The walls were quaintly decorated with vintage floral paper. Two identical sofas sat either side of the sash window. Two children under five ran up the steps from the kitchen laughing and playing. She asked them to keep quiet so as not to wake the baby in its pram. Both children acknowledged her request.

She took me down the steps and into a large kitchen diner with French doors that led out to the cottage's large garden. The whole scene was idyllic but perhaps a little plain. As she took me around the cottage's sparse but functional space, I felt they had the home working well, yet occasionally I noted a bag or stuffed box poorly concealed. This made me feel someone was hiding something under our noses. Indeed, it became clear that this was the problem! The second husband had been sighted by several friends in the bookmaker's although he swore no knowledge or understanding of betting. She said he was always buying jewels and gold yet they were struggling to meet the mortgage payments. She opened one of the hidden boxes to show me his collection of diamonds and trinkets.

The second husband was very different from her first, the lady explained. He was hands-on with the kids and great at DIY. They had their own business. He was a handyman and she dealt with invoices and the girls. He cooked Mediterranean food. So, what was the connection between the semi-hidden jewels, and the gossip? Why was he hiding these items? What risks was he taking to buy them? And if I could not help would they lose everything?

In folklore, a magpie is attracted to shiny objects and likes to hold on to things. It seemed to me that her husband was a magpie. I suggested that they put up fake but pleasing crystal chandeliers and add some luxury items such as glitzy fabric cushions and eiderdowns. He should start a scrapbook with her and collect pictures of the many jewels he was buying. He should stop actually buying them! This way they would keep their treasured home and she would help him to get off the path of gambling to buy his shiny things.

Returning months later, I was pleased to find they'd taken pictures of, then sold, the jewels. The scrapbook was already full of interesting jewels that they collected and now he could share his passion with his family instead of hiding it. The daughters were making papier mache` of sparkling jewels, displayed in the living room.

He used to lie to his wife about going to the betting shop and he did still enjoy the occasional flutter at the bookies but now that cost him little more than his time. This allowed him and his wife to enjoy trips out with the children to the many museums where he could touch and feel objects without having to buy them. They started a relationship-journal and set aside time each month for sharing a romantic evening out. They enjoyed open communication where they both could keep an eye on the family finances such that a balance was struck around the family priorities. She shared finances with him so that he was fully responsible, lifting the burden from her shoulders.

He had realistic targets to meet that meant keeping and enjoying what they had before taking risks that could ruin the family.

The mortgage payments and self-expression have become the focus of the husband's work. In fact, the whole family are more self-expressed and stable. We may not have all the material wealth we think we need or deserve but if we fully engage – and love what we have – we can find joy in simplicity.

Key actions: add glamour to the home with chandeliers and luxurious fabrics; scrapbook objects of interest; sell gems to pay for the treasured home; prioritise finances together; have creative communication with crafting and use relationship-journals; see official advice on gambling. (Listen to the song *I Know A Guy*.)

19. A School's Room Plan

Key themes: Room Plan for schools; letter to the head teacher of Dupree Government School in Mauritius:

Mind-reading rooms is useful for any environment and here is an example of its application outside the home. Perhaps you would like to start a Room Reading group at your school? I wrote this letter to the headteacher so that, over time, she could address the issues. It was my way of thanking the school who had educated my sons whilst they stayed in Mauritius.

Mind-reading rooms develops school communities and can easily be set up and run by the PTA.

Dear Soochita,

Please find here my observations and suggestions for using Room Reader in Dupree Government School. Mind-reading rooms is a new concept that promotes and energises any space by cleaning, ordering, colouring and creating co-operational structures. (In your case 'co-operational' is between parents, teachers and pupils.)

The school is oversubscribed (at least by Western standards) with 40 or more pupils to one teacher. I understand there are approx 300 pupils in the school, ages 3 - 11. The school has had problems with litter-dropping, parents' willingness to trust the judgment and direction of the School Principal and Deputy, and teachers who set out what they want to achieve but often don't manage to deliver.

Pupils discipline is left to and managed by you alone. Your office is open on all sides in the main play area. You are exposed. The children constantly pop-in. (These interruptions are polite but inappropriate.)

The security guard looks miserable and this misery greets all who enter here! The school has been promised a re-build of some parts and, whilst waiting for government funds, the paintwork is long overdue. The children want to play with balls and shuttlecocks but they sometimes get stuck on the roof leading the children to climb up to retrieve them. You have had to stop children bringing balls in as you cannot risk their safety (for example, a child falling from the roof).

Space is limited with children having lunch in the same room they study in. You have two assemblies going on each morning both of which you make a huge effort to attend. The parents appear dissatisfied with the school's management of their children.

The children sometimes show a lack of empathy to the younger ones. You have to travel very far to the school and are coming to the end of your four-year term. You enjoy the challenge of the Mauritian system whereby principals move around every four years but would like to learn how mind-reading rooms can be utilised in this school and – on seeing the results – perhaps others.

Room Plan:

Your security guard is the first person a visitor sees when they attend your school. He/she must, therefore, smile whilst being professional and diligent. His smiling face and smart presentation must become part of his job description. Often people are unaware of how they present. You will find by asking him to smile each time he opens the gate that his whole demeanour will transform. The impact will be that people coming in to visit the school including parents, teachers and pupils will feel welcome, warm and at ease.

Welcome sign:

A 'Welcome' sign that has long-faded sits on a wall far from the entrance. How about a refreshed sign painted on the front gates?

Plants:

You have many wonderful plants at the school. This is a positive contribution to pupils. As a visitor, I would like to know what kind of plants you have and what they are useful for. (Aloe vera, for example, is a natural healer). This can be done by adding some water-proofed signs under the trees.

Vegetables:

All children should know how to grow a vegetable. The world is changing and people from all backgrounds are now growing fresh vegetables for the health of their children. Please explain to parents how this improves knowledge of the earth and teaches self-sufficiency. Children may never grow a vegetable as an adult but just knowing how to, empowers them. In England, many primary school children grow and eat the vegetables in school.

Crafts:

Young adults, boys and girls who can sew on a broken button before an interview are more likely to get the job! Teaching simple crafts may seem a waste of time but children do learn how to manipulate their fingers (sewing, cooking, making crafts) and produce practical results (clothes with buttons, delicious foods, baskets, paintings).

Litter mouth:

The litter bins in the school are not child-friendly. Can you turn them into hippo mouths with papier mache`? Then the children can enjoy throwing in the rubbish and keeping the school clean. They can also write litter-poems and drawings. The best one can be used to post around the school? Example: When you unwrap a sweet, keep the school neat, think Litter Mouth or Send your litter south, think Litter Mouth.

Keep Britain Tidy campaign:

Why was this rubbish campaign such a success? Because it was a doubly positive message. Firstly, we are keeping Britain, we have it in our possession. That's a comforting thought and we're doing this by keeping Britain tidy. Secondly, keeping Britain tidy is an easier activity than what British people have had to do in their recent past to keep Britain at all.

In Mauritius, I was astonished to see people throwing rubbish out of windows and onto the streets. Why? It was because of a lack of bins in public spaces and no attempt at positive messaging by the government. Although they have many other positive and effective messages on simple boards, they failed to use this idea with the rubbish problem.

Pre-primary Park:

It seems like the school could make greater use of this park with other children using it. The equipment could easily handle a six or seven-year-old. I suggest you extend the use of this area.

Water Sign:

Please ensure children can always drink a little water as hydration means they remain alert.

Sunrise:

For the stairwell starved of paint I suggest a sunrise theme that swirls around the first, second and third floors using deep orange, yellows, pale creams and ending with sky-blue. If you would like some help with painting the sunrise walls, please contact my nephew (a former pupil and art student) Billy Matombe his mobile number is: 0571 xx xxx

Outside Classroom Walls:

Each class should share the things they care about whether it's a plant display (as we've seen) or something else the class just loves. A class can impress parents and visitors with a special group interest. This can change yearly or termly.

Drawing/Maths/Language/Science/History/Geography:

I see the teachers have good intentions that often fail to materialise. Therefore, the teachers need to think how they can multi-task lessons. The teachers need to identify the key lessons of each subject and develop combination subjects so that two subjects are dealt with at once. This way the teachers are empowered.

I am concerned these children are not able to physically express themselves at school. They must engage the body to stimulate the mind and ensure knowledge sticks. Many of the children looked bored in the classroom. Some were half-asleep. This is a real shame as they all have the capacity to learn. I believe that levels of attention can easily be improved with more active participation in groups and outside use of space for lessons.

Each class could be divided into four lots of 10 with one team leader (a pupil) for each group who leads the team in a specific subject. Then each group will develop and share the expertise with the rest of the class.

Start an art bin for empty cereal boxes and other used containers to be used to create art. Encourage children to recycle all packaging. Even clothes can be recycled for sewing practice.

School Rules:

The school must draw-up a five-point system of expected behaviour: set standards for others; be grateful for opportunities (remember those with none); treat other people how you want them to treat you; Listen before reacting; ask for help.

Prizes:

Each class can win stars and prizes for Hot Topics and Top Team Player. Stars are given out over a term with the winning team sharing a prize like a cake or fruit or a small item. (It's the thought rather than the amount.)

Classrooms:

Given how many children are in each class, these rooms need as much airing and natural sunlight as possible

Outside areas:

Don't waste these spaces; they ought to be used much more than just for playtimes. For example, the children on the top floor use the outside for classroom activities on Mon & Tues; children on the second floor, Wed-Thurs; ground floor, Fridays.

Toilets:

These need painting in a pale green which could be a sea theme – darker at the bottom and lighter at the top.

Balls/Playtimes:

The 6 – 7-year-olds need to use the park as well as pre-primary.

Basketball hoops should be added to the enclosed central area for children 8 - 11. You explained that the children bring balls; this could be allowed at least one day a week on a class by class basis. The class who are bringing in the balls that day may want to play with other classmates. That's fine as long as the class who is on the rota for bringing them in and taking them home is responsible for the good use of the balls.

If anything happens such as a ball goes onto the roof, it must be reported and dealt with by the caretaker. This section above could be made into a poster and put in the netted play area with space at the bottom to write which class is responsible for balls each day.

Assembly:

Daily assembly including the national anthem, prayer, then the day's agenda sets up the school day. But this takes too much time especially – because you go to both – every day. It needs to be quicker and the Deputy can attend one so you and he alternate involvement. Business of the day should be 10 minutes max. Have time-monitors to increase the speed of assembly until it becomes the norm. Reducing assembly by 10 to 15 minutes gives more time for learning.

Food/Hawkers:

Encourage all to bring in only healthy foods such as homemade dall, fruits and natural foods. Food should be eaten outside unless it's raining as this is another chance to change the environment from the long day in the same space. Children can bring in a small cushion or mat to sit on outside. (They can even make a mat or cushion from a craft activity.) A lunch space can also be allocated so that play can happen without disturbing children who are eating.

Principal's office:

The Principal's Office is to be closed any time the children are playing outside. No children are allowed to enter the principal's office without an appointment nor can any parent speak to the principal without one, unless it's an emergency.

Head office:

The Principal should allocate year teachers. A head and a deputy for each year should take difficult children for half a day. The class who has the difficult child will lose stars.

Your deputy should liaise with head and deputy year teachers on management of discipline. This way, if a child is acting-up in a head of year's class, they can be sent to the deputy and vice-versa. The year heads and deputy heads ought to have a specialist subject where they can be used by other teachers as a resource.

I would like to see a monthly lesson-planning meeting with all the teachers and yourself working together to improve the outcomes of lesson-plans. Lesson-plans should be angled to tackle two or more subjects in one hit. Your monthly teaching meetings ought to try out ideas in 'role play' so that you and the teachers find workable solutions to doubling-up topics and adding in physical activity. (Children learn better that way as they are indisputably involved).

Principal's Office Layout:

The layout of tables is OK. However, the room needs painting and less clutter. Bags ought to be locked away; flowers, plants and/or fish could bring some life to the heart of the school, displayed on the Principal's table and in the room; I'd like you to have new curtains in a calm but rich colour such as deep emerald green or royal blue. I think the school ought to celebrate each Principal – how about starting with a school photo. This can be displayed on the walls; achievements and significant events ought to be in a school yearbook.

The Principal must see the packed itinerary as an opportunity to excel through close planning with the teachers and integration of subjects whenever possible. This will always be possible and will ensure your teachers are winning the game of education whilst having fun. This, in turn, will ensure that your teachers stay longer at your school, and have less illness (as illness is often caused by stress). Your Deputy must play a much more active role to allow himself to grow and maximise the knowledge and expertise of the Principal. And he should be the first point of contact unless the Principle requests otherwise.

The pupils seem very willing to co-operate. Harness this energy and pupils will exceed current expectations (which are not high due to their social class).

The teachers seem well-educated and open to new ideas that will have them achieving more than they have done before. They deserve teaching to be as stimulating and challenging for them as it is for the children. They will look forward to attending school and becoming skilled at working with teams and team-building as key to active participation and growth. Head of year teachers and deputy year teachers offer a voluntary opportunity to those who show a commitment to the school. They may not get extra pay for these titles but it will inspire them to take on leadership and to be the best teachers in Mauritius.

Parents must be sent a copy of the "School Rules" created by the children and the Principal's structures in a simple yearly policy document such that they have agreed (by signing and returning it) to what you plan to do and how you plan to do it. Any parent questioning school system should be invited to join the school committee to discuss their concerns and be directed politely but purposefully to school policy.

A Parent-Teacher Committee ought to be encouraged with the aims of supporting the school, raising funds and creating activities for the school's development. Two parents from each class ideally should meet each term to look at the school's needs. This could be simple things like homemade food sales for school fund-raising or selling crafts to buy craft materials for the school.

In England, many parents help teachers daily so pupils can learn more. Parents attend to assist with reading, writing and if they have a special skill like cooking or art, sewing or science, they can offer a valuable contribution to their own and other parents' children.

I believe that some of your parents may not know how to read or write themselves. A parent support group can be set up by, and for, parents who want to learn with their children. These activities will foster understanding between the school and the parents. Teachers and children must empower parents to start developing the school by actively participating.

A School Library:

I only saw books that the children are working with in class. I have noted a lack of books throughout the whole of Mauritius. Is it possible to start a small library? This is a place where children can loan a book for a week and take it home to read. This might have to be managed – perhaps funded – by your new parent committee.

The school has been at breaking point for years and it is time to empower the teachers by enrolling the parents to participate. Subjects should be multi-tasked to achieve key outcomes rather than set objectives that can only be – at best – partially achieved.

All this is a challenge but, with implementation, your school would be a shining educational and social light for others. Please keep me informed. Best wishes, Hannah

Key actions: Decorations; presentation of school; staff smiling; better use of space; sharing plant knowledge.

And I hope this detailed Room Plan created for this school inspires you to set up a Room Reading group in your school to strengthen links between parents and teachers.

20. Sequins and MS

Key themes: overusing body; impact of poor diet; looks over love.

The next story is about a wonderful lady who used to be a showgirl at the London Palladium. I visited her and her fiancé at their home in Clacton-on-Sea. My client showed me many pictures of her in sequins and feathers, she was a beauty and still is, but her multiple sclerosis was debilitating. In MS, an autoimmune disorder, the immune system mistakenly attacks the layer in the brain or spinal cord – called the myelin sheath – that surrounds and protects the nerves. This scars the sheath, and some underlying nerves, disrupting messages travelling along those nerves. There are predisposing factors that contribute to MS. These are your genes (if your sibling or parent has it, you've a 2% chance); lack of sunlight (if you live in a country far from the equator, or wear a burka, you'll have low vitamin D levels); and smoking (if you do that you're twice as likely to develop MS compared to those who don't); and I have a fourth…

She told me she knew of many dancers who now have MS. Excessive use of the body over years takes its toll. In mind-reading rooms we believe that excellent nutrition such as organic vegetables and meat, along with herbs and supplements, can make a huge difference. Conversely, it can also take years to recover from long-standing shows that last hours, eating a poor diet, and dancing in heels.

This lady's flat was heavily coated in nicotine. It seems my client spent most of the day enjoying the fact she could still lift her fingers to her mouth and inhale. It is deeply distressing for her to have MS after such an active lifestyle. I could not ask her to stop smoking but I did ask her if she would meditate as I knew this would reduce the number of cigarettes she had each day. Her fiancé was always present. He is a loving partner and she explained to me that they were due to marry in April. Her friends were coming to stay, and she was embarrassed as her partner was busy looking after her and her many cats, so he had little time to properly clean.

In late January, we provided a deep-clean and declutter service for the whole flat. We found items of food dating back 10 years in the cupboards. We applied organic compounds to the carpets to remove the smell of nicotine and cats. The lady had a double entrance into her flat. The two entrance points – one to the front and one to the back – each had a set of stairs. "Given your star status," I said, "one entrance was never going to be enough."

She smiled. In fact, even though she was struggling with her MS, her past was very present.

Sometimes we think we need to have all the looks, glamour and shimmy to find lasting love. But this lady had found her love when she was most in need of help and wasn't looking or feeling great. Her fiancé loved her despite her physical difficulties and this genuine care between two human beings is quite the most touching thing I have seen. Isn't it obvious when we are young and active we will be loved? Admired? But these attributes fade and all we have left is our personality, our generosity, and that's when we shine from the inside.

We provided my client with a few vitamins and proteins to build her strength, ready for her visitors. And she was well enough to marry in April. She will keep her independent mind even if her body is dependent on someone else. So, as we all are, she is independently dependent. Unless we live alone, self-sufficient on a mountain top, we all like to think we are independent, but none of us can be and few of us really want to be.

Key actions: organic carpet cleaning; mindful decluttering; deep-clean; vitamins. (Listen to the song *Independently Dependent.*)

21. Twin-set and pearls

Even if we struggle outside, it's generally accepted that most of us are comfortable at home. Yet I have found many clients find being at work is easier than being at home. We express facets of our character at home that can be easily hidden outside with the attention on – or distractions of – work or school. We may not like who or how we are in our personal space at all. Then we'll spend less time at home or hide away our home for fear of how others might react. So, it is easy to become disconnected from our real self both in and outside of our homes. I have a good relationship with several people whose homes reveal this disconnection.

My lady, a coiffured, pearl-wearing, immaculately turned-out woman, was highly successful in her business and social circles. She was also a confident speaker. We attended a management course together and over a year became close friends and we still are. She invited me to her home and I imagined it would reflect her 'top-of-the-rangeness' in every way. Surely there'd be pristine bookshelves lined with intelligent novels? Soft leather sofas and walnut parquet floors? I was looking forward to hearing classical music on her Bang and Olufsen speakers (no doubt embedded almost invisibly into her designer walls). Then she'd recite poetry or share her latest floral arrangement whilst we enjoyed cucumber sandwiches and green tea.

Not quite. When I arrived at her flat and she opened the door, despite my years of looking at homes, I was shocked. The disconnect was so dramatic in terms of who I believed she was from the outside appearance and how she was living inside. Filthy, badly-laid carpets; a lounge stacked floor to ceiling with magazines and paperwork, holding years of dust; a kitchen with a quarter inch of grime on every surface; when I opened the bathroom door, I swear the whole lavatory moved like a mirage oozing yuk. The only saving grace was her Bone China tea set – her pride and joy – housed in a catastrophic kitchen. She offered me a sandwich but it was so far from the cucumber delicacy of my imagination that, sadly, I had to decline.

I suggested she participate in a Room Reading group although, currently, she has not taken this up. Any type of plan we embark on is going to be a challenge. Mind-reading rooms can only be a success if the participants are willing to try the suggestions. I never push my services because even if I get into the house, a forced outcome would make me less sensitive to the needs of the space and thus the occupants. I can only hope that one day she'll recognise how mind-reading rooms could help her and her home.

She was trying to do too many things in that small space without any order. Her office took up the living room, from floor to ceiling. She also rented her extra bedroom, meaning even less space for her. Her business success had kept her from managing anything else but her business, which had outgrown the living room, reduced the hallway, kitchen and bathroom to dirt, decay and misery. This had compromised her health; her internal body space was decaying with cancer and this thwarted opportunities for her to have a social life in her personal space. The cost to her health and environment could never compensate for her invitations to chair meetings and her growing her bank account.

Room Reading groups can help you research your needs to get your whole life back in balance. Such groups can create a Room Plan for the 'client' setting out exactly what you need to do. Then it's up to them.

Are you disconnected from your home? Do you have a significantly different persona outside? This could prevent you from spending time in your own space. You're likely to eat out much more than if your home is a reflection of you. You may have difficulties keeping a partner or even getting one. To deal with this, join a Room Reading group and make small changes. You will very likely need some help if the place you live in requires deep-cleaning. Don't worry, maybe 85% of a thousand houses I have visited need deep-cleaning. As we know, domestic or light-cleaning a room or a home isn't enough. Most cleaning companies do not offer proper deep-cleaning. This art has been lost over the last 40 years. Room Plans provide structures and guidance so that the deep-clean becomes routine maintenance throughout the year.

I know how easy it is to thrive and fail at the same time! And it's going to be hard to let go of those things that are working. However, if you can - with the help of Roomies or a Room Reading Group - see your life as a whole rather than as separate pieces, you will join the dots. This will have you making better choices and once you have moved beyond what you're dealing with now, you will find your home, health and work start to balance.

I heard that my lady business friend has (since my visit) waded through the several mountains of magazines, and thoroughly cleaned the living room. She's moved her business out of the home, into a proper office where it continues to thrive. Her cancer is being better managed with nutritional changes.

22. Unplugging the Kardashians

Kim Kardashian had a lucky escape when she was tied up and robbed in her Paris apartment in 2016. I am glad that she – and her two innocent children – escaped unharmed. But how did she/we get to this point? How did we become so fascinated with someone else's life at the expense of our own? How can we unplug the Kardashians without robbing or harming them or others? Let's look at this as Kim gave us an unintended break from her unending onslaught of sexual media supremacy.

In Kim's nightmare wake-up call, she realised the real price of her wallowing in luxury and exhibitionist behaviour was a danger to herself and her two children. Yet her manufactured beauty that sets her above most other women on the planet was also shattered due to her assailants' disinterest in it. We ordinary mortals were more shocked - 'though relieved - by the fact that Kim in body was untouched, safe with a gag over her mouth, simply shoved into her rented bathroom whilst they escaped with her very real bounty, her flaunted excess of diamonds.

Kim Kardashian was briefly humanised by this event. The impact on us is we finally get that she is just another helpless human being. The robbers stole her million-dollar sexy image. True professionals, they weren't even tempted to take the clear chance to steal a kiss on Kim's cheek. This complete disinterest in her constantly promoted sexual image was as damaging as the lost diamonds.

For a while Kim faded from the limelight, dropped the rocks, and her rarer appearances in the media showed her dressed down, covered more and even slightly humble. The Kardashians were victims of their own *sexcess.* They struggled to recover, even tried a re-brand / re-shuffle (swapping Kim with Kendall).

However, the Kardashian machine has done an amazing job of its sexually dominant pecking order with Kim firmly at the top. Could they still fix what had been unintentionally broken by those thieves?

Kim bounced back in April 2017 with airbrushed / photoshopped pictures of her largest asset. That scandal lost her a few hundred thousand followers, but with 50 million followers on Twitter (then Facebook, etc.) to play with, her strategy of returning to sexual prowess form lost a genuine opportunity to be a real person. I am certain Kim is highly intelligent and would be a great role-model for women of colour beyond her now dented image.

Unsurprisingly, then this re-emergence of sexcess perpetuates the pressure in women to have plastic surgery or just focus on their sexual appearance rather than the totality and complexity of a human being. A young woman's dream isn't to help change the world but rather to have a very large bottom and top with the tiniest waist imaginable. This can be achieved by pumping silicone into your butt and boobs whilst starving yourself. The Kardashians have made millions from this look, helped by their team of experts. We gave these female icons the power to set the rest of us mere mortals up for failure. Why did we buy into these unrealistic ideals? We have been duped again. As well as the silicone implants into our breasts and bums, we've absorbed the poison – drip-fed by magazines, TV and Internet – into our brains.

We're now addicted to what Kim ate for breakfast or what knickers she is wearing. Really? Isn't it time to laugh at ourselves? I can promise you the Kardashians are laughing all the way to the bank. Let's get interested in our own wardrobes and drawers, not Kim's! Look at the impact on ourselves and our daughters of buying into such pointless plastic people! How do you feel after you have read that latest celebrity gossip? Better or inadequate? Unless you can promise yourself that you view such plasticants as mere objects of curiosity, the answer has to be 'inadequate'. And this marketed inadequacy often leads to depression.

So, put down the prettified pictures designed to stop you thinking and acting for your own life and start getting connected to real people around you, people who'll help you change your environment. Stand up for the transformation of how women are depicted in the media by supporting better role models starting with you, your own daughters and sons. Remember, the power given to the Kardashian consumer-addicted formula to stardom can be unplugged by you and yours starting in a Room Reading group. Here are some ideas for unplugging in your group:

Do not look at celebrity magazine covers unless it is to criticise what is being touted as news! For example, did one of your adult children recently give birth? What a joy to have nurtured them and surely much better to share and talk about them than a pregnant star?

Do not read celebrity gossip unless it is to voice and recognise the mediocrity of so-called news.

Discuss the impact of trivia touted as news versus real-life issues that you and others are dealing with (these can be good/bad stories).

Look at the impact on our young people, especially young women of plasticants. Discuss and create activities that celebrate local young men and women as role models.

Acknowledge your satisfaction when a media star or dodgy politician is shattered by their own excess. Recognise that your schadenfreude is derived from the unnatural influence they have exerted over you, and that you can release yourself by unplugging from fake media influences.

Support role models who benefit you and others locally.

Celebrate local women's achievements by creating awards and writing articles or blogs about them.

Apply mind-reading rooms in your homes.

Switch off your screen whenever you find yourself watching rubbish.

Plan how you can improve and transform your life daily.

Create and action your own ideas and seek others to work with.

Do not look outside of yourself for quick-fix answers.

Quick-fixes don't exist; even recognised leadership forums like Landmark (formerly EST), or similar programmes, only work in a vacuum. Thanks to such training, you will contact people with whom you had a terrible relationship and get it resolved. Yes, you will tell them you love them... and more. But, within days or months, the status quo will resume - as it did with me - over years of Landmark training. Many of the good intentions fall by the wayside because it's mostly talk and there's few agreed actions between the parties. The reignited relationship dwindles even if the memories are not quite so bitter. Landmark is full of inflated gimmicks that will last about as long as one of its programmes. I remember a photograph of Will Steel, a great course leader, in an African state smiling broadly with two participants, I like Will, and Landmark Leaders may well have good intentions, but in the photo's background was a shanty town of poverty and misery. If only Landmark really did turn the lives of millions rather than just turnover millions.

Landmark and courses like it work on the basis that if you have spent hours on their phones (as I did) selling their programmes (as if your life and the person you're talking to's life depended on it), you're most unlikely to come out later (as I am doing) saying it's all a lot of positive talk that creates nothing more than participants selling to future participants. Oh, isn't that pyramid sales without the financial incentives?

We thrive or survive in the trivia of family fallouts and feel that our family is always worse than everyone else's. But what if you just relied on people you meet who have a shared interest and common created goals? Since you can't choose your family – just your friends – if you have both and it's productive, fantastic. But if either isn't working, you can take some new actions. Don't question yourself. Accept that you will make mistakes. I am a master of mistake-making! But one thing I realised is that making mistakes is actually having a life. You will not get it right every time. And, anyway, what is right?

Mind-reading rooms is all about finding a balance, no matter what you are dealing with, so that you can create new environments and new ways of being and doing that don't suck you and your loved ones into any particular way of being. How refreshing to let go of your and others' expectations. Live more instinctively from moment to moment. Teach those around you how to share and enjoy the ups and downs of life together. Set up a Room Reading group and start building your support networks. Skill-sharing and listening will develop your skills better than any expensive self-development course. Mind-reading rooms will provide results in your homes. Surely, feeling a buzz when everything else is falling apart isn't going to be enough in the longer term? Invest in time alone; invest in a conversation with others and create a Room Reading group. Invite people to skill-share and care. Watch with amazement as you all collectively empower each other and how your whole life will be transformed little by little. No crazy promises, no expensive targets, just people mind-reading rooms.

(Listen to the song *Show-horse.*)

23. Mind-reading environments with an edge

The young men who are likely to carry out knife crimes on the street are already involved in other criminal behaviours. According to the British press whose reports reached a peak 2016 - 18, this centres around the street sale of drugs and protecting or controlling patches, and not street gangs (as we are often led to believe). These young criminals want fast money and are in a different league to regular kids who persevere through education and work. We are making the lives of the former easy! They know 'good kids' won't be armed because 'good kids' have a fear of knives instilled in them by the current system. That's an open invitation to rob or manipulate young adults who have little confidence or chance of defending themselves. Also, vulnerable young adults – somewhere between 'good' and 'bad' – may slip onto the wrong path, ending up with a criminal record and all the long-term disadvantages that bring (plus the seduction to persist down that path).

Contrasting with British studies, an earlier WHO (World Health Organisation) report on knife attacks noted that these crimes are not as prevalent as we might think and are more likely to happen at home. The latest WHO and UK press reports now say we have a youth epidemic of knife incidence around the globe. And I'm sure we do. Either way, this information isn't addressing how to reduce the fear of knife misuse for worried teens and parents or those involved in educating and protecting young people. Each time we hear of a stabbing death, we fear that our son may be encouraged to carry a knife to protect himself or, worse, be the next victim.

I am not suggesting we allow kids to carry knives on the streets (even though that happens in Mauritius and some other countries, as I'll explain later). I did not know about WHO or the recent studies until after I had written my story, which is set in a third world country with boys who come from poor, working families and who are subjected to corporal punishment in secondary school. Despite this experience, knives are used positively in Mauritius and other countries and that translates to a low incidence of knife crime.

My approach encourages the use of knives in controlled activities to build confidence and trust amongst the youth. Playing with knives to cook or practice stage-fighting or unarmed combat techniques will offer much-needed skills and a safe outlet for knife use. We all know that some people will always want to harm others. This tiny minority will stand out more if the general youth population is confident and empowered. Scouts and Guides use knives in their character-building activities, and they are generally known to be considerate, confident children and adults. So, we ought to be promoting them more.

Demonising the knife and young people can't be the answer since we have demonised - we are demonising - them, and now we have an epidemic. I hope that parents will encourage young people to take up the knife with confidence in appropriate environments. Deal with conflicting messages on inappropriate knife use by having conversations about knives. How to help young people to distinguish between fantasy or screen-life and real-life uses of the knife is another crucial conversation. These dialogues and activities could be done within several settings in the community: school, police cadets, scouts and guides, or Room Reading groups.

When I returned to Mauritius to pick up my children, I went on a boat trip with my 14 and 16-year-old nephews, Marcel and Yohan. They're typical Mauritian teenage boys. Their parents are together and working in low-paid skilled jobs. Mauritian schools still use physical punishment fitting the WHO-profile of teenagers likely to use knives in inappropriate ways. But these boys don't use knives inappropriately. In fact, I'd say 70% or more of the youth population fit the WHO profile in Mauritius, yet knife crime there is very low!

I boarded the canoe-ish boat (it had room for two or, if others hang their legs either side, six). As I sat, a machete sailed past me. I was far too late, but instinctively jerked back, horrified. Looking to see who it hit, I heard the machete land harmlessly – perfectly – in the boys' mother's washing basket (borrowed by them for collecting stuff). I turned back to the boys as Marcel casually threw his knife equally close to my head and equally accurately into the basket. Because – coming from the UK – I associate youth and knives with extreme danger, these three or four seconds were terrifying for me. But the teenagers might as well have been throwing a soft ball. And 'soft balls', like machetes or large knives, are equally in regular use by young men in Mauritius.

On this day, our knives would help us hack down branches, cut away shellfish from stones and spear fish; on other days, the boys made kites from bits of materials found whilst out and about, or safety adjustments to surfboard-foot-holdings and they'd gut fish for their mother to cook. These boys used knives with skill and care. Merely an object for them, they had no fear of the blade.

Back in the UK, it became clear to me that informing our young adults of the facts will provide empowering choices and may reduce the temptation to buy drugs on the street. Knowing that your local drug dealer is highly likely to be carrying a knife might make you think twice about buying even a legal amount of cannabis. He's probably under pressure due to the threat of being robbed or usurped by other dealers, and he's going to be using all kinds of drugs he sells, too. Add to that the fear of undercover police pouncing with a 'stop and search', revealing his knife and, in his drugged state, you have a ticking bomb.

Also, doesn't this recent report highlighting the connection between drug-sellers and knives, demand more legal forms of buying recreational drugs? I mean, if our young adults can go to a vape store or a supermarket, why not a hashish or cannabis store or section within any shop, if it's legal? Surely, it ought to be controlled like any other activity such as tobacco, alcohol, prostitution and gambling?

Craft activities, stage-fighting, archery, building camps, and cooking, or making things where knives are handled by our young people – so they see knives as helpful tools – would reduce knife crime. It's clearly evidenced in Mauritius and Guides or Scouts. Governments in the West are incorrect and damaging youth confidence with their variations of the message: 'A knife is bad and dangerous in the hands of a young person.' Full stop. This purely negative thought ensures more young people take up the knife as a mode of self-defence on two levels: firstly, reacting to the association of Government to young people being only bad; and secondly, the message that knives are bad and dangerous is translated to: 'Knives can protect me because, when I have one, I am bad and dangerous.' So, let's have a new message: 'A knife is safe in good hands.'

24. Life and death

Key Themes: using mind-reading rooms to alleviate trauma; manage changes and celebrate life.

Over the years, my appreciation of good tradespeople has grown. Good tradespeople will always be needed to maintain the home, and it's vital you check they are properly trained and competent (by verbal or written references). One family had the unfortunate experience of poor tradesmen who they brought in to install a lift for their mother who had cancer. Alethea lived with her mother. It was she who called me for help. Alethea, the eldest daughter, is the rock in this family. She was determined to utilise Room Reader and ensure all her family were supported in their times of illness, birth and death.

The builders had failed to cover floors and furnishings. They had shown no respect or care for the work, leaving the whole house thick with dust. Simply put, the house had been abused with poor building standards at a time when the family needed care. We provided a deep-cleaning service for the whole house.

The second service the family requested from us was dealing with a lost room in the house. The room had become a dumping ground full of junk and very dirty. Misuse of the space was acknowledged by the second daughter and, after decluttering and deep-cleaning, the space was healed and ready to receive her own daughter's new baby. Before the birth, they invited us to provide The Nesting Instinct Service for the expectant mother in the flat they had moved into; the nesting instinct is the driving force just before the birth when the expectant mother wants everything meticulously cleaned. We dealt with that property, too. Just before her death, the new great-grandmother was delighted she got to see her tiny great-grandson in a clean, comfortable home.

Seeking intervention typically involves removing oneself from the root (the home) buying more objects or engaging with various therapeutic services. We often want to escape from where all the dramas, upsets or repression are being played out by doing other things that can escalate rather than resolve the issues. Alethea chose to deal with them head-on (in the home) and the benefit for the family was a clean house and the associated mind-reading rooms results that bring closure and completion. Alethea felt the love of my team in soothing the wounds of the family homes.

I was touched that my team and I were invited by the whole family to the funeral of the great-grandmother. The head of this family had closed her eyes peacefully for the last time. I stood in the church and was certain this woman's soul was free. Despite many calls and emails between us, I never did meet the family. Nor could we meet at the funeral as the church was packed-out to celebrate this lady's life. As the service ended, I slipped out with my team knowing we had played a small part.

Key actions: deep-cleaning to heal abused home; preparing a home for a birth; decluttering the past to create a future.

25. Room Reader time-warp

This next Room Plan moves beyond the boundaries we've seen so far. The idea is for you to learn just how creative your Room Reading group can be. Many skills combinations will emerge from your group, which may include people with DIY skills or skills developed in other professions.

We have looked at a teacher stuck in a 'time-warp'. Houses can also be stuck in time. A time-warp can be related to a person's age or, as in the following case, a mixture of times within each room or space in the house that is creating mental chaos. I tried to bring the house to a cohesive point in time and used the space to empower the owner. This house was built 100 years ago. Mena's grandparents owned it in the 1930s, approximately 20 years after the first owners; then her parents inherited it changing one or two rooms in the style of the 1950s. During the 1970s the parents moved out leaving the house to Mena and her sister. They brought students into the house turning the whole property into bedrooms. Over years, the students and Mena's sister left but possessions from every person dating back 80 years remained. Each room had a strange mixture of uncoordinated eras; the house – like its owner – had a lot of excess baggage. And it was too dark.

The problem is that the house has just been added to with each wave of occupants; it had not had any consistent ownership so existed in a strange time-warp. I had to stop the time-warp and get the house rooted so that Mena could enjoy it and move the relationship forward with her long-term boyfriend, Stevie.

I started with a reminder of the definition of mind-reading rooms. This was her Room Plan:

Mind-reading rooms – long definition: The transformation of a group or individual consciousness through cleaning, rearranging or changing of furniture, products, pictures, ornaments, people, pets and space in the home.

Mind-reading rooms – short definition: Movement of space.

The house needs stripping back to create a more solid base. I would like to reduce wallpapers and rugs to the minimum, plaster as many rooms as possible ready for painting and stencil work.

It's time to invest your money in this space as a priority. It will add value to the house and comfort both of you.

Who does the house belong to? Make it yours, if it doesn't belong to you, buy it? But please do something with it!

Stop buying clothes and start window shopping for new sofas and light fittings. You can buy fantastic lights and furniture on eBay but decide in advance what your budget is and do not forget to include a man and a van if your item is 50+ miles away. (The transport can be costlier than the item).

Divorce proceedings and commitment:

I understand Stevie is still married? What are his intentions? What do you want? I don't wish to step on any toes but, after three+ years, isn't it time to declare your relationship in some way?

Remove...Declutter:

Before decorating or cleaning please sell or give to charity your two large brown sofas; the flimsy pine wardrobe in the master bedroom; 60% – yes, sixty percent – of all your clothes and shoes; any rugs that are old or that you don't like; superfluous wallpapers; odd bits like cheap pine shelving; and remove carpets from the bathroom or loo.

Holdall style bags. Use the side cupboards as some wardrobe space. Remove files to new office space after sorting unwanted files.

The house needs connecting, as many of the rooms are disconnected. This can be achieved by having a main colour running from the top landing down the stairs into the hallway and outer room. You can keep your cat wallpaper but the rest of the walls need to be painted after plastering in one flowing colour. This could be any shade of orange with cream stencilling (cats?) or cream with orange.

Arrange a plasterer to come and have a look at the house and give you a price; you could paint yourself or let him paint too.

New light fittings such as crystal or glass that match in the hallway, landing, stairs and outer lobby.

New light fittings for each room to complement above.

I would like to see you take over the master bedroom to become you and your partner's.

Only one wall can be wallpapered so choose the wall in front of your bed?

Keep the little leather sofa in this room.

Plaster and paint the remaining walls in complementary colours.

Your current bedroom to be a guest room.

The small room to be a neat little office and library for Stevie.

Bathroom and loo:

Tile floors, tidy plaster and paint, maybe add colour with towels in any orange or lemon white.

Master sitting room:

Make this a dining room with your lovely table and wicker chairs, and have a flowery three- to five-seater sofa and office table in the same space.

Plaster walls using mocha browns, creams and stencils.

Cosy sitting room:

Use the hatch to pass tea and toast or freshly washed fruits through.

Have a comfy large sofa in a fabric finish in gold, cream or soft green (but not brown).

Replace the pretend fire with a real one.

Plaster walls. Have one wall with wallpaper, the rest painted in soft lilacs or rose white.

I would like to see a long pile carpet in this room.

Mena:

I've found short meditations Get recordings so you can meditate a few minutes every day. It helps me to quiet my mind and relax. I have one session every two or three weeks. Each session lasts around one hour and twenty minutes. I think you'd greatly benefit, too.

Declutter, this time with deep-cleaning

Do a 3 - 6 monthly deep-clean of one or two rooms all year round.

This can be done when you're away or at home.

Living room/dining room & kitchen deep-clean, add declutter x shelves and x drawers.

Office/bedroom deep-clean add declutter x shelves x drawers.

A bathroom deep-clean

Your bedroom deep-clean (add declutter x drawers and x shelves)

A single bedroom deep-clean, add declutter x shelves x drawers

Hallways/stairs deep-clean

Rugs/carpets deep-clean using organic compounds

Organic deep-cleaning is a meticulous clean of all areas we can see and reach, inside and out.

This includes paintwork, doors, upholstery, floors and windows inside.

Beds can be turned (mattress) and vacuumed, and bed linen changed if required.

Declutter of any drawers or wardrobes; This service can include simply folding or sorting out what you want and don't want, or ordering to manage clothes by colour, style or season.

Identify the service levels in each room; deep-clean alone or deep-clean and declutter. Count how many drawers or rails or shelves you want decluttering and put the number next to the room. You can put a little sticker on those drawers/shelves/rails that need sorting or ordering.

Water filters/juicing/foods:

Proper hydration from oxygenated water filters fitted for the whole flat, then you can simply fill a bottle. For a small fee, suppliers change cartridges and ensure the system is kept well. I'll arrange this for you or you can go direct.

Organic juicer. Twin gear juicers for organic carrots & apples daily.

Organic meat has much lower levels of chemicals. Eat less meat but organic. Vegetables and fruits – organic – eat as much as you can with every meal.

Enjoy full fats such as olive oil and grass-fed butter, full-fat unprocessed cheeses; eat minimal factory-farmed red meats and more oily fish. Reduce refined sugar to the minimum possible and avoid main meals of white pasta or pizza. Focus on quality vegetables and full-fat unprocessed foods, not on counting calories.

Salads and sprouting vegetables. Soups and gluten-free bread.

Clothing/storage/repairs:

I noted that you both like clothes! Excess clothes increase likelihood of moths and reduce usable space, can also block energy flow.

We recommend each person has around 8-10 base items; these can include trousers, dresses, skirts, suits, jackets.

Two coats, one winter, and one raincoat per person.

6 pairs of shoes include 1 pair of trainers, 1 pair of boots, slippers or flats; smart shoes x3

8-10 pants/knickers, vests or bras. A tracksuit, swimsuit and a bikini.

Seasonal packaging will help store clothes not in regular use.

Activity:

I feel that you and your partner would benefit from dancing together. Dancing is your passion and though you may struggle with the splits, learning a quick step is a fun way to keep fit and have a shared interest. Ballroom dancing classes can be found in your area or nearby.

Swimming at least once a week would be a good way of keeping your joints and muscles moving in weightless space. A sauna afterwards relaxes you and releases toxins.

I hear you grow vegetables together; grow more, add fruits and salads.

If you have too much, have a weekly sale of seasonal vegetables and fruit for neighbours. It's a great way to develop community spirit.

Yours, Hannah

(Listen to the song *Light in the Gloom*.)

26. Desperate DJ

Key themes: renting; filthy homes; impact on well-being.

The next space was so filthy that the professional woman living there was demoralised by it.

My client had to isolate herself from her friends and colleagues in a bid to hide the forced squalor she is living in. Perhaps you will relate to this story. Are you living in sub-standard rented accommodation? A Room Reading group could help you transform this space. It probably won't be perfect but, as in this case, it will be habitable. We can understand from this story the importance of deep-cleaning our spaces. A Roomie group can easily be set up with just three people. I am sure you will have some friends who are willing to participate and help you regain your life. We have been conditioned to think it is wrong to share our difficulties; we fear being exposed to others. But be brave, reach out and share. Be authentic. You will be amazed at the love in the world. When we are authentic and empower people to action, we bring out the very best in those around us.

Look at the fund-raising activities that raise millions for worthy causes. Your life and home are equally worthy of dedication and creativity. If you're unhappy or your space is unmanageable, how can society work? Understanding ourselves and our space is key to everything. It is your responsibility to yourself and others to take action. Of course, putting pressure on negligent landlords is vital. Our role isn't to address this specifically but to transform the environment in the belief that this will impact everything long-term.

Bibi is a DJ and journalist. She had just moved into a filthy flat that she was embarrassed to bring her friends to.

Key actions: deep-cleaning, re-arranging furniture, adding plants; introducing an activity.

We carried out the following Room Plan.

Dear Bibi,

I am sorry to say that we are unlikely to make much impact on this drab flat. We cannot move the mould behind the pipes, we can't re-plaster and paint the walls, hang lovely curtains, put in a new bathroom and kitchen, add decent light-fittings, etc. because this is a rented flat. We can clean the kitchen, scrub oven and fridge, and (except behind the pipes) all the above. It'll be less unhealthy for you.

Living room/dining room & kitchen deep-clean:

Add declutter x shelves x drawers. We will bring some coloured plants for every room in the flat.

A bathroom deep-clean, plus the cleaning of bacterial mould and re-silicone round the bath. Add a new shower curtain.

Your bedroom deep-clean (add declutter x drawers x shelves at each and half-rails at each)

A single bedroom deep-clean, add declutter x shelves x drawers at each and half-rails

Hallways/deep-clean

Moth-proofing drawer liners infused with wonderful oils that you will love and moths hate. Deep-cleaning is a meticulous clean of all areas we can see and reach, inside and out. This includes paintwork, doors, upholstery, floors and windows inside.

Mattresses can be turned and hoovered, maybe bed linen changed,

Declutter of any drawers or wardrobe per drawer or kitchen cupboard or shelf. This service can include simply folding or sorting out what you want and don't want or ordering to manage clothes by colour or style or season.

Identify the service levels in each room; deep-clean alone or deep-clean and declutter. Count how many drawers, rails or shelves you want decluttering and put the number next to the room. Put a little sticker on those drawers/shelves/rails that need sorting or ordering.

Organic meat has fewer chemicals. Eat less meat but organic. Vegetables and fruits – organic – eat as much as you can with every meal. (We've already discussed organic juicing with the right juicer.)

Salads and sprouting vegetables. Soups and gluten wheat-free bread.

Clothing/Storage/Repairs:

We recommend each person has around 8-10 base items; these can include trousers, dresses, skirts, suits, jackets.

Two coats, one winter / one summer.

6 pairs of shoes comprising one pair of trainers, a pair of boots, slippers or flats, smart shoes x3   8-10 underwear, & bras.

One tracksuit, one swimsuit, one bikini.

Seasonal packaging will help store clothes not in regular use.

Activities for Bibi: Rock climbing. This exhilarating skill will give you strong arms and legs, tone your abs and get you out socialising with people who like having fun. It's also mentally challenging, to ease the worrying about your situation; when climbing you'll only be thinking about reaching that next rock!

Best wishes, Hannah

In this Room Plan we transformed what we could to make the space habitable for Bibi and got her out doing an activity that brought mental and physical power. The results led to her interviewing me on her radio station Bibi Does Soho.

Many of us are living in cramped or below standard accommodation. I have a friend who shares a studio flat with her eight-year-old daughter. They have one bed and all their home is in one tiny room. My friend expressed her deep unhappiness at being stuck in such a place. She felt trapped. I suggested she join a Room Reading group. Through this, she has managed to transform the resentment into a creative challenge. In this spirit of creativity, she has started to look for better accommodation.

Another Roomie was sharing a flat with her partner and their daughter, and another family. They all shared the kitchen and the bathroom as well as the communal hallway. The living room was a bedroom for the second family. They had minimal natural light due to the flat's small windows. The furniture in the bedroom/living room was dark and heavy, the hallway was blocked with unused stuff such that everyone tripped over it and had to quietly, resentfully, fight their way in or out to work or school.

I suggested the hallway be de-cluttered and furniture could be swapped for lighter pieces. Then the group added natural pictures in the bedroom to lighten and brighten the space. The communal kitchen was deep-cleaned, simple house rules were created and – for the first time in two years – the space was enjoyed by the occupants.

Within three months of this transformation the woman's partner got a dream job, they bought a house, she closed her business and started to provide foster care in her new home. All the frustrations and obstacles – once dealt with in the space – released the occupants to full self-expression. They got married, too! So, mind-reading rooms is more than just making a happy place; creating a creative space can be about changing your place in life.

What is your dream? And how can that be translated in your space?

What seeds of that dream can be planted in your space?

Are you stuck in your past? This may not be something you are fully present to, but take some photos of your space to share with a Roomie group. What issues are you dealing with that indicate you're in a 'time-warp'? Discuss this and start to plan small changes including collecting memories or drawing pictures in a scrapbook. This helps us bridge gaps in time. Do not rush the process. If you do, you might find yourself returning to your past.

Managing objects to enhance relationships.

A woman did not want to part with her dead mother's broken TV. She already had a working one in her bedroom. The two TVs made the room cramped and irritated her husband. I suggested she create a personal scrapbook to put pictures, draw or write about her mum. I asked her how important her marriage was. She removed the broken TV and decluttered her house by setting up a Roomie group. This reminded me of Mary and Janice from earlier. If you or your partner is holding on to a problem-causing object, join a Room Reading group.

27. The Dog Woman

Key themes: reverse-anthropomorphism; over-identifying with pets; filthy homes; limited expression; limited kitchenware.

You will likely know someone similar to the Dog Woman. Perhaps you have too many pets or find them getting in the way of a relationship? On the way home from seeing this lady, I shared her story with a taxi driver who then explained that he and his wife were going through a divorce over a Yorkshire Terrier. I thought they were fighting over custody of the dog, but the dog was actually the cause of the separation. The dog had been bought by his wife. He never imagined that over the next three years the dog would become the centre of her world. He said she ignored him when he came home from work because she would be busy with 'Little Fella'. The dog took over his armchair and would growl when he came to relax with his newspaper. He had to spend a minute or two persuading Little Fella to vacate his seat – gently does it – so as not to worry his wife that the terrier might be upset. The wife then brought another armchair for the husband so the dog would not be disturbed. At night, he would find Little Fella curled up on his pillow on his side of the bed.

I realised that many people may be faced with animals who have taken over spaces or relationships. This next tale highlights another strange scenario and a good outcome.

We are a nation of dog lovers but the dog must be suited to its environment. When you choose an animal, you have to work out how it will be managed. If you don't have outside space, it's even more important to define the areas and management of any animal you have. Discuss with your family the (dis)advantages of having the animal before going ahead.

I had a client who had over-identified with dogs. She's an aromatherapist and had the most incredible sense of smell. At 32, she wasn't an unattractive lady so couldn't understand why she had not attracted a suitable partner. Trouble was, her long, shaggy hair hid a lot of her face, and her strong dog smell would have put most two-legged suitors off. As an aromatherapist – especially one with a sharp sense of smell – I'd have thought she'd be more self-aware. (Later, I'd check this.) She said she wouldn't consider a man who had cats as "I don't trust them." She'd been known literally to chase cats along whichever street a client might be on.

She sometimes liked to be alone with her dogs, and had bought a strange-looking cottage in the middle of nowhere. The cottage was made of wood. It was very low and had a large front door with only a small window on either side. The front door had no knocker or handle, but a gentle push opened it.

To me, it was simple: her home was a giant dog-house!

Secluded as she apparently wanted to be, she ran into difficulties when cats kept appearing near her home. She was allergic to them and chased them away as soon as she saw them; when she couldn't see them, she'd try to sniff them out. She had unintentionally moved next door to a cattery.

She wore nondescript baggy clothes all in black and a dog collar. (That's the canine type not the vicar's). I was invited to dinner along with two of her clients and a friend of hers. The two clients thought she was great as they had both had allergies and sleeping problems that she had helped with aromatherapy. The friend wore similar clothes to her. He was a gardener and dog-lover.

She served the meaty meal on flat, metal plates waiting for her guests to finish before slopping her meal onto her own metal plate. Then, she disappeared from the table down onto the floor sitting with her knees folded under her, and leaned forward to scoop up and swallow her food by hand. She spoke with a deep throaty growl yet seemed unaware of her sounds. Her favourite books were about the similarity of humans to dogs. Her doggish house was filled with pictures of humans and dogs, dogs chasing cats and other animals. All her ornaments were of dogs. She had several dogs in the house: a Great Dane, two retrievers (mother and son), a Pekinese, and three mongrels of varying sizes. They seemed content to lounge on the very large dog-bed during the meal. She said she had "already fed the family."

Her bathroom was filthy and only contained dog shampoos and the oils for her aromatherapy. I noted she had a toothbrush but it was a dog toothbrush so this and the toothpaste were also for dogs. (Having said that, while the dogs sauntered around me after dinner – although I am no expert – I can certainly vouch for their fresh breath.) In fact, I couldn't see much evidence of her belongings apart from a Parka coat and a pair of walking boots. There was no wardrobe and not many items in the kitchen for cooking and eating. (And, since her culinary skills mainly catered for canines, there were few complaints.) Her cupboards were packed out with Pedigree Chum and Bono biscuits. The fridge was similarly full of dog bones and pigs' ears. The meal she had made for us was mostly meat, and I wondered if I had been treated with pedigree hotpot.

My thoughts were interrupted when a cat appeared near the kitchen window. The dogs charged out of the swinging front door encouraged by her with a growling "go get 'em". I'm sure I wasn't the only person who found her demeanour and her home unusual. But, as is often the case when faced with unusual circumstances, our defence is to ignore oddities or pretend everything is fine.

Her two clients left at the same time as me. I asked them how long they had known her. She'd treated one for several years, the other was more recent, lived in the city and intimated that country folk could be a bit different.

My client slept on a king-size mattress flung in the corner of her room (like a dog bed) with all her dogs. She also kept a pushchair for her Pekinese and one of the mongrels. The dogs all had jumpers knitted by her for winter walks.

I suggested that she had mixed up her dogs' life with her own. Initially, she couldn't see it. I pointed out details covered here so she saw that some of her life had impacted her ability to get a man. She recognised this for the first time but confided that her parents had dog kennels out in the yard and used to put her in the 'dog-house' when she acted-up. Trouble was, they sometimes forgot she was still with the animals.

We started by defining her space and the dogs' spaces, then we did a deep-clean to remove the years of smell and dog hairs. She replaced her 'dog bed' with a new solid bed and mattress. She removed the dog collar, replacing it with a rather nice fake pearl necklace. She started to wear her favourite colours and fabrics which we identified together. She also underwent hypnosis so she'd stop chasing cats.

We organised her bare kitchen. We arranged her home with plates and cups, limited to 10 sets of each. (More than this just takes up space). Due to her diet, she already had sensible cutlery. Cutlery ought to be good quality, easy to hold, and usable. Knives that look like knives but can't cut butter are a waste of money. Buy items that work.

To avoid contaminating carpets and floors with outdoor mess, I recommended a dog foot bath and slippers for my client.

She still likes to eat on the floor but her taste in foods has developed beyond meat dishes. The deep-cleaned bathroom now has a basket that houses the dogs' smellies and one smelly for her (with a different smell, thank you).

Her aromatherapy business has grown with her home organised and her more colourful demeanour. Though she still can't stand cats, she's stopped chasing them (hypnosis was successful) and turned her attention to chasing a new man. Since he phoned for a chat while my team and I worked at the cottage, she's sure – in contrast to the cats – he'd like to be caught. She'd humanised her dogs such that when they growled and hunted amongst themselves, she felt part of the pack. But she also needed human contact, someone to take her hand.

Her dogs are getting used to not sharing the big dog bed with her. They enjoy forest walks and chasing stray cats... without her help.

Key actions: deep-clean, defining personal space, new bed, transforming appearance, developing a balanced diet, hypnotherapy.

(Listen to the song *Waterfall*)

28. Steve Jobs – L.I.S.A.

Key themes: adoption and impact on ego; control and relief; objectification of daughter - Lisa - to relate/control; emotional design; contribution and resistance to it; Apple after death.

I'm guessing you know someone like Steve Jobs. Are you a Jobs type? Do you stop at nothing to get to the top? And, even if your success comes from a shared effort, do you take all the credit? Do you decide whether to allow that other designer to bring his/her products into your sacred home (thus endorsing them), or would you prefer to live sparsely? Are you such a control freak that you can't even think about adding another vegetable to your two-veg family diet, even if you're dying of cancer? What does it take to recognise that we all have a bit of Jobs in us? This story may help you – or someone you know – to re-evaluate how you live, change your job, eating habits or whole life. One thing we all know by now is the price we pay for our life and work choices will show up in our personal space. And, of course, money can never buy your health back. Ask Steve Jobs.

I love my Apple iPhone. I love all Apple products. Why? I'm not the only one who willingly paid a lot more for an Apple computer with no CD-writer in the early 1990s. I fell in love with the designs, the jellybean-coloured exteriors or slim-line, weightless, transparent workings of computers that I knew nothing about. For me and many Apple lovers, it was the emotional connection that made other (probably technically superior) products pale by comparison

Why are Apple products so beautiful? Steve Jobs. He created Apple as a brand name in personal computers for the home. By designing those early products, the home was the setting in which they would be unwrapped, revealed and live. He wanted the Apple machine to be a dominant part of the furniture. With soft lines and vibrant colours, he achieved this. Jobs worked with the best computer designers and technicians. They acquired star status for working with Apple. And Apple was Jobs. But his need to control every detail lost him his position with the company he created. Apple fired Jobs after his decisions – against colleagues' and the board's advice – meant huge financial losses and missed opportunities.

Steve Jobs then hung out with the film animation company, Pixar, buying a large share and producing computer animation programmes for box office hits such as Toy Story. But Jobs still hankered after Apple, and Apple did not do so well without Jobs. (His loyal customers stopped buying Apple products when the main man wasn't around). The two were eventually reunited and the love affair began again with greater passion and intensity than in the first flush, when Jobs had given birth to the company. On the cover of every magazine that mattered, and shortly afterwards with the unveiling of the iPhone, Jobs' fans went wild. Apple sold millions.

Steve Jobs was a brilliantly creative man. I became intrigued as to how or why someone obsessed with design – sometimes at the cost of technical substance – could have had millions of dollars of personal property without a stick of furniture. Really. He had more than one mansion but slept on a mattress on the floor. It wasn't that he wanted to live frugally, and he was no philanthropist, so I can't say he felt guilty for his extraordinary wealth. I think Jobs felt he deserved to have created such a unique concept as Apple. Something had left him hungry to ensure a part of him would be remembered and loved. He would not give credit for any aspect of an Apple product, even the technical genius was owned by him in his eyes. The thought of anyone feeling that he, Jobs, was only part – or even most – of the whole was unthinkable. He had little actual involvement with the technical details; he saw himself as the director of materials (people), they merely realised his creations. His relationship with the Apple objects was like a parent to a child: he would play with and share his baby as long as it came back to him with everything intact. Whatever Jobs thought he had missed out on in life, Apple fulfilled at the creative expense of colleagues, and the love of family and home. But as an adult, he didn't allow himself to choose items other than Apple(s) he created for home.

Steve Job's adoptive parents held back from telling him about his real parents until he was a teenager. Till then, he lived a regular life and his teenager's bedroom was filled with stuff you'd expect to find there. However, as Jobs heard of his adoption in tandem with creating Apple, he became increasingly isolated. This showed up in his unwillingness to have anything less than his vision for Apple products and, later, no furniture in his own homes. The adoptive parents always adored him but, somehow, their endearing loyalty wasn't enough for Jobs – what was described by him as – "the giving away of a beautiful gift," (being given away by his biological parents).

A millionaire at 21 – and worth four million just a year later – he started to treat the individual as a throwaway part, only necessary to create the whole. He was the one who, through others, created maximum impact in the world. His home computers (the market he designed Apple products for) would have meant he thought a lot about the home. It was a business decision for Jobs to tackle the home market. IBM had such a stronghold in the commercial market, even Jobs felt he couldn't compete at that early point in Apple's life.

Within three years of his being told he was adopted, his first love became pregnant. He threw her out of their home. The baby, Lisa, wasn't in his plan... he wasn't in control. And he ignored Lisa for her first seven years. He denied he was the father and refused to pay a thing until DNA tests proved there was a 95% chance she was his.

Development of the Apple's L.I.S.A computer began as Apple itself started to boom but, more tellingly, it was in the year of Lisa's birth. Jobs claimed his new computer name was just a 'coincidence' as it was an acronym for "Local Integrated Software Architecture". He even swore – lied – in court documents that he couldn't be Lisa's father since he was "sterile and infertile, and as a result thereof did not have the physical capacity to procreate a child". Several years on, Jobs admitted to his biographer: "Obviously, it was named for my daughter." It's interesting how he tried to turn his daughter, Lisa, into L.I.S.A., an object he could develop and control. It was the only way he wanted to manage her existence.

A breakthrough for Jobs was due to state intervention, medical proof and his eventual admission that L.I.S.A. was named after his daughter. This allowed a human relationship to begin. Despite his need for control, with the right level of input, he could have evolved.

The US state in which Lisa and her mother lived sued Jobs for the years of hand-outs on which they'd had to exist. L.I.S.A. was discarded by Apple as a failure; Jobs was fired. During his time out, he spent time with Lisa, but they remained estranged. The whole scenario mimicked his biological parents and the enormous sense of loss and anger he felt at being rejected by them. The irony was when he faced a similar dilemma to his biological parents, he abandoned his daughter as he had been abandoned. Jobs continued to objectify his emotional relationships in Apple designs.

His empathetic designs fitted perfectly in our homes and pockets like personal keepsakes. Boxes designed to hold the iPhone are avidly collected for the love that has gone into every shape, texture, fold and finish. You can be certain Jobs approved it before you received it. Jobs agonised over the thickness of the paper the iPhone was wrapped in, the colour, the precise size of the box.

Jobs later married a new woman but at home he, his wife and approved baby still sat on the floor to eat their vegetarian meals.

Far more than mere packaging, Jobs was aware of the impact on the consumer of every detail inside the box ... a sliding versus opening package for an iPhone, or the exclusion of a compact disk – irrespective of a massive loss of sales to competitors – because he didn't fancy a slot for it. He was obsessed with the emotional impact of an object on people and space way beyond the norm.

He defined himself by becoming a genius in the art of design of personal computers, then iTunes, iPods, iPhones, iPads and then every item in the iStore followed. Despite having the power to partner several technological advancements with the likes of Bill Gates's Microsoft, for Jobs it was less about technical function than it was about the look and feel of a product. Even though the iPod was technically created by a Chinese company, Jobs' design for it has dominated the music sales market, closing record stores down with its capacity to allow you to stream and download endlessly.

Apple never gave away its design edge to another. Steve Jobs ensured he was one step ahead by buying what he didn't have then turning it into an icon with his design-mastery. And knowing he had the exclusive rights to Apple - in his head - who could touch him?

He and his wife often considered buying furniture but, when it came to the final decision, he just couldn't commit. His wife had to sneak-in beds for their children. This indecisive almost obsessive need to control and define space with only his creations meant he would not allow any other designer a chance to get any emotional credit from him. Jobs found it very difficult to work with other people. It took his being fired from Apple for him to accept that he was not a one-man show. Also, Apple had grown up and he had to learn to work with others if it was to survive beyond his lifetime.

He was equally controlling with food. Most of his life he lived off large quantities of a few select vegetables. When he became a father for the second, third and fourth time, he did not mellow; he still resisted buying a sofa or a rug. The home remained void of the most basic comforts; even a washing machine took months of analysis between Jobs and his wife before he settled on one that met his almost impossible standards. His clothes made by his favourite designer were a black cotton turtleneck jumper and plain beltless trousers. He had 100 of these outfits.

Jobs died of cancer probably brought about through his nutritionally deficient diet and self-imposed empty home. But beneath the vegan exterior of a man hailed as a computer whizz, his real genius was in his choice of collaboration – as long as he controlled the result and received the recognition.

He loved his adoptive parents, his wife and children. He bought them luxuries, but his inability to create a family home (as opposed to buying a big house) was something he could not overcome. He denied himself and his family things we all take for granted. This was because he could not fully complete with his parents rejecting him, even knowing who they were and meeting his sister, wasn't enough.

Room Reader would have created a new beginning for him and his family. Like the twice-abandoned boy who burnt down his house to pre-empt the perceived threat of rejection, we would have needed to work with Jobs on slowly putting in objects. It would have meant him acknowledging his anger and pain and the impact of his unwillingness to participate in family life for his family to thrive. He would have been encouraged – at least helped – to design his home furniture. Although the process would have taken time, the urgency of completing such a project for the benefit of his beloved wife and children could have driven him on. Jobs hardly recognised how he and his family lived, nor was he present to the impact of his lifestyle on his health and those around him. Room Reader would have helped him and his family address this impact and provided a structure to ensure Jobs could have expressed himself fully with everyday comforts to enjoy with his family.

Any sign of normality was perceived by Jobs as a weakness. He hid behind a non-existent sofa; we could never see more of him than he permitted. He kept himself from loving and being loved through his minimal engagement with objects in his home that represented the void in his emotions. His resistance towards engagement with his past and present ensured he always felt alone. The only way Steve Jobs could live was through loving a series of his created objects that would love him back without judgement.

Jobs created – or at least perfected – for his worshipping millions: iMacs, iPhones, iPods, iPads, iTunes and put them in his iStores. Yes, he was iAll but iSolated... a lone star in a dark place. Although he basked in the bright lights of commercial success, he lacked the light of love from his natural parents. People around him became unseen shadows. Who knows what else he could have invented or brought to life from other's backyards? He once said in an interview: "I put the spirit of creativity into objects." So, the pancreatic cancer that finally controlled the ultimate creative controller would have shown him the limit of his legacy…like it showed us the extent of it.

As his wife responded when asked why he refused the surgery that probably would have saved him: "The body exists to serve the spirit." So, Jobs would be content knowing his spirit could never be given away as he had been. He'd have found some spiritual meaning when evening falls. Brash or assertive, control freak or perfectionist, credit-stealer or businessman, cold bastard or cool-headed, mean-spirited or magnetic, he'd know he could rest in peace. Having never heard of Room Reader, he couldn't have regretted missing out on it. He would only know that in so many family homes around the world – as in his two near-empty houses – he'd left us all some Apple.

Key actions: resistance to furniture; recognising the power of objects; Room Reader's potential. (Listen to *When Evening Falls.*)

29. Jane Eyre and the sex box

Key themes: children encumbered with adult emotional turmoil may have a deficit in sexual maturity in adulthood; suppression of expression (often seen in young girls) manifested in adoration of unrealistic body images may mean an inability for them to fully express themselves; how these things can be addressed in the home.

I have a client; I call her 'Jane Eyre.' Imagine a woman and a home that show aspects of this classic story. My 'Jane Eyre' also has characteristics of the second woman, Mr Rochester's 'unhinged woman in the attic'. The garden has a tree struck by lightning left crashed on the ground and symbolises the foreboding nature of the relationships in the classic. And here, the husband of the house (like Jane Eyre's fated lover, Mr Rochester) casts aside both women at one time or another in favour of other women's attentions, leaving our 'Jane Eyre' exasperated and lonely. If your life story was a novel, play or film, who would you be, and why? Discuss in your Roomie group.

'Jane Eyre' has three children aged 10, 14 and 17. The youngest child had the largest room next to mum and dad. He could hear their constant arguments. His room was expressive, and he had some great toys and games. But it was lacking a good quality bed and, anyway, the room was far too big, given the turmoil of his parents' relationship. Because of the combination of his seeing the imbalanced relationship between his parents and having a bigger room than his older siblings, the scales tipped against him being contained, and towards him feeling responsible for his parents' marital problems. If you consider that his room was next to his parents, you can imagine the youngster hearing their arguments and – in his large room – feeling a sense of overwhelming helplessness.

My own childhood experience tells me it would have been damaging for the boy to have such a burden, one he has no experience of handling.

The long-term impact of too much space in emotionally unstable environments is an inability to connect with self and others. The personal impact of forced maturity is likely to manifest in extreme behaviours like addictions (alcohol, gambling, drugs) or sexual immaturity in adulthood. Children are incredibly flexible and generous creatures, but when they are overburdened with a close adult's emotional relationship, they suffer their own childhood's emotional deficit that may become permanent.

I suggested he move to a smaller room.

The daughter, aged 14, had an expressive room at first glance and everything appeared 'normal' but her posters indicated a predisposition for perfection: ballet dancers and unrealistically thin models adorned the walls. Her belongings lacked order; she had too much stuff, with clothing in a shelf-space that covered a whole wall, the clothes unfolded and falling out, showed she wasn't taking reasonable care of her belongings and likely herself. Her mirror was so slim that when you stood in front of it, you filled it. This, coupled with little expression outside of her room, concerned me.

I suggested that she be encouraged to organise her belongings and take more of herself into the rest of the house. I wanted to see her books, paintings, and stuff around the home. Young girls who are more focused on unrealistic images and living in a cold, loveless home (which you'll see it was) are likely to develop low self-esteem and control issues. Although she might achieve academically, she is likely to be influenced by drugs/low weight and other issues if her social skills are not expressed in the home. So, I encouraged them to buy a new bed made from solid wood with lots of colour on the covers to replace the one she had which was lifeless, hard, yet weak in structure. I wanted to see fewer clothes on her shelves and more care taken of them.

If you have a nice dress or suit and you want to buy that gorgeous other dress/suit ask yourself: Do I need this new outfit or do I have enough? If you really can't live without it, give one of your outfits to charity or as a gift before you replace it with a new (or even second-hand) one. I can assure you the process will slow down your buying habits. You can do this with everything (shoes, bags, hats, coats, suits, shirts, underwear, sofas, beds, kitchen items...).

A good basic wardrobe aims at having eight to 10 complete outfits for males or females with seasonal items stored or replaced. Sports kits, swimming costumes or specialist items can be limited to essentials. Unless you're professional, one spare set is adequate.

When I started giving items away before replacing them, my spending went down by more than half and I was able to take my four children on a once-a-year £5,000 holiday that, until then, I never could have dreamt of. I now appreciate the clothes and furnishings that my family has. We choose items with much more care, my children are tidier and more appreciative of personal and family possessions; and we are all more willing to give and to share.

Mirrors in the bedroom must be wide enough to take in around a third of the room, less width than this will make anyone look large because they are not looking at themselves in the space of the room. Slim mirrors make you feel fat! The mirror ought to be taller than you so that you don't have to stoop to see yourself. A mirror can be placed near natural light to capture your most natural reflection.

My 'Jane Eyre' client's daughter ought to be encouraged to have house parties. Cooking and eating with her friends in the house would help to develop a healthy socialising culture. The parents' relationship – especially the mother's with the father – is crucial. If you want your daughter to have a wonderful family life and later a contented sexually-fulfilling relationship, then address your own relationship issues in the home. So much of our lives are lived outside in created but unfixed environments... cafes that look like living rooms, bars that look like stage sets. These are fine for occasional use, but we are turning into more than a cafe culture; we've started to live in these spaces. This is a financial burden, and we're escaping from our homes. Let's turn our homes into our dreams, invite people in and take responsibility for our most expensive and nurturing expression of ourselves.

The third child, the eldest, was centrally placed in the house and identified by me as the rock. Despite being autistic, he was the only stable element for the family. Everyone has a place in mind-reading rooms and people defined as having low-level autism have a thought-rhythm that allows some to tune-in on higher, more defined frequencies. They often like order and sense beyond the daily trivia of 'news' and 'fashion' by which the rest of us are encumbered.

Interestingly, he was also the only member of the family with a good quality bed! Now you might think a bed-change is a silly way of dealing with emotional imbalance. But in my official and unofficial years as Room Reader, all my clients' happiness tells me it works.

The family home had five large bedrooms, three bathrooms, three or more living rooms, a giant open-plan designer kitchen and a beautiful garden... all the elements of wealth but little expression of the family. Filled with office-style furniture, the house had too many hard edges, no warmth on the walls, several pictures of twisted, skeletal naked humans, and a conservatory in the garden smashed by a fallen tree. I was amazed that a highly qualified interior designer had been intricately involved in this overall creation.

'Jane Eyre', our lady of the house, had felt a little overlooked whilst the husband had enjoyed the female designer's full attention and approval for the bleak and lifeless interior.

The lady had retreated from the marital bed to the attic. She confided in the interior designer that she was having an affair. My client initially felt her disclosures were supported by the designer and went into the details of her secret relationship and why she did it in the first place. She was relieved to be able to share.

Weeks after the revelation, the designer wasn't so friendly. She threatened my client that she'd tell her husband about the infidelity.

I realised these threats would add to her chaotic state of mind. It wasn't the designer's place to tell the husband and she'd have known that. I suggested my client reassure this woman that she was intending to tell her husband and ask her to allow her to do this on her own terms. Also, to state to the woman, that ultimately, she could do what she wanted. My client could only do what she thought best.

Many people have affairs. Often it is done if a need isn't being met in the relationship. However, the stress caused to all those involved never justifies the affair; it's far better to identify what changes you could make in your home and relationship. Starting a relationship driven by sex, addictions, violence, or money, is bound to fail. If you think that money could keep you happy for life, you will have limited your self-expression. I mean, if you marry a guy you love and he's rich, great; if you marry because he's rich, not so great. On the other hand, if the relationship was genuinely good for a while, I believe it can be recovered. Affairs can be with money, drugs and alcohol as well as the more obvious one we see in this case.

This strategy I posed to my 'Jane Eyre' of telling the designer she would admit the affair to the husband herself, was enough to put the designer off her proposed course of action long enough for my client to regain control. She did admit to having an affair and her husband initially reacted with hurt and anger thus things appeared worse.

In time, the husband would have to acknowledge that his lack of care and warmth had driven her from him. My client would need to accept that her unwillingness to confide in her husband and make clear requests had led him into a false sense of security, and led her into justifying her affair. It wasn't going to be easy for either party but they had enough in common. The marriage had once been a loving one, plus three lovely children, in a big house (albeit one in need of self-expression of all members). I believed through mind-reading rooms this couple could create something new.

My client had relegated herself to the attic after the affair. And, once it was revealed by her, she remained estranged from her husband.

The marital bed occupied on the floor below by the husband looked like a used ashtray; it was king size and low. The whole bed from floor to top of the base was only six inches; there was no headboard; the mattress was surrounded by a deep wooden border in a flat, grey finish; worn sheets; it was unmade and housed in a room without character. They had pictures hanging directly above the non-existent headboard. The pictures were probably securely fixed to the walls but hanging pictures over your sleeping area will create a bit of stress. "What would happen if it fell on my head?" Better to put pictures or other potentially dangerous objects such as swords, drums, mirrors elsewhere in a room.

The bedroom is the place where I see many issues, yet it's the most important room in a family home. The bedroom is supposed to be a place for love and rest. Lovemaking is a vital part of a relationship. Physical communication must be given space and time. I recommend that partners don't go to bed just to 'sleep', they should allocate time for 'love-making'. Sex is an activity that can make or break a relationship. You prepare mentally and/or physically for any other activity so prepare your bedroom and it will surely reward you.

The bed must not be moveable when you give it a shake. A great mattress on a poor base isn't going to work long-term. Don't compromise on either. I recommend a bed that isn't low or overly ornate. Brass beds can look nice but catching flowing locks on a brass pole is excruciating. This happens when you're sitting in the bed with a bit of static in your hair; the static attracts the hair to the metal. Try to sit up on a bed before you buy it. If the headboard has pointy carvings or hard metal, you risk feeling much worse than the princess with a pea under her mattress. But, more importantly, a bed that sits comfortably in the space neither too big or too small, with a mattress that suits the sleepers, will ensure you don't wake up feeling grouchy. A bed needs to have some space underneath so that air and light circulate it; energy can flow in your room. Avoid beds that leave less than a two-inch space between the base and the floor. If you have a bed with drawers or underneath storage, think carefully about the contents. I'd limit the use of storage or drawers to hold only items related to the bed, such as bedding, duvets and pillows.

Do not put boxes with paperwork under the bed. The emotional content of your under-bed filing system will ensure you never fully rest even on a perfectly balanced bed, mattress and frame. I have a client who had not slept well in two years. She had dark circles under her eyes, aged skin, and low energy. I noted she kept boxes containing files of her bitter divorce under her bed. She couldn't let go of the past nor create anything new until these files of negative energy were removed.

Let's return to my 'Jane-Eyre' client: Under a stark table – the type only fit for a prison cell – was a heavy, carved wooden box with a keyhole. Inside the box were the couple's sex toys including handcuffs and whips (you can guess the rest). The sex box had initially been created by the couple for fun years earlier, but due to the lack of expression in the home, and in particular the ashtray bedroom, all the fun had long since evaporated. For her, this sex box was symbolic of being trapped in a game and only the husband – chairman of a FTSE 100 company – had the key. The industry leader thought holding this key would hold his wife. No. The lack of natural love played out in this loveless room had hurt them.

The woman in the attic had strayed, desperate for some warmth in the arms of another married man. There was no compassion in her marriage; no love, just a slightly unhinged woman, with cuckolded husband and two out of three children at unofficial risk. But was this obvious from meeting them outside? Absolutely not. Although we hide behind illusions and position, is it worth it?

The current position of the 'Jane Eyre' family is that the smashed tree and conservatory have been removed. The lady has ended her affair and is back in the marital bedroom, with a different marital bed. Some furniture has been replaced with comfy patterned sofas and new beds. The twisted naked paintings have been removed and warm vibrant colours now cover the walls. Two of the children are swapping rooms. The future is looking more expressive and less stressful for everyone.

The unhelpful interior designer is no longer relied upon for any confidence or service. The lady of the house has removed the sex box. She and her husband are working on the home and the relationship. The children are calmer, more content and having friends around.

Key actions: Room changes; bed changes; encourage social cooking gatherings for daughter in the kitchen; address relationship issues in the marriage; add colour with fabrics and paint; replace slim mirror with a good-sized one; family to be more expressed in the home (personal items in shared spaces such as books, artwork or other loved items); form Room Reading group with other parents; swap ideas and furniture; create social events; start photo scrapbooks of rooms; discuss issues and changes – planned or made – and share results; remember to seek medical advice if needed. (Listen to the song *Plastic Flower*.)

30. The Cookie Queen

Key themes: fat women; thin women; media manipulation; kitchen sizes; obsessions; male balding; misdirected energy.

The next story tackles the impact of 'perfection' on two women's lives. The daughter – until joining a Room Reading group – was drowning in both extreme dieting and gluttonous consumption of fairy cakes. These should be called 'dead cakes' as each one is light, pretty as a fairy but dead nutritionally and deadly to our waistlines. While being 'perfect,' we must also be the sexy mistress of buttercream baking delights hoping someone else will eat our efforts to save us from a bulging waistline and rotting teeth. Here, two generations of women battle for 'perfection' in different ways with life-threatening consequences for one. We have all at some point been 'too fat' or 'too thin.' We've all been 'wrong.' Encouragement to eat more, or not at all, has never been so pronounced. The impact is in schools with girls and boys either stuffing calorific fast foods and being fat and proud, or experiencing terror at touching a morsel and being thin and too weak to be anything.

The time to teach our children and reduce unhealthy fast-food consumption or fear of eating is now. Encourage a balanced diet at home, school and outside for our children. Every other shop is a café or take-away marketed as fashionable to our kids. Over-stimulation of senses means we either opt-in and over-indulge (resulting in a lifetime of yo-yo dieting) or opt-out with desensitisation, resulting in poor appetite, low body weight, and poorer physical and mental health –

especially for our highly-susceptible teenagers. Parents, teachers, carers and chefs must understand nutrition and suggest foods that provide wholegrains, starches, fruits and vegetables daily. Limiting factory-farmed meat and increasing wholefoods (brown rice) or starches (white rice), yams, sweet-corn and any vegetable mixes will provide energy and nutrition. We are going to have to fight for our children's right to delicious satisfying foods that will keep them healthily into adulthood. I know how hard it is with cheap quick-fill foods at every turn. But we are the customer and if enough of us make a stand for better foods we will find them available and affordable. Perhaps you are a great cook? Please share your skills with your Room Reading group, you will be helping change eating habits for what all of us know is the way to eat – it's just that some need an arm around the shoulder whilst looking in the right direction.

Imagine a future where we have no advertising on packaging and where we have scoops and containers that can be refilled with foodstuffs. The cost to us – and the planet – would drop significantly. We'd know when we are being manipulated into buying food that isn't good for our health. We would buy based on the quality of the food rather than that of the packaging.

We could grow basic salads at home. Schools would have vegetable-growing sites for kids to manage. This way they'd understand, appreciate and enjoy what they harvest.

Your Room Reading group can discuss the impact of issues here. Create scrapbooks of healthy balanced images, environments and foods. Enjoy cooking and sharing healthy dinner events at home. Involve your children in these discussions. Food-growing and group-buying organisations can also be involved in your Room Reading group. Foraging and other exploration with foods generate an ideal environment that will transform high streets and cafes, supermarkets and, in time, the media. And it all starts at home in our kitchens.

But how big or expensive do our kitchens need to be? What foodstuffs do we need to store, and in what quantity? How big do we need our cookers, fridges and freezers to be? Do we need these things at all! Please discuss and share your kitchen dilemmas ready for action.

Martha only just managed to attend my seminar; squeezing herself through the single door was difficult. She had brought in some pictures of herself, her family and her kitchen. In the second half of my talk, I asked whether she would like me to analyse her home-space with the group. She wobbled over and distributed her enormous bulk onto a single chair next to me. She was not a timid woman and although it was clear she wanted help, I don't think she really believed that a Room Reading group would be any use.

Martha started her story by explaining to us all that for 15 years she had starved herself. In the stunned silence that followed, we heard Martha's chair creak under the strain. The pictures we were looking at were of an unrecognisable version of herself when she was almost skeletal with her family at home for the holidays during her university days and of family gatherings, parties and weddings. Her mother was very slim but baked at least three times a week. At the time, Martha thought her mother must be able to eat whatever she wanted without piling on pounds. With hindsight, she understood her mother indulged others – especially Martha – but only ate the crumbs herself.

As a child, encouraged by her mother's homemade pastry and cakes, she had a sweet tooth. At five, she was chubby, and everyone thought she was cute so it hadn't mattered. But then, she explained, the Government started to advertise healthy eating habits and her primary school had stopped her having cake and custard at lunchtimes. This had angered her, especially as the other children teased her for being deprived of what they were enjoying.

What was even harder, Martha's childhood home had a very large kitchen full of ingredients to make the fatty foods she loved. So, whilst at home, she would eat mountains of homemade cookies and cakes. Then her mother had a letter from the school telling her to put Martha on a diet! Her anxious mother complied by giving her salads and putting the goodies on ever-higher shelves. Martha hated having to eat what other people said she should.

Mixed secondary school was a nightmare with constant name-calling, especially from other girls. Martha lost her appetite for all foods. Her weight plummeted from 85 to 51 kg in just six months. But it didn't stop there: the fear of being teased again was so intense that any food was unbearable. She wasted away to 38 kg. Her periods stopped at the age of 15 and, by 25, she was told that her chances of conceiving were zero.

Her thin university-era lasted five years then she went further down to 30.5 kg. It was, she explained, a protest against being deprived of her favourite foods when she was younger and that this rage had deepened with the media messages of young women being too fat, too thin or just not good enough. She said she felt that her basic rights had been taken away. The only thing she could do to rebel was to starve herself so that those who starved her of self-expression would be disempowered. I wondered how many other children had been either forced to eat – or not to – at school or home.

Martha starving herself for 15 years turned the (empty) tables, maybe, but a little late. Her periods had stopped and never returned to normal. Her bones had become weak and her heart had developed a problem. Her mother seemed lost to help and it was likely she, too, had struggled with being the perfect size mother. She was warm and loving, an excellent cook and hostess, with a waistline that lesser women would envy. Yet this had been managed by off-loading her own desires to eat onto her daughter.

Martha was physically unable to finish her degree in business management but she had met Tim. For the first time in her life, she wanted to eat healthily to get her periods back, and she wanted a family. At first, Tim was supportive, but as she blossomed to a size 10 UK / 6 US (54.2 kg) for the first time in years, he asked her to stay as she was. Martha felt the anger returning; even Tim was dictating her weight, dictating when she 'looked right'. She made this clear that was how she felt so I mentioned how his 'dictation' might have in fact been a sign that Tim cared and wanted to reassure that her struggle was over, that she'd now found the right weight for the right man at the right time – and for the rest – of her life.

Now married to Tim and living in a comfortable home she had an extension built to house her dream kitchen. It would be enormous. Here she would make wonderful food for Tim and her friends. Martha started to put on weight. The larder was always full of her homemade cookies just like the ones her mother used to bake.

She felt in control. Cookbooks, especially about fairy cakes and the intricacies of craft baking such as sugared balls and sprinkles, coloured buttercreams and icing took hours of her time and kept her mind off having no children. Then, alone with the buttercream and chocolate fondants, she would make herself large pots of tea and tuck into the hugely calorific delights. Decorations for these cakes filled her lines of shelving; her favourite TV show was The Great British Bake Off. She was free to indulge. She said she felt free especially now the media liked fat women! She bought into magazines about women and admired the new trend in fat female models as her weight grew and grew so had her confidence in her 'choices'.

Then my question was: if she felt so free, what help did she need? That is when she explained that she was suffering from depression and that the number of foods she was buying had cleaned out her finances. She was now so large that she had to have tent-like dresses made. Tim left her for another woman. She hated men, hated the media but, most of all, she hated herself.

Her new boyfriend enjoyed her size and even encouraged her to eat whatever she wanted. In fact, he became unhappy when she wasn't eating. (Some men enjoy the partner's powerlessness that obesity brings.) Martha knew she was a victim of conflicting and extreme ideals. She could not be who – or how – she wanted to be because she didn't know where to start. She ditched the food-pusher. This left her desperate to find a way through the lifetime maze.

But my immediate problem was that this was all equally confusing to my seminar attendees. They expressed concern over Martha's health, focusing on her eating and not eating throughout her life. Many women in the group had similar (though less extreme) issues to Martha. Even the guys felt they had to live up to media-standards.

Let's weigh this up: a child is encouraged to eat large amounts of cakes and sweet foods; then is deprived by those who encouraged it;

she grows up with large full kitchens; she starves herself to punish those who sought to 'control her' or to 'regain her control'. This whole dialogue was highly influenced by TV and magazines that define and re-define what we all should look like.

I suggested the following actions: I asked Martha to collect every slimming and cooking magazine she had and put it in the garbage! I asked her to take out half of her kitchen units so that she limited her food storage space to 25% of what she had now. I asked her to wear clothes that made her a little less comfortable so that she would want to eat less to wear what she had comfortably. I asked her to take up walking, indeed, to forgo any transport and walk everywhere, except the supermarkets. No supermarkets. Instead, she was to buy ingredients from small shops. She protested this would take much longer as the small shops had less variety. I countered that buying from specialists would encourage her to buy less (remember, she had to carry it home) and walk more. I asked her to buy new cookbooks on healthy whole food eating and follow those recipes. She could still eat cakes if she wanted to but healthy versions with fewer fats and sugars and more fruits... that's fruits in or out of the cakes.

Ten months had passed by the time I heard from Martha via Skype. She had lost enough weight to improve her health without having to diet or go to a gym. She had also started a scrapbook with the things she liked. This had kept her from being overly influenced by the media. On her walking trips she had connected with a walking group. She had met a man called Henry. He had been depressed and was balding. He felt under pressure to be so much more than he was, and this had him retreating into food and beer. An early heart attack had woken him to take responsibility for his health and finally accept he was bald. The two now enjoyed healthy cooking together and occasional treats. They kept a journal of favourite walks; taking pictures and sketches of these trips brought both a lot of pleasure and helped them get fit gently.

For the first time in her life, she could see how her personal space at home in the kitchen – and during her education – had impacted her behaviour such that she became a terrible expression of it. This manipulation had harmed her for years. Now she was truly free to play with her food without it controlling her whole life. Her sensitive nature had always found its answer – for good or ill – in her food.

Key actions: reduce kitchen units; buy ingredients from specialist shops; walk; use scrapbooks; remove weight magazines; buy healthy eating cookbooks.

Throughout my adult life, meditation rescued me from what Landmark calls 'the morass' and what Sam Kogan called 'the sewer.' Yes, the subconscious mind is a sponge for rubbish and, if you do not meditate, be sure it will stop you from taking actions that help your life. If I was the Prime Minister, I would insist that all schools do a daily 10-minute meditation to calm the mind and focus on the day ahead. Meditation also stops 'the sewer' from flooding into chaos, anxiety, nightmares and addiction. A simple meditation is nothing more than a breathing exercise that you and your family can do any time of day or night (even in the car). Simply breathe in through the nose, filling up an imaginary balloon inside your tummy and lower back; hold for three to five seconds then release the balloon through pursed lips, slowly and with intention. When exhaling like this you can imagine your breath is a flame hitting a chosen spot ahead of you. Children love this daily practice. It helps activate the vagus nerve which easily becomes over-stimulated if you're predisposed to stress (like me). Meditation's a life saver! So, here's my friend with his story and how he now changes others' lives. Enjoy!

Meditation and the Art of Chillaxing by Simon Paul Frost

Ask most people if they meditate... the answer would be 'no'. Ask most people if they want to feel calm, relaxed, be free from tension, anxiety and be happy about life... the answer would be 'yes'. Why is it then that most people don't meditate but desire the mindset that mediation provides? Wouldn't it be great to chillax? (Chill = to be calm, free from tension. Relax = to be happy about life, anxiety free.)

We have concerns – or even fears – because of our old associations. After all, what does meditation mean to you? Orange-robed monks sitting in silence for hours on end; chilled-out hippies or even an anti-religious practice that is more witchcraft than prayer...?

Modern meditation teaches you that time-saving/fast-track versions can very easily become part of the manic life we all seem to be living. If we feel limited by constant restrictions, we can lose hope. If, however, we remain calm then we enter a place of better understanding and flow. With this new objective perspective, we can create and see the opportunities for our desired changes.

How often have you been in a place of regretful hindsight? Wouldn't it be great to be in a place of productive foresight? Then you'd focus on the things you do want rather than waste energy on things you don't.

We all love to feel calm, we all love to relax and we would all have our lives happy and positive... so what are you waiting for? If you learn to meditate (like a workout for the mind – the more you do, the quicker and faster you become) not only will you be able to understand what meditation is, you will be able to share the art of chillaxing!

I was fed up with being fed up, not enjoying me at all. I wanted to feel good about me. I wanted to feel I had some higher purpose and try for the first time in my life to see myself equal to others. So, I started to be present to me and live fully in this world – with me as I truly am.

I admired others to avoid failure in myself; finding excuses from my past, I avoided the risk of failure. My actions were a Catch 22 of karma.

I remember thinking: My actions have all dug this self-wallowing pit where I sit, alone. Instead of filling the pit with steps of hopes and desires, I allow insecurities to lay a roof across the top and keep me buried. The drugs I take build fantastic ladders but, in the cold light of day, disintegrate. Why doesn't a ladder of ideas, as vivid as my dreams flowing teasingly through my mind, find the exit route? Not outside, but within me is my new story. Starting on level ground, it could – I could – become the new story. Yes, my story could become a mountain to stand me high.

My wake-up call: when written down it seems amazing to me that the past patterns of denial were so strong, they pulled me to self-destruct. Thankfully, I am here today to tell the tale and it is death that made me finally ask questions and opened me to want to 'see' more.

I was in my late twenties at this point, and during this time I did not have the clarity or strength of thought to move on and create a more positive life. I 'fell victim' to blame and excuses and self-abuse. I put myself to the very back of my priority list and found illusionary solace in drugs. Cocaine was the only thing I could rely on and be there for me in my time of need. And as Elton John has said: 'I wasn't in charge; the white lady was'. Cocaine gave me the illusion of confidence.

I was in a relationship with Andrew. He was a genius/madman of Stephen Fry intellect (actually, they had spent time with each other

– I'd have loved to have been a fly on the wall when they spoke) but he found life just too hard and always thought from a young age that he just did not belong in this period of time. He always felt over-exposed to the world and so used drink and drugs to try to seal the defencelessness that made him constantly question his self-hatred and worth. He worked as an agent and a casting director in the mad show business world so his crutches (booze and drugs) could go unnoticed because of the prevalence of both being used by those around him. After many attempts at suicide, he finally died from a heart attack at 37 brought on by an asthma attack. (Andrew hated to exercise, he smoked at least 40 strong cigarettes every day, and his heart was further damaged by his daily cocaine.)

His death shook me. My mind was muddled with what was good and what was bad; the light and dark all blended into a perverse viewpoint. Everything I had known was blown to smithereens. I had loved him, and I had told him, and I had shown him, but still he wanted to die!

Thus, I was forced into a place of deep thought, of deep wanting; I truly wanted to know the answer to life. I was lucky enough to know that deep inside me there was a good man desperately trying to find his way out – even though most days I hated him. However, I treated 'him' with such disrespect that I pushed, shoved and blocked a loving and peaceful world coming anywhere near to me. I'd created deafness towards all positivity. Andrew's death made me start to truly live. How could someone who I thought was so intelligent, seemingly fun-loving and confident, hate life so much that he eventually destroyed his very existence on this planet?

Don't take your world to this harsh lesson before you choose to get to know who and what you are. I had no idea I was choosing a 'poor me' mentality and always being a victim of circumstance. I was attracting negativity into my world.

I finally opened to a new self-understanding – a place where all that I believed to be true was questioned and could start to truly see the illusions of our world of control. Meditation was the tool which opened me fully, enabling me to declutter and restructure my sense of self. The physical me, my physical soul home, became nurtured and cared for, releasing past fears, bringing a vibrant and clear energy into my world.

Your very own bubble: in meditation books, one of the aspects I don't warm to is, when they are describing visualisation techniques at the beginning of the prose, they say shut your eyes… What I am about to write, please read fully before you attempt to close your eyes. (Or just record the instructions on your smartphone.)

Once your eyes are closed – focus your intention to the middle of your forehead (just above and right in the middle of your eyebrows). Try to create a sense that your perspective is sitting right inside of the large physical self. One of the scenes in 'Men in Black' had 'aliens' going through some kind of customs. One was a large creature of extra- terrestrial physicality but once challenged by the authorities was discovered to be a tiny alien sitting inside the forehead of the larger body, driving and steering the whole being. This is how I started to see me and how I was with myself once I was willing to look within.

Once connected with this place, the third eye area of your forehead, think about your entire body being in a bubble. It's your protective aura field. Visualise your entire physical self in this bubble. Allow a moment or two to think about you right in the centre of the protective bubble.

Imagine, or just feel the bubble is two feet above your head, two feet in front of you, two behind you, two below you and two around you on both sides. Try to send your mind around your body trying to notice the two feet rule. Once you have given yourself a chance to know where the outside 'edge' is then you can start to use white light.

Now, imagine your bubble is filled with white light. This space (the aura field) is being filled with the purest kind of light you can possibly think of; a blinding white light that seems effervescent, alive, and almost liquid in form, as it fills the intentional space around you.

One of the ways I started to understand the 'white light' was the same kind of feeling I got when in the sunshine. I mean, the sense you get when your eyes are closed and you point your face towards the sun. It can feel as if your head is filled with light and you're part of that light.

Give yourself a couple of minutes now to 'bathe' in this light – allow yourself and your aura field to be calm and centred within it... I promise with this brief exercise you will start to connect to a new level of YOU!

x x x x x

Add a meditation to your Room Reading group (at the start or end of a session). You can also practice simple breathing meditation at home with your children. It's especially good for preventing younger kids' nightmares, calming anxieties and soothing teenagers' hormones or exam nerves. So, meditate yourself and experience the benefits to pass on to your loved ones.

31. Elton John and David Furnish
My heart belongs to Daddy

Key themes: completing past hurts; impact of bitterness from parental splits on the child; ways of managing obsessive behaviours; same-sex parents; managing large collections of objects.

Gay men don't necessarily make better parents than straight couples, although I do admire Elton John and David Furnish. They are role models for the future of gay parenting. I recall a time when I would have been very much against the idea, but that was coming from the first 14 years of my life when I was immersed in Catholicism. I still agree that religion can be a useful tool if used responsibly to guide us but, like Elton, I also believe it often causes more harm than good especially when – however hard you pray – God has seemingly condemned you. Elton was mortified to be lost to God because of his sexual preference.

Setting aside the issue of sexual legitimacy as long as it is within the law, we must utilise the skills of all people to thrive and certainly ensure every human is valued enough to be accepted by a god of any faith. Those faiths that reject homosexuality cannot educate children because the religion is prejudiced and discriminates against choice. Thus, if children or parents want to follow any specific religion, it should be sought outside of schools to ensure that schools remain authentic to the rule of law and the most modern thinking. From the position of Room Reader, balance can only be found within all major religions taught equally in all schools. It is not enough to have a

Christian or Muslim school offering a cursory history of other religions.

Attending a Roman Catholic primary school, I believed all I was taught. St Michael's Church was full of iconic paintings and statues. This led me to be prejudiced against many people and a little conceited because I happened to be the same colour as all my religious icons. My world, my religion was white. Homosexuals and those who had (or advocated) abortions were abhorrent. Going through the rites of passage as a Catholic girl with my three sisters, this was simply, to us, the normal way of life. I worry about single faith schools now. Because even after going from the primary to the secondary Roman Catholic school, where we all received a multi-faith education – since we had already been indoctrinated – our minds were fixed on what we thought we knew best.

Another problem that arose for my mother and I was the 'no sex before marriage' idea and 'no contraception.' This means women in such religions are likely to have early or unwanted pregnancies and for homosexual men to have shameful sexual encounters where condoms would not be asked for, then the women would be vulnerable to men in straight encounters, men would also be vulnerable to other men in homosexual ones, as well as open to depression after so-labelled 'murderous abortions' or 'homosexual acts.' Both groups are likely to experience further stigma as carriers of a myriad of sexually transmitted diseases. All religions must modernise to ensure a society where humans are treated with respect and equality. Denying people sexual protection and choice, making same-sex relationships criminal or forcing women (like my mother) into early marriage or being a single parent is clearly counter-productive to modern society.

I believe that parents wanting their child to follow a religious path should do it outside of the tax-funded school system if we as a society are genuinely committed to shared empathy and natural choice. How beautiful it must be to have found a seed of faith in religious education that grows with us into adulthood by choice rather than design.

Having been raised to think that gay sex was abnormal and against God, it took me 12 years to undo my prejudice, to understand that the creativity of humans is such that we explore and create with our partners.

It has never been more important for us to communicate directly with each other in a non-judgemental way, to focus always on the collective good. This insight has helped me to understand that Elton John and David Furnish are OK to parent their kids.

Anyway, in the next 20 years, we will drop the term 'gay parents' in the West because there will be so many. There'll just be: 'parents.' And that will provide many children with caring role models, children who'd otherwise be stuck inside the care system. Of course, many LGBTQI+ parents will want to have their own biological children. I still think that thousands of such couples should be encouraged to adopt foster children because the state 'care system' has a poor record of positive outcomes for so many children who would benefit from loving parents.

Should our progress sacrifice minorities for the sake of traditional roles? We all agree that love starts at – and often leads us back to – home.

I haven't seen many gay parents that are given credit for their great job. And with the trappings of drugs, fame, promiscuity and immense fortune, Elton John is hardly likely to be no.1 of anyone's parenting top 10! But I think being a parent has made Elton blossom as a father and an artist. We have seen him take control of his addictions through sheer honesty and hard work. Still, the source of his tendencies to excess warrants further analysis. And some Room Plans for the star and his family.

Over the years, David Furnish has provided Elton with a stable love, one that Elton craved as a child. David Furnish took a big chance on this relationship. Furnish was a successful advertising executive on the board of Ogilvy & Mather, thus it took some consideration to really wear his heart on his sleeve. Coming out to his parents and announcing his love for the international star was a step he went on to fully embrace. Since then he has had very much a 50-50 relationship with Elton producing the video 'Tantrums & Tiaras' in 1997 and working with Elton's Aids Foundation. David and Elton exude warmth when they are with their sons (Elijah and Zachary). It's lovely to see. I know the sons will need security. Elton stepped this up, influenced by the premature deaths of Princess Diana and Gianni Versace, but I would advise that less is more. They have security guards inside the gardens of the home. This may impact the children's self-expression... and their own. Privacy is important for new families who need to be surrounded by caring people who'll support them through the early years of parenting when they are likely to make mistakes. I can imagine that David is the one who gets up to change the kids' nappies at night and Elton sings them happy-nappy songs.

These two boys will thrive in the balanced environment created by David and Elton.

A playroom where anything goes ('messy play') is vital for children to develop tactile skills and physical confidence. I know this was an issue for Elton as a child, and still is. It's good for him to put structures in place so that his children develop body-confidence. This can be through 'soft play,' or baby yoga. Both the boys and the parents wear natural textiles and comfy shoes. I hope they have a good diet of organic veg and meat, with reverse-osmosis filters for washing and drinking to purify their water. Juicing with a cold-press juicer is another way of ensuring a young family gets a fresh supply of vitamins. Twin- or single-gear juicers are also better than masticating juicers; masticating juicers have bigger engines which heat the elements and destroy vitamin content.

Our children give us a chance to relive our childhood. Elton's mother, Shelia, was a big influence on him especially since they left his father, Stanley, when Elton was just six. (They went to live with Sheila's mother.) Sheila may have projected a lot of her marital upsets onto Elton about Stanley who was often away in the military. On his visits home, Stanley and Sheila would argue and she'd highlight how she disliked his parenting of Elton. This may have made the young boy feel his father was wrong to try to instil guidance. And Sheila may have interpreted this parenting as unfairness towards Elton.

The other issue is of his father, Stanley, not attending his concerts which offended Elton, but I would remind him that his father knew his genius. He would have heard him playing at home from an early age. And it was he who bought Elton his first piano.

When your parents have negatively said that "you're just like your father", or "you're just like your mother," this kind of remark is used to put down the other parent. But the impact of cutting comments between parents that relate to personal traits is on the child. The child carries the genetic makeup of both parents and thus understands he/she is deficient in some way. Not only that, but he/she can do nothing about it. For a child, the impact is low self-image, self-loathing, and a tendency to aim for perfection but never attain it. (As if they're faulty materials.) They are likely to have cosmetic surgery, take drugs or alcohol to escape from themselves, struggle to accept or receive love, overachieve or be critical of themselves and others. They are also likely to try to control their urge to hide away by hiding behind extrovert clothes – including glasses – that can create distance between the wearer and an audience. But, if the glasses are over the top, they'll actually add to the sense of awkwardness.

Elton still needs to address the impact of his early years and Room Reader would ensure a reduction in his wardrobe from hundreds of trousers, shirts and other items to just eight to ten sets of clothes. I would allow him to have more clothes for his performances, in fact, as many as he wanted as long as he was using them. Elton must find himself less distracted with his image and more at peace with who he is and what he stands for. So, meditation would be useful; we recommend short meditations to relax. This would ensure his attention was retained long enough for him to benefit.

It's been a long hard fight for him to work out who he needs to be. His exaggerated wardrobe draws him back into that chaotic state of mind that once led him to a dark place. Furthermore, he must complete all unsaid conversations with his father and mother. It matters not that the father and recently his mother have passed away; completion lives beyond the grave in mind-reading rooms. It's a golden opportunity for reflection and acknowledgement of the past.

Elton is an obsessive collector of porcelain and photography. Again, I would look to pare down large numbers of items in the home. If Elton wants to open a collection room, it ought to be separate from his main home. It would make sense to ensure these expensive items are kept well out of reach of the two boys. Children are naturally curious and love to test boundaries, so seeing how daddy will react to a thrown porcelain doll may be too much of a temptation.

The choice to stay in Berkshire surrounded by nature and local people who have known Elton as an occupant is certain to encourage protective feelings for the family. This is important to Elton especially for the boys as they grow up. I think Elton and David have set the bar for same-sex parents, and it's good to see them participating in activities for the boys. Far from retreating into the intoxicating world of showbiz, Elton has embraced fatherhood as a new beginning and is thriving as never before.

At times when our lives are in balance, it's perfect for addressing past imbalance. Mind-reading rooms isn't just about addressing issues when you're in trouble. It is there to help you grow and create more structures and sensitivity to colour, shapes, light and comfort. Elton John has lived much of his life feeling solitary because he was trying to please his mother by rejecting his estranged biological father. He couldn't have had both because very young children do not have enough emotional language to assert themselves. He was a child prodigy and his music-making comforted him from the age of four.

He would have still been a child prodigy if his parents had had better communication, but would he appreciate the love he has with David Furnish?

I wonder if he would have recognised what it takes to love without manipulation. Elton can understand now, as an adult, how crucial it is to have someone love you without conditions.

Elton will always be the hardworking professional who produces music we love. It's time for him to embrace himself as David embraces him, as family and friends embrace him, as his children embrace him... as his father and mother still embrace him. And I think he has already accepted - long ago - that there's some whose beliefs will ensure they never can.

Key actions: reflect on position and understanding of relationships to encourage empathy; put in structures for the boys; reduce wardrobe; consider putting statue collection in a designated space; reduce obvious security presence around children. (Listen to the questioning song *Amazing Greats*.)

32. The broken (door) knob

Key themes: passive vs active lifestyle; impact of passive sex; desensitised societies; extreme behaviours; broken objects and their impact on male sexual dysfunction; socialisation supersedes genius; normal life is key to fulfilment.

Many of us may have heard of the term 'bread and circuses.' Well, the next story touches on the idea that we are being distracted to the point that our behaviour is extreme. We are encouraged to indulge in fast-foods or poor nutrition (bread) and hyped-up games like big live football matches where high levels of aggression become the norm; we'll obsess about a pop-star or soap-opera where we'll cry or fight over the idol; porn, especially using violence or depicting women in a derogatory way; and many other distractions that help politicians stir up the masses with racism or religious wars on the basis of false information or biased morality (circuses). Led by the nose, we lose our capacity to physically function with our SAD (Standard American Diet) and are at best only partially engaged with what matters in our home-life and the wider community. This story looks at why people might end up homeless and what activities can be done at home to address addictions to porn and desensitisation of society seen through a man's behaviour.

I had seen my client twice outside his home. He was a professional actor, unmarried, childless and reluctant to fully open up to me. He had been down recently as he had experienced major disappointments in his life, at one point being suicidal. He had fought through this low point with Facebook chats and some online dating sites. But, in real life, I could see his problems. He had poor posture. Although physically fit, he often dropped his head a little which curved his upper shoulders. He also had a variety of habits such as nail-biting and picking spots. Wearing shorts one day, he seemed to be able to find the smallest pimple on his inner thighs and scratch at it. He removed the surface and applied a drop of alcohol. This, he said, rid him of the tiny "itchy heat-spot" and then he proudly showed me the equally tiny scars of his previous conquests. He had intermittent mouth ulcers which he treated with salt. Although the ulcers were uncomfortable – since he always tried to look on the positive side – he'd "prefer the stress to come out rather than be internalised and lead to far worse nasties". He swallowed air which led to barely-hidden burping. This was obviously because – to use the cliché – he needed to get out more. He occasionally hit himself hard on the legs. He said this was to "gee myself up" although he didn't look like a horse. In fact, my client was a handsome man, clearly intelligent, but seemed to have no clue about how to behave despite being well over 35, educated to degree level and reasonably well-travelled. He was unaware of the many disruptions, habits and hurts he was acting out. This is what happens when you leave a guy in a room alone for too many months.

After the second home-meeting, I suggested he send some photos of his flat or allow me to visit. He agreed for me to attend his flat in east London. He was reasonably well-presented although seemed to be attached to a worn plastic Costcutter bag in which he'd carry his lunch, often fruit and bread. This hardly looked professional for his acting auditions. He listened to music when he was out, so he had little verbal engagement and limited awareness of his surroundings.

Overlooked and lacking social engagement through work or relationships, he liked to take risks in traffic as he crossed roads, rarely waiting for approved signals as he felt they took too long to appear. This made his life more exciting by increasing his risk of being knocked down by a bus.

He had a lot of energy the way he touched – almost attacked – himself whilst scratching, nail-biting and road-crossing recklessly (often on a hopeful journey). This misdirected energy was complemented by his watching porn. Although he did say that he learned women-pleasing tricks from fantasy screen-life – and we all listen to fantasy love in our pop songs – there was no doubt when I first met him that he was full of theory.

We live in a world of sensationalism; many of us feel we cannot compete with those who seem to have more than us. This results in dissatisfaction or depression. Working and having relationships can feel futile compared with the lives of those played-out and hyped-up in the media or even in the school playground. The impact is desensitisation of varying degrees from low-level impact such as extra-marital affairs, recreational drug-taking, regular gambling, over-consumption of alcohol, sexual perversity, right up to religious fanaticism where young newly-converted Western-born Muslim women seek religious adventure with jihadists...

It's all out of balance. Religious leaders must modernise and promote the best aspects of their religion. It's their responsibility to make religion work with society not against it. The time for the media, governments and people to take responsibility for hyped existence is now. Inclusive everyday activities need to be at the forefront not overlooked as trivia. It is the nuts and bolts of daily life that provide us with a smooth and steady existence. Promoting the normal ways of being and doing leads to satisfaction and reduces the likelihood of extremes.

My client's flat had several years of dirt. He advised me he had never touched many parts as he had an aversion to cleaning; his mother had made him clean and polish the taps and knobs of a large property every time a potential buyer had come to view. He was now "off cleaning for life". I said that many people wanting to sell their house did make an effort and that his mother was merely anxious that they sold the house. The family had been very wealthy but had lost everything through no fault of their own. My client had gone from a luxury life to poverty, moving from private to state school, and needing free school dinners. The family home had been seized and they moved out of a mansion into a small council flat.

He had found my company, Spotless Organic, whilst searching for help online. His late mother had a copy of Mrs Beeton's Household Management, the aforementioned 19th century book. It remained popular amongst middle-class women throughout the last century. His mother had relied upon the book to manage staff working in the home, so he had a vague memory that good household management was important. He wanted to have a deep-clean using natural products and a declutter. Spotless Organic was one of the few companies that provided this.

He did wash dishes after making a sparse meal (with his broken-handled pan). I could see the future for my client was going to get worse as he had retreated into a world of painful rituals and mind-numbing porn. He could easily lose hope and slip outside the home onto the streets. We wonder when we see people in such circumstances how they could have got there. When your home is a painful reflection of how you live and it's unbearable to be surrounded by your failure, the only way may be to get out. I think my client was on the way out. Many people who live on the streets rarely return to a home after giving up the most precious space we have. It's like we had a chance and blew it. Disempowered, we cannot face the same decline again. For some who end up on the streets (and of course we cannot discuss every single situation) the friendships formed with other street-people offers companionship and business collaborations such as selling or begging. It may be a preferable environment for lonely souls who have a home and nothing else.

Sadly, we never really can disconnect from, or complete on, the past unless we face it. I was asked by my client: "What is completion for Room Reader? Is it the same as a resolution?" Mind-reading rooms completion doesn't provide an answer as resolution does. Mind-reading rooms completion is about accepting the way things are and the way things aren't. Such acceptance isn't about putting up with stuff, it is about recognising what it meant – or means – for you, and that it can or has passed. We can take incompletions with us no matter how far we travel. The impact of not accepting situations or people the way they are or aren't, includes heart attack, cancers and nervous breakdowns. These incompletions are likely to be numbed with addictions. We all suffer in life, but we can learn to suffer less by facing ourselves and working things through so that we do not carry a growing burden. This is completion. Room Reader allows us to alleviate this little by little with cleaning, clearing a drawer, changing a cushion, painting a wall, collecting ideas in a scrapbook and sharing this process with others. One thing that becomes clear to me on sharing this story is our need to form relationships. So, reach out and get connected with groups or invite your library to set up a Room Reading group for other local people. Smile and say hello to your neighbours and share your skills and experience.

My client seemed to pick up after the first two meetings; by the third, he was willing to confront himself and his habits. I was pleased that the wannabe actor was the director of his life and he could perform a new scene.

He said he had been without a woman for two years, and that he liked to watch porn – masturbating over it – on at least three occasions weekly. Despite claims he suffered from erectile dysfunction, it seemed to me that this dysfunction was largely a confidence issue as, when he heard he might get a part in a big show, he had no problem getting it up. The only issue was he had no-one to put it in. He was desperate to have his flat deep-cleaned so that he could bring his new girlfriend home, but deeply worried that he would not satisfy her sexually. I asked him why he felt that way. He said he had tried with her and been unable to perform.

He had recently met a lady with whom he was in love, but he had not been able to be honest with her or express his sexual feelings. He had practically destroyed the opportunity by constantly pushing her away, telling her he did not fancy her, he wasn't wanting a relationship, and any other negative thing he could think of. Luckily, his natural actions – holding her hands, kissing, calling three times a day – spoke louder than his protestations. So, she stayed around.

If you find yourself relating to these people, start to observe yourself. Bad habits are usually our way of ensuring rejection so that we are left in peace, alone, desperate, but intact! Positive habits can be nurtured; similarly, awareness of the poor habits will reduce them over time. Try eating a piece of fruit instead of a chocolate bar, being especially helpful to a neighbour or friend, cleaning out a drawer, arranging to pay a bill, start an activity that develops you, such as gardening, cooking or another craft.

My client had been unable to invite his lady to his flat due to its filthy state. And when I attended, I noted the knob on his bedroom door was broken. Though the flat was filthy, he pointed out that he swept the central areas of the room, cleaned the fridge for my visit, and had always kept the inside of the filthy shower unit clean.

His life was full of broken ends... The handle to his bedroom was broken; handles on kitchen cupboards were missing; the frying pan handle was loose and floppy (it needed a good screw); just a string was hanging for him to put on the bathroom light (the knob-end had disappeared); and he often dropped his head. I agreed he needed to have a deep-clean of his flat, a declutter of his cupboards then, once every handle had been fixed or replaced, he could have one-to-one Pilates lessons in his flat to improve the connection between his shoulders and his head.

I asked him to stop watching porn, as porn desensitises and numbs our natural sexual desire. It makes us use passive imagination to the point where we become lazy and inactive when we have the opportunity to engage in normal sexual relations. He would find any normal woman a disappointment after seeing the perfect models on the screen. His confidence had been smashed due to the perfect men whom he said had much larger penises than his. The porn had drawn him into a make-believe world that meant he had no time or inclination to improve his life.

I also asked him to stop masturbating so that he could allow his new girlfriend to please him. He had in the past popped a Viagra but, as he did not seem to have any biological dysfunction, I wasn't happy for him to use chemical stimulus if he could stimulate himself naturally. For some men in balanced relationships and homes but have some minor biological issues with blocked arteries causing erectile dysfunction, Viagra may help. Use such medications mindfully and in combination with improving diet and lifestyle.

My client has started basic sexual relations with his new girlfriend. They have not yet had full, penetrative sex but are building towards this. It's amazing how many of us are living alone, relying on the internet to socialise. The impact of this is lots of passive sex and the difficulty of appropriate behaviour when in a real relationship. I suggested hypnotherapy sessions to improve his confidence and develop an ability to become aroused by his partner.

My client has to be re-socialised with the help of his girlfriend. It will take some time for him to become sensitive to real people and fully engage with sex. He has a new canvas bag for his lunch. You may think this man is unusual, but I can assure you his presentation is nowadays quite average.

Humans need to participate in activities to be fully self-expressed, whether it's throwing a ball, swimming, walking, cleaning, organising, cooking, painting, gardening… knowing our bodies provide for us and others in a thousand ways. Sexual encounters are the development of physical and social engagement with others.

My sister worked with people with mental and or physical challenges. She said the major issue was her clients had become passive, too disempowered to tie a shoelace or boil an egg. My suggestion is that social services stop playing mother and start empowering people with skills.

Millions of us should learn practical life skills to enhance engagement with the self. Schools must incorporate life skills, cooking, growing vegetables and herbs, making natural remedies, meditation, yoga, cleaning, organising and sorting.

Maths, English, history and science ought to be incorporated around aspects of daily life. Otherwise, what is the point of knowledge? Society must ensure the development of socialised beings over geniuses or experts. We're shocked when we hear about deviant behaviour from people in positions of authority, from politicians, presenters and even religious leaders. Then there are the ones you haven't heard about! The underlying deficit of that person remains undiscovered because we step over it. We overlook basic human skills required to be grounded in favour of ever-greater heights. Abnormalities are generated through ignoring the need for social skills required in favour of disconnection and ultimately a passive race that follows rather than leads from within. The ideal is socialised experts found in the majority as opposed to the minority of people.

Imagine the joy of growing a vegetable in your own pot or patch then washing and cooking it to eat! Schools are trying so hard that they have missed the basics. There are too many disconnected children, lost in computer screens, in make-believe passive worlds. Don't get me wrong, make-believe can be creative, using your imagination for writing or – even better – role-play. But with the passive make-believe on offer, is it surprising obesity/anorexia and depression amongst children and young adults are increasing? Literally, we're disconnecting from our bodies, lost in the speed of a Tweet, or a Facebook 'Like'. Who wants to clean or make a sandwich when fantasies are instant? Normal activities become obsolete; we reject ourselves. Yes, often it's easier to 'Like' others. Amazon has just bought Twitch. The site has around 100 million people a month who watch other people play video games. And I thought we were passive enough when we were playing them ourselves! We have become a voyeuristic nation, sending bitchy, or even hateful texts to strangers whilst the texters enjoy live streaming and attention... any attention. Fantasy worlds take us away from engaging in reality. They allow us to hide behind created images and give free rein to anonymous and often offensive communications.

Young women are stumbling around the UK's major cities on killer heels in their thousands every night wearing provocative tiny outfits, freezing in the cold and rain to attract male attention. We have all got numb to normal life, normal people. Normality seems too dull. We spend our time on meaningless passive activities. We develop extreme and abnormal behaviours and life's beauty is lost.

We have the opportunity to turn this around like my client did. He now had a girlfriend to take his hand. This was no thanks to him with his initial expectations of fantasy straight from the screen into his reality. But even though she would take his hand, he would have to take action to secure another reality else he would be bound to fail again. Whether it's the anxiety – the beautiful pain – of embarking on a relationship or the anxiety – the beautiful fear – of having sex for the first time with someone, there are many storms in our hearts and heads. It's all about sharing. And this my client would do. He did not want to rely on theory anymore.

Key actions: Deep-clean whole flat; limit use of porn; take care of appearance; replace broken knobs; physical activity to improve posture; enjoy real relationships; hypnotherapy and Pilates.

(Listen to the song *Full of Theory*.)

33. The Priory Lady

Key themes: mental health problems; addictive behaviour; low weight; exhaustion; kids not sleeping; lack of love and self-expression in relationships; wanting perfection; magazines with created interiors; underusing space.

The next story tells of a family led by interior design magazines - and so lost - that the whole family's life was hidden away in the darkest recess of a large underused house. At least they were brave enough to share their situation and to seek help. The mother had already had extensive mental health treatment, and this just reminds me that, without the shift in the environment, little changes. As a family unit, they needed lifting out of the basement. Be brave and set up your Roomie group today. Be a detective in your own space. Always seek medical advice if you or a loved one need it.

What you will see in this story is the maximising of unused space; the gentle stimulation of appetite through home baking; using bread-making to explain the need for sleep to a young child; the development of a husband and wife's relationship through personal positive journals; and creating messy play, art, reading and yoga areas. Mind-reading rooms is all about communication and transformation of spaces. It can be used as a tool to enhance therapeutic interventions or simply empower you to take action. It's always better to do this within a Room Reading group.

I approach a beautiful family house at the end of a smart road in a London suburb. So far, so perfect. I enter the hallway. Greeted by the lady of the house with a faint smile, she's a shadow of a woman; petite with little flesh housed under baggy clothes. An overweight Labrador walks behind her. I hold the woman's bony shoulders lightly to give a polite kiss on both cheeks. Then I hesitate. Suddenly I'm scared to let go, fearing the bag of bones in my hands might collapse. The dog growls. We all walk down the large hallway. The dog leads, side-glancing me, daring me to touch his mistress again. There are a few vintage pictures of nothing in particular on the hall walls. The contrast between the large Labrador's over-protectiveness – voiced by his low growls – and the lady is stark, although it doesn't surprise me. She is around 35 yet frail and, of course, the dog understands this. As he continues to threaten me, he has to be locked in the living room.

She leads me into the kitchen; the cupboards are large and almost empty. The glass display is spread out on a shelf with only two small hinges that seem on the verge of breaking. The lady has two very young boys but they are not at home. The children's play area is below the glass-laden shelf (clearly a hazard). More than this, the boys cannot play in a relaxed way as a sense of danger has been created by the position of the poorly built shelf and the glass. It isn't something that they are fully aware of but, still, would you feel relaxed playing directly under a weak-looking shelf with 40 or more glasses above your head? Have a look around your home and check that shelves are properly secured if holding glass or heavy items. I would never advise putting a shelf like this in a children's play area in any case because it would be better placed where the children are less likely to knock it down and/or, worse, get injured.

The lady gives me a full guided tour. As we walk, she explains that the boys each sleep in their own rooms alone. But neither is sleeping well. She herself has had several mental breakdowns over the years.

On the top landing, a leaking roof window drips rainwater into a bucket. I ask how long it has been like that. "Six months or more," she tells me, but her husband doesn't want anyone to fix the leak. He "definitely will do it one day" she quotes. She shows me the boys' rooms and I note very few toys in these cold places with their bare white walls. Downstairs, the living room is dishevelled on one side. A large incongruous sideboard appears untouched. On a shelf are unopened gifts from times long since passed. I guess that some of the presents are marriage gifts (the wrapping paper tells me so). I ask how long she's been married. "Six years," she says.

She has very few pictures of her sons aged four and five, and even fewer of her and her husband. She tells me she hates this room. Her friends have no children and they have a perfect house. She wants "to have a house like the ones in the magazines". She has piles of expensive interior design magazines. She spends her days leafing through them and resenting her space that cannot compete with the monthly glossy images.

One of the largest rooms in the house is a guest room with a big, bright en-suite bathroom. I ask her if they have guests. She said, "Rarely". It seems a huge waste of light-filled space.

She tells me they travel miles to take the little boys out but she gets exhausted. The cleaner only comes once a week for two hours. I am amazed! The house is over three or more floors and large. How can the majority of the space look so immaculate with two youngsters and a large dog?

Despite being a great place for the dog and boys, the garden is little used. I ask if we could unlock the doors to it. She can't find the key. OK, the garden needs some work – it isn't as clinically perfect as the house – but is another wasted space.

She wants to practise yoga but has not created any space in the spacious home for this. She and her husband do not go out because she drinks too much. They have not been out in years. The relationship has been dying for a long time. She says her therapist helps but when she comes home, she is drawn back into the space. She can't face eating or cooking much. I cannot find any normal dust levels anywhere apart from one very high cobweb. This large house appears empty and unused. Her glass collection is her fullest expression of her fragility. She does not know where to begin, or how.

In the basement, I find the only real evidence of this family in action. The husband has beer-making equipment. She explains he retreats down here after long days in the office. The basement ceiling is low, the space is packed with unused toys, laundry, washing and drying machines. The whole life of this family seems hidden away in here.

This was my Room Plan for her and her family to emerge from this dark, restricted space:

Your energy levels must not be compromised with physical over-exertion to the point you put yourself under mental stress. I want you to put your physical health as a priority above anything else. Build up your duties with strong support systems so that you do not get overwhelmed ever! Learn to make requests (clearly, verbally and in writing of those who you are paying or who can help you).

You might find the play 'The Glass Menagerie' interesting. It's based on memories as opposed to facts of the characters in it. One character is as fragile as the glass ornaments she collects. I think it would be a good exercise for you to see how – if – you are different from the Menagerie's Laura.

The minimal use of domestic help tells me your house is underused. I want that to change. I want you, Conrad and the boys to engage with your home and manage the space at the same time. This is all doable, but you will need to trust other people to get you delivering family life in a structured, controlled way.

I have a chapter called 'Keeping up with the Joneses.' No-one on this earth is in any way like your family. So, please stop comparing yourself to the incomparable! Trust in yourself and Conrad and those around you to deliver and have a life that works. Be a leader, not a follower, don't buy lifestyle and interior design magazines to see if you're getting it right... Don't compare yourself to couples without babies or even those with! Repeat this mantra daily: I am unique, my children are special to me, my husband is caring and helpful, my family does their best always. Anytime your mind tells you otherwise, acknowledge this is merely a thought, as opposed to fact.

You need a housekeeper 3 times a week, each for 3-4 hr session.

A gardener to come and oversee garden once a week for 2 hrs.

Employ a babysitter or part-time nanny depending on what you decide to do regarding work. The hours would be to manage the family's requirements.

Things are out of balance right now; you either have too much or too little to do. You and Conrad decide about the future and create structures with a few different service providers that will ensure you have at least three people paid or unpaid to manage things with.

You could also use a dog walker so that neither you nor Conrad has to walk the dog twice a day every day. Allie is quite a big dog, try to split the dog walking between the housekeeper, you, Conrad and you and Conrad. If Allie is trained, take him out alone but I think it's a lot to manage two young kids and a dog on your own.

Housekeeper Schedule:

The Housekeeper must be given a run-through of the expected service. Talk to Conrad about what is manageable for both of you. There is no point in either of you taking on more than you can cope with. Be really honest about what is working and what isn't so that you can both put people in place to help. You having breakdowns tells me that what was happening was lacking, putting you under too much pressure. You must ensure this doesn't happen again or that the risk of this recurring is dramatically reduced. This can only be achieved through putting in structures at home and work such that you and Conrad and the children are fully empowered.

There is a lack of vibrancy in the house. I would like you both to slowly inject some colour into your clothes, walls and fabrics. Make a scrapbook for you to collect colours and images that inspire you to action. Ask your husband and the boys which colours they like, which fabrics they like to touch.

You and Conrad need to identify tasks based on your needs. The only thing I have not included is a nanny. This is because if you're not working and you have the suggested housekeeper and maybe a dog-walker and babysitter you will not need a nanny. If you're working, then the nanny will take over your duties. You might consider working part-time and having a part-time nanny with all the above in place.

A meditation expert can also help you connect your energy and focus your mind. He or she can teach you two-minute meditations. (I found this helpful when I couldn't escape from negative thoughts.)

The children to go to bed at allocated times whenever possible. Jess isn't sleeping well. This will change when he shares with Joe. Do the children spend any time with their grandparents? Please arrange at least one weekend every month for them to stay with grandparents or aunties. You can also alternate so that you and Conrad have one of them and the other one is away for that weekend. This way you have two weekends per month with only one child instead of two. I would have a babysitter at nights so that you and your husband can go out at least one weekend a month.

Deep-Cleaning and Declutter:

We recommend a 3 - 6 monthly deep-clean of one or two rooms all year round. This can be done when you're away or at home.

You have a shelf filled with glass ornaments directly above the children's play area in the dining room. I would like this moved or enclosed, even if the shelf is completely secure. Having so much glass on an open dubious-looking shelf in a play area is a hazard.

Make bread with Jess at least once a week and, when Joe can join in, him too. Let Jess make his own shapes and show him how to put his dough to bed. When you awake, the dough will have grown in its sleep. Tell him sleep helps us to grow strong. Share the bread with guests.

Basement declutter and order plus deep clean:

Clean all accessible areas including beer-making equipment, take unwanted items to charity, clean all pipe works of dust and remove or organise what is left. The living room (the cluttered side) needs a 50% percent reduction of stuff. I would like this room to be a more obvious library for yoga books and music, but the shelves look like they are collapsing, so need to be replaced. Simple wooden bookshelves in either wall coving can be built to house your, and children's, books, CDs and a quality music system.

I would like you to move the desk and table, get rid of that whole cabinet on the other wall and put the desk and table there. Create a large, cosy reading corner with bright coloured cushions and a bright rug, low shelves for the children to read with you and your husband. Make this space usable for yoga with the kids. The other half of the room can be focused around the fire and TV as well as reading space for you and your husband. This room can also be used by you to practice yoga. I would put a heavy curtain or a folding screen to reduce the space as and when you want. Please arrange a family photo shoot and have three or more printed and framed for the living room, the kitchen diner and the boys' bedroom. I didn't see any pictures of you and Conrad together.

The bedroom that is currently Jess's ought to become the guest room. The room that is currently Joe's should become an art room for you and the boys, including Conrad. (I wouldn't mind if you choose to do it the other way round, too, so Jess's bedroom is the art room and Joe's bedroom becomes the guest room). Or put both the boys next to you and make Jess's room the art room keeping the guest room where it is. The most important thing is the boys are better sharing for the next two years. Whilst you're evolving, they need that extra sense of security and can get it from each other.

The New Art Room:

Buy paint-boards, chalk blackboards, white/coloured papers, clay, blue tack for hanging pictures in this room and the kitchen diner. Keep this room for you and the children to express and have fun in a contained space. Keep designated areas to reduce spillage between rooms or spaces. Tell the children that activities are defined by the rooms they happen in. So, no painting in the living room or bedrooms, for example. Create simple rules such as: always wear your apron to do art; wash your hands when you're done creating; let your art dry before showing to mummy and daddy; have a container to carry items to the nearest sink after use for washing (paintbrushes and pots, etc).

Top Floor:

I think the boys should be moved to the big double room with the en-suite bathroom. These rooms give them more space to play and more space for toys. You can put a child safety lock on the bathroom door. Put a curtain between the two sections of the room. The curtain (easily openable, of course) should be made of a fun material that will inspire creativity. If you decide to have the boys' together in a bedroom on your floor, the other bedroom could be an art and playroom.

Guest or staff are not your priority. You and your family must always come first when deciding about the rooms. Agree a timeframe with Conrad to have the leaking window repaired. If he cannot do this and other identified work, then get someone in to do it! I can arrange a builder to give a price.

Family to have at least one planned outing a month (parents and kids). But don't force yourselves to travel miles. Hampstead Heath is on your doorstep. Jacksons Lane Theatre is a great family space with lots of kids' shows and a café. Keep your outings local so you don't have the stress of travelling with young kids. City farms and walks within a five-mile radius as well as London zoo should keep them happy for the next five years! Longer trips can be made when you're going on holidays.

Parents to have allocated time with children using a written timetable. Time allocated must be at least 4 times a week 1 - 2 hrs for each child or both together. This can include painting, messy play, reading, bread making, bath-time, dressing or cooking.

One of these sessions must be outdoors at the park or softplay with you and Conrad together. Ideally weekends. Conrad to have a class a week outside, e.g. rock climbing or other physically challenging activity.

I don't know how far away the children are from nursery or school, but if you can have more cleaning and ordering of the home and kids, take them or pick them up on three occasions weekly. This is on the basis you have someone helping you to get them ready to take or pick up, or someone else is managing the house so that you don't have more than two children to handle on school runs.

Family coaching session once a month: You and Conrad to have at least one walk a week together outside the home for one hour.

One other activity together per month: this can include dinner or visiting an art gallery, or any activity chosen by both of you. You can take turns if you find you can't decide or agree. Really do your best to enjoy the activity chosen by your partner.

Monthly planning: You and Conrad to spend at least 2-3 hours creating and diary-filling; ensure your planned dates are actually done. Both of you should keep a reflective journal or diary of dates you have had with each other and the times enjoyed with the boys.

Try to keep a track of your off days too. See if they coincide with your periods. If you feel that things are going downwards, communicate with Conrad and those around you to reassess levels of support. I had terrible PMT. I used to hide it or try to fight it. Now I manage it, I take time out, I rest, I share with my partner what I am dealing with and I allow myself to make mistakes when my body is under pressure. Making these changes have reduced the symptoms and the impact on me. It's increased my love of other people as I allow them to fully support me when I need it. It's made me more capable of providing for others when I am well.

Clothing/Storage/Repairs: I recall that you have a wardrobe on one of the landings with clothes you don't wear. Give these to charity. We suggest each family member has around 8-10 base items; these can include trousers, dresses, skirts, suits, jackets.

Join a Room Reading group with Conrad; you'll start sharing with others and help each other achieve goals. Mind-reading rooms is a practical, unique concept and if you and your family fully engage with your Room Plan, you will find, six months from now, your home and family will be in a very different space.

Yours, Hannah

Key actions: developing warmth in the space; creating rooms for activities; room changes; bread making and baking; keeping a relationship-journal or scrapbook.

34. Tracey Emin – My Bed

Key themes: twins' connection; impact of double life on children; excess vs normality; created sensationalism for social reflection.

Much has been written about Tracey Emin's *My Bed*. It was recently sold for £2.2 million to a Dutch count. My Bed apparently tells the story of her breakup with a lover and subsequent 'sleep-in' in the bed. She retreats into a world of vodka, cigarettes and takeaways. Her bloodied underwear and several other objects are left on the floor; two suitcases – joined together by chaotic string – sit off to the side. In a recent interview, Emin shared how My Bed still held the scent of her life then. But that was ten years earlier. She was no longer the same person. Many people across the world have seen My Bed; artists have played on it; others have stolen bits of paraphernalia. Art critics either love or hate it. Emin became famous and infamous because of it.

The honesty of the human condition in all its self-absorbed, broken-hearted idiocy has given My Bed glory beyond our own emancipated sheets, broken hearts, hangovers and bloody periods. Isn't this, according to Emin, how we live? However, here, we are not interested in the merits of My Bed as a work of art nor its current perceived meaning. We are exploring whether My Bed is a true reflection of Emin and her life. If I can provide scope beyond the obvious, she – and we – can find a new perspective in My Bed.

How could Room Reader have prevented My Bed from ever needing to be made? Sorry, I mean unmade. (Although in Emin's case, given the fame and fortune that followed, she may not have thanked me.) Room Reader doesn't rely on the assertions of the speaker or her many observers. We look to the subtleties of the objects. These include a soft toy, a mixture of white and soiled sheets, used condoms, and all the other detritus of loose living. At one installation, a noose hangs over the bed and a wooden coffin is nearby. I have not seen the latest installation of My Bed but I believe it's a decoy: the heartbroken lover, getting drunk and eating takeaways is so surface.

Emin is a twin, her father is Cypriot-Turkish and had another family (a legitimate one). This situation – unknown initially to Emin – often had her waiting days for daddy to come home from long 'work' trips.

She has always been close to her twin brother, Peter, and she says they had a connection bound together in the womb. The twins also shared a wooden cot and comforted each other when one wanted soothing or milk at night.

The father's double life soon became known to Emin and her brother. Emin fought defiantly for her father's attention. She was also very angry that they (she and her brother) had been dealt such an unfair hand. As an adult, Emin confronted her father saying: "Having two families isn't right". He claimed that his wife Sheila and Emin's mother, Pauline, knew about each other and were fine with it. But Sheila blamed Pauline for becoming pregnant with twins when she (Sheila) already had three legitimate children with Emin's father. Emin had an adventurous childhood travelling with her twin brother, Peter, and the father on work trips. They also went to Cyprus where they spent some years living with relatives. Pauline, Emin's mother, ran a cheap hotel so they were socialised and confident in two languages and two cultures between here and Cyprus.

I see Emin between the lines from the media persona she has created of being a rough, fag-smoking, vodka-gulping slut. For me, all this is an image created by her for sensationalising excess.

I see My Bed as the bed of two children. This is shown by the mixed male and female items such as the bloodied knickers, the underpants, soft toy, soft drink, the used condom. There are two suitcases wrapped in chaotic string (twins in the womb) two pieces of luggage ready to be picked up by a third person linked together. Their fate is inseparable, and they must wait until they are collected. But who are they waiting for? Who will collect such awkward – illegitimate – suitcases? Emin was expressing a life situation, one where she absorbs herself in triviality, alcohol abuse and overt sexual exploitation, but My Bed is a bed for two children not lovers; the lover, if there ever was one, is merely a pastime while she and her twin wait and hope for Daddy.

Emin is an artist, she understands the need for aesthetics to encourage (sexual) pleasure although My Bed inspires nothing but self-loathing of the bodily excretions (she and her brother couldn't help being born, being human, being bloody and producing – or at least being involved with – semen). Interestingly, the condom could have solved everything, if only her father had worn one.

The bed base looks like nothing more than hardboard; the sheets are plain and dirtied; the covers crumpled in a roll, looking like a large wave in a turbulent sea of dubious moments; the soft toy (childhood) present but left unattended on the floor; the deep blue rug next to the bed is terrifying. I feel that when I stand on this I am going down into the depths of despair. Why? If these are two adults as Emin and her critics claim, is it really so bad that you would want to hang yourself?

Self-loathing, self-abuse and exhibitionist behaviour are common in children and adults who are angry with irresponsible parents. Children must be given the respect they are owed, respect by those who choose to create them. Tracey Emin is a traditionalist. She believes in traditional family values like: don't share a father, don't blame your kids for being born, and do expect them to blame you for your selfishness that left them angry.

Emin has denied herself children and, after her operation for endometritis, can't have any. She raises concerns about adopting because she is single. Pauline struggled as a single mother and Emin felt it. Her brother, Peter, followed the father's line and has three children by three mothers.

I see an opportunity for Emin to complete on her past with her deceased father, and for her to get involved with her brother's children. Then auntie Tracey would get joy out of allowing herself to do a more consistently committed and responsible job than her father ever did.

She also recognises that nobody's perfect and ensures to portray herself as far less than perfect. She can fool us into thinking she is nothing more than a sluttish fag-toting, drinking vodka in buckets and shitting for millions. Really? I think she's a perfectionist, not controversial at all. She understands the need for normality and teaches us to crave normality through depictions of excess.

Key actions: exploration of My Bed to uncover reality versus public persona. (Listen to the song *Defiance.)*

35. Porcelain doll

Key themes: ever-increasing disconnection with black roots seen in four generations of a family home.

Through the creative medium of Room Reader, I have shared some of the world of our influencers. This story highlights the generational impact of media messages. Are you a white woman that over-relates to black culture? Are you gay pretending to be straight or straight pretending to be gay? Do you feel trapped in your body? What is it that makes you feel that way? I believe that mind-reading rooms can go some way to addressing such imbalances. I am not suggesting that we must only engage in our own culture or sexual identity, but that we are aware of choices so that we know our spaces truly reflect what we want to be.

The woman in our story can never be a 'white woman' because her skin is black. The result of her trying to be something so different was an inability to accept herself as seen and experienced by others, including her husband with whom she was becoming increasingly distant. Another impact of this disassociation from herself was that all three of her children coveted white partners. Many of you will probably ask what is wrong with mixing things up? I agree. There is nothing lovelier than children of mixed heritage. But what we are looking at here is the impact on three generations of a family influenced by white supremacy in religion, fashion and culture to the point of colouring the choices of the woman's children. In other words, they felt compelled to take white partners over black to please their mother who lived and breathed being white even though she wasn't. As you'll see, when the mother made changes and began to connect and enjoy who she was, her children's choices also changed.

You might think this woman was an extreme case, a 'one off,' but have a look at many black stars and see how they, too, are emulating whiteness. In mind-reading rooms people are everything, nothing exists without our say-so. It is time for us to work together, transform our lives and be proud of our identity.

It was two years since my last visit to Mauritius. This time, I was supposed to be on holiday. I had three of my four children with me visiting their father and all their adoring relatives. Danwantee's health, though fragile, was stable after support from her Roomies, and her home – including the immediate surroundings – remained clean and tidy. Most importantly, my ex-mother-in-law was happy. I couldn't help calling at the Dupree School that I'd analysed to see how the kids were getting on. The headmistress to whom I'd sent my report had since retired and taken the recommendations to her daughter's school in Canada. However, she had time to make some changes: I noted the plants now had written explanations, the Welcome sign had been re-painted, and the children were sharing the park and managing ballgames on a rota.

The Mauritian family I was staying with had a close friend they wanted me to advise so I felt obliged to help. I was told the lady was suffering from severe anxiety about going out, and high blood pressure. Yet, when I reached her villa, her life appeared steady and stable with a 20-year happy marriage producing two handsome sons who lived with her, and a daughter now living in France. It was a beautiful villa set by a blue-water river that stretched out to meet the Indian Ocean. The client's mother and grandmother lived within walking distance and the client, Anna, made wedding bedding and wedding dresses. Her husband was a full-time engineer and part-time fisherman. They had their own boat and the boys were doing well in secondary school. On arrival, I thought there had been a mistake. Why would a successful, perfectly pleasant looking, black woman still in her thirties have such serious problems? I could detect no signs that would account for a condition that left her housebound these last two years.

We had tea in the open-plan kitchen-diner. The room was simple and highly functional for cooking and eating at the kitchen table. The views from the windows were of little, multi-coloured river houses dotted above the banks. Fresh herbs in plant pots showed good use of the spaces. Boats bobbed gently on the water's edge. A large TV was the centre-piece of Anna's dining room. A computer, chair and a daybed for naps doubled as a sofa for guests.

Whilst I was there, Anna's mother arrived; she was a lively woman in good health and well-dressed in European-style clothes. She busied herself making divine fish curry. The boys came home from school. What a handsome and polite pair they were! And the last piece of the puzzle, the father on his moped returned from work.

Anna showed me some of her bedding creations: these were special one-off items. She made them by hand with intricate details such as individual petals to make one flower, and then a hundred more! Indeed, I have never seen such a committed seamstress. She also made gorgeous white wedding dresses, white bedding christening robes and holy communion outfits.

I could not relate to her issues. How could these anxiety attacks and her escalating blood pressure be manifested in such a balanced space?

I left early and agreed to return when Anna could show me the rest of the house. Days later, she gave me a guided tour of the bedrooms and her workstation and I met her grandmother who was also there. Anna's bedroom was tidy, functional but a little exposed as it had openings into the main dining and living room. This could be causing some stress. On the other hand, if these openings were closed the couple would have no natural light from the dining room windows.

The bathroom was basic by Western standards but a perfectly functional space. The teenage boys shared a king-size bed. Their room was full of white soft toys. Along its white walls, the only picture was a life-size, colour print of a white baby wearing a nappy and a straw trilby hat. Underneath this baby, it said: 'The face is the index of the mind'. Why a white baby when the whole family was black? Of the infinite number of pictures and quotes she could have had, she chose one that emphasised appreciating the white face. The boys' wardrobe was full of smart shirts, trousers and shiny black shoes but no hint of their own ethnicity. Then we went into her guest dining room and living room. These were rarely used spaces. A selection of porcelain ornaments caught my eye. She also had some porcelain ornaments in her bedroom. Many people collect these quaint characters. They depict pretty, white ladies parading in flouncy dresses with pink parasols, couples relaxing on benches, or angelic boys playing harps or with hoops. They are clearly white European in style.

A large statue of the Virgin Mary above eye-level looked down upon us with her bright, blue eyes and milky, white hands open wide. (It never occurred to her that the Virgin Mary and her Middle Eastern Jewish son would naturally be olive-skinned with black, curly hair and dark brown eyes.) I could empathise with Anna on this as she could not have bought an authentic statue. In my youth, I was surrounded by only white religious icons that were clearly not based on the ethnicity of the people. Even visiting other countries and churches, I cannot recall an authentically ethnic picture or statue of the Virgin Mary or her son.

This over-emphasis of white religious art shows how we are all being sold the line 'White is best', 'White is purer', but it's based on a lie. Thus 'White supremacy' is inauthentic. We can change this with some authentically ethnic-religious art in our homes, schools and churches. But, for now, we'll probably have to make it ourselves.

Meeting with her mother highlighted how both women dressed only in Western-style clothes. And to confirm this was not a one-off, Anna's wardrobe revealed no interest in traditional African dress or colours. Moreover, Anna had no pictures or ornaments connecting her or her family with their culture, not even a family photo. I asked Anna how she felt venturing out of her own space. She said that when people looked at her, she felt "dirty"; they were "judging" her as a "failure".

Before I could be certain of my analysis, I wanted also to see the homes of her mother and grandmother. The mother had many pictures of her family on the walls, unlike her daughter – my client – who had only the white baby. And the grandmother had some pictures of relatives on her walls. The overall impression reflected three generations of deepening disconnection from their ethnic and cultural identity in favour of white culture and identity, as seen by Anna's created environment. I wondered what the impact of all this over-identifying would have on the fourth generation, her two teenage sons and daughter in France.

For the grandmother and mother, I could see no problem with this in the sense that they appeared not to suffer. Mind-reading rooms is designed to address an imbalance between the mind and the environment or objects. Anna clearly had an imbalance between these two, thus mind-reading rooms was needed.

We wandered around the house and I pointed out the white toys, porcelain ornaments and white baby. Anna was stunned. A few minutes passed. I patiently, silently, held the space and her emotions. Her eyes welled-up. "I think you're right," she eventually whispered.

I suggested that she start to relate to her ethnic roots by adding some family photos, images of African women in traditional dress and that she collects things related to her culture that she liked in a scrapbook.

I stayed in Mauritius for a month and three weeks later – the day before I left for the UK – Anna phoned and asked me to go out with her. I was surprised to have such an invite from a lady who had not strayed beyond her village boundary for two years. When I arrived, I was delighted to see her wearing a turban! "Wow," I said, "you look beautiful!"

She beamed. With no hesitation on her part, we went out into town. She bought materials for some bedding she was making. The white baby had gone, some of the porcelain ornaments had been removed and replaced with culturally-connected pieces. Her blood pressure had now stabilised. She told me that her appetite, sex-life and sleep had greatly improved, and it was obvious her agoraphobia had vanished; she was in town on an almost daily basis and meeting people with greater confidence than she could have imagined. She also informed me that her sons had only ever had white girlfriends but now – just in the three weeks since I advised the house changes – one of the boys had started talking about dating black girls and the eldest was looking forward to his second date with one! And Anna's husband was overjoyed that the newly-appreciated ethnicity meant greater self-expression in the bedroom.

So, once Anna got who she was, she could relate to being 'a white-winged dove' as in the song. Anna is no longer owned by whiteness. She can fly wherever she pleases. Now, *that* is authentic.

Key actions: remove 50% of white ornaments; start a scrapbook of black fashion and culture and bring in ethnic ornaments, family photos and dress. (Listen to the song *Never More Than Tonight.*)

36. The Fish-man

Key themes: alcohol addiction; wrong job; loneliness; communication skills; connection to own home; Barbara Wren; Sadghuru; Roomies.

I have very little knowledge of, or interest in, fish. Still, when I came to Exeter in the county of Devon, I inherited a large pond full of beautiful Koi and some 'invisible' little catfish. But between us preparing to move in and actually arriving, someone had ripped out and sold the filter system. After about a month, the first catfish floated up dead. Then another. I spent weeks trying to rehome the lovely koi – ironically much sturdier than the catfish – for fear I would lose them through ignorance. Despite best efforts (like putting buckets of fresh water in the pond) one did die. We rehomed some early on. And catching them was tricky.

Also, each time the boys went to play in the garden, I worried that they might fall into the pond. So, I decided to empty the pond and save the last few fishes. My son's friend said he had an uncle nearby who would take them. I was really relieved to conclude the issue of fish welfare and child safety.

Knee-deep in increasingly stagnant pond water, the boys delighted at netting out the last fish - yuck! I happily plonked the fishes into a mop bucket and hoped the uncle would oblige by taking on the orphan fish. Soon, around 11 am, the nephew, Jet – my son – and I were ringing the uncle's doorbell whilst standing next to his gleaming, top-of-the-range sports car. He took a while to let us in and, as he said 'Hello', a strong scent of alcohol hit me.

Mick soon revealed he was an alcoholic (people tend to share such issues with me even when I have not been invited in as an expert). Whilst inquisitive Jet found many lovely garden things to examine, I listened to Mick's story as we wandered out into the most beautiful garden I have seen. Japanese ornaments and sophisticated waterways housed the Koi he kept so well. Our fish were released gently into the water and immediately looked very much at home.

I heard that Mick was lonely, having lost two long-term relationships due to his drinking. I could not comment on that issue specifically but could look at his space and objects. I felt compelled to offer my advice as he had kindly rehomed the Koi. He accepted my offer. Yes, the garden was breathtaking with oriental trees and little pathways leading to a shady nook at the back, ideal for a rendezvous or intimate dinner party (although he said he had few friends). However, on closer inspection, I noticed he had three large (well, up to my hip) statues on the right side of the garden. All three were of a grotesque and judging nature making eye contact with the viewer. I suggested these gargoyles were a reflection of his judgemental mind and, if he wanted to ease his burdens, he ought to get rid of all three.

He saw the connection to his darker side and agreed. I also noticed a Buddha figure with a beautiful woman statue that was turned to walk away from the Buddha. I suggested that Mick was representative of the Buddha as this statue was housed atop his garden although it was also off to the right as opposed to a centrally imposing or egotistical position. The Buddha had a slightly hidden, gentle reverence (very like Mick) for all his wonderful work and thus the woman ought to be turned towards the Buddha, not away from him. To ensure that when Mick found another partner, she would not walk away but work with him, a gardener in rehab would be a great match because they would help and inspire each other to growth and peace.

We went inside the house. It was closed off from his creative garden. In the living room was an almost wall-to-wall TV screen with a black background surrounded – or enclosed – by sofas that seemed to keep me in this space. This meant he was as far away from his beloved garden as he could be, and trapped by the sofas. The other side of the living room had a cold glass and metal table surrounded by four chairs which he would rarely use. The vantage point was lost by these tables and chairs and ensured he rarely looked back towards the garden because of the cold hard reminder that he was alone. He never had dinner parties to attend to his guests. I noted the kitchen and other areas limited his view of the garden's expanse and beauty at every point.

Mick's job was surveying damaged buildings. He hated it. He had lots of money wasted on expensive cars and TVs. He owned all but 10% of his large property. He said he had paid thousands to participate in alcohol-reduction programmes but rarely completed them due to his shy nature. He always struggled with dancing and holding hands with others.

He complained his last girlfriend left after 15 years. (She said it was the alcohol long after she'd gone). I explained that most people do not have great communication skills and that is why using space and objects can help so much.

Sometimes we look beyond the obvious issue – in this case, alcohol – to the wider context as a way of changing our lives. You might find starting with space and objects leads you and yours to a greater level of understanding without the need for a degree in therapy.

Life has become so comfortable yet so complicated. Do we have too much luxury but too little gratitude for it? Practise gratitude for those around you at least twice as much as you practise unhappiness! (We Brits don't only complain about the weather.) And ensure your spaces and objects are utilised to heal by cleaning, clearing and ordering when issues arise.

I left Mick, but that night woke restless thinking of the fish-man alone and even disconnected from his vitality (the garden). I knew that his gardening skills could free him and soothe him into finding balance and maybe a new partner. The fish-man's life was in the balance. He had to plant himself in his garden. I rarely suggest such drastic measures, but when first looking into Mick's eyes, I could feel the approaching heaviness of death. I suggested he change his job, become a gardener, that he made his living room area in the dining room, and that he opened-up the views into the garden right across the back of the house to connect him with his creativity and calm. I also recommended the naturopath, Barbara Wren. A visit to her would help assess if he was lacking any nutrients or vitamins as I know this can sometimes lead to alcohol or other addictions. I advised him to take up meditation with Sadghuru. This wonderful Indian mystic offers free online meditations and worldly insights for everyone to grow. I know that the fish-man now has some tools to get his life and home working in a way that he might not have thought of before.

This is the beauty of sharing Room Reader. Mind-reading rooms really does give people more options than they ever thought possible and actions that do not always revert to medication but support practical and accessible efforts to regain balance. Plus, Mick has three beautiful fish to inspire and remind him of my suggestions. I do not know if the fish-man will take up all my suggestions. I only know that the three garden gargoyles are gone, and the lovely lady statue has been turned towards him.

Key actions: remove grotesque statues; turn the female towards the Buddha; new job; re-arrange living room and dining areas; open-up views from the back of the house.

Epilogue

Room Reader goes into the 'revolving door' of interventions.
Because
for us to truly shift our mind
everything in our space must shift in tandem.
Otherwise
we are stuck between the mind's willingness
and the physical environment that remains unwilling.
No matter how hard we try
to spend less, love more, eat better, or sleep deeper
– even with outside expert help –
we repeatedly return to our rooms
that have been constructed on our issues.
So
the larder remains full of cookies, the bed still creaks
the wardrobe stays stuffed with our impulse buys and
once more
we must return to incomplete treatments.
Mind-reading rooms
– Room Reading –
allows you to finally exit that revolving door.

* * *

48614347R00166

Printed in Poland
by Amazon Fulfillment
Poland Sp. z o.o., Wrocław